ROAR OF THE HEAVENS

ROAR OF THE HEAVENS

~~~

STEFAN BECHTEL

CITADEL PRESS
Kensington Publishing Corp.
www.kensingtonbooks.com

CITADEL PRESS BOOKS are published by

Kensington Publishing Corp.
850 Third Avenue
New York, NY 10022

All Kensington titles, imprints, and distributed lines are available at special quantity discounts for bulk purchases for sales promotions, premiums, fundraising, educational, or institutional use. Special book excerpts or customized printings can also be created to fit specific needs. For details, write or phone the office of the Kensington special sales manager: Kensington Publishing Corp., 850 Third Avenue, New York, NY 10022, attn: Special Sales Department; phone 1-800-221-2647.

CITADEL PRESS and the Citadel logo are Reg. U.S. Pat. & TM Off.

First printing: June 2006

10 9 8 7 6 5 4 3 2 1

Printed in the United States of America

Library of Congress Control Number: 2005938602

ISBN 0-8065-2706-4

To the victims of Hurricane Camille—may they
never be forgotten

And to my beloved son Adam—may he
find the greatness within

FOREWORD

In the fall of 2004, we thought it couldn't get any worse. During the height of the Atlantic hurricane season, the Fearsome Foursome—Charley, Frances, Ivan, and Jeanne—slashed across Florida, unleashing tropical energies that tallied a damage bill exceeding forty-two *billion* dollars.

Now, in 2005, much of the United States' Gulf Coast lies in ruin. Hurricanes Dennis, Emily, Katrina, Rita, and Wilma—all of them at least Category Four storms, and three of them rated Category Five—exploded out of the Gulf of Mexico with lethal wind, storm surge, and freshwater flooding. One of these storms, Wilma, established a new Atlantic record for lowest atmospheric pressure and underwent one the world's most rapid rates of deepening.

It seems that the threat of hurricanes has shifted into hyperdrive. With the unimaginable Katrina catastrophe that unfolded in New Orleans, nature's Pandora's box of tropical tempests now yawns wide.

But was the past a prologue to this nightmare?

The book you hold in your hand contains one of the most frightening accounts of what the weather can do to human beings. *Roar of the Heavens* documents a tropical cataclysm known as Hurricane Camille. In August 1969, Camille carved a tremendous arc of devastation from the Gulf Coast of the United States, up the Mississippi Valley and into the Mid-Atlantic. During her lifetime, Camille's total energy equivalent exceeded several thousand megatons of TNT, making her a storm of superlatives. Wind gusts approached 200 mph, the absolute upper limit for the strongest hurricane that nature can conjure. And the ocean was heaved into a three-story-tall battering ram that surged rapidly inland with the force of an Indonesian tsunami.

Camille and Katrina were both incubated by the warm waters of the Gulf of Mexico, springing into Category Five monsters and taking dead aim on Louisiana and Mississippi. Frighteningly, a mere thirty-six years separated two storms which by all rights might only be expected to recur once in five hundred or more years. But what made Camille so different from Katrina?* Camille possessed a dual personality, an occult side that bordered on the unnatural. Camille first slammed into the Louisiana coastline, swiftly snuffing out 175 lives, then rapidly weakened while moving north up the Mississippi Valley. After two days, the tropical tiger had tamed into a pussycat, as meteorologists would normally anticipate. But as the remnants approached the Mid-Atlantic coast, forecasters did not predict the sudden opening of a second dark act. This one claimed an additional 150 lives during one horrific night deep within the hollows of central Virginia's Blue Ridge Mountains. In just eight hours, the tropical tiger roared back to life, unleashing biblical torrents of rain—enough to fill three-feet-deep oak barrels to the brim. The rains fell so astoundingly hard that it was nearly impossible to breathe, or to hear anything above the deafening roar. So much water crashed from the sky that the entire veneer of a billion-year-old mountain range simply sloughed away.

Roar of the Heavens is a meticulously written and dramatic narrative of one of the greatest natural disasters in world history. Presented herein is a succinct reconstruction of the atmospheric events that gave rise to a perfectly oiled, super-efficient rain-producing machine—a nearly unimaginable synergy of steep mountains, tropical moisture, and energy. Numerous survivors provide riveting testimony about what it was like to be swept headlong several thousand feet down the mountainside, tossed among mud and trees and boulders the size of homes. Ultimately, this book provides one of the most riveting accounts of extreme freshwater flooding, which remains the number one hurricane killer in the western hemisphere.

In many ways, Hurrricane Camille was the prophecy of Katrina. Camille occurred during the end of an especially vicious cycle of Atlantic hurricane activity, the deadly years of the 1950s and 1960s. These tropical cycles wax and wane on the order of several decades. Now the relatively quiescent period of the 1970s and '80s has given

---

*Katrina was officially downgraded to Category Three some weeks after the fact, as evidence was reassessed.

way to a resurgence, commencing in 1995. Now, in 2005, for the first time ever we have run out of names for Atlantic storms; our lexicon now embraces the Greek alphabet. We can expect another ten to fifteen years of heightened storm frequency. And recent scientific work has suggested that hurricanes have even grown stronger in the past thirty years.

With more people than ever now living along U.S. coastlines and cities tucked deep in the Appalachians, our vulnerability to the hurricane threat is approaching the red line. If Katrina reveals to us the horrors that are now possible, Camille should have sounded a blaring warning cry.

—Jeffrey B. Halverson, Ph.D.
Associate Research Professor of Geography
University of Maryland, Baltimore County/
National Aeronautics and Space Administration
Goddard Space Flight Center
October 27, 2005

ACKNOWLEDGMENTS

For their help in understanding the science of hurricanes in general and Camille in particular, I would particularly like to thank my "science advisor" and collaborator, Dr. Jeffrey Halverson, Ph.D., assistant program scientist at NASA and the Goddard Space Flight Center. I'd also like to thank former National Hurricane Center director Dr. Robert H. Simpson, who granted a very long interview despite his more than ninety years; New Orleans meteorologist extraordinaire Nash C. Roberts, who also granted a long interview despite advanced age; Virginia State climatologist Dr. Pat Michaels; former NHC director Bob Sheets, for his excellent book *Hurricane Watch*; and Dr. David E. Fisher, for his book *The Scariest Place on Earth*, which nicely combines atmospheric science and plain English.

I would also like to thank all the people of Nelson County who helped me reconstruct the scene before, during, and after the great storm, including Warren Raines; Sheriff Bill Whitehead; Cliff Wood; Tommy and Adelaide Huffman; the Reverend John Gordon; Bobby Ray Floyd; Junior Thompson; Jake and Colleen Thompson; Frances Fitzgerald; Florence Dawson; Mr. and Mrs. Dan Payne; Phil Payne; Dr. Robert Raynor; the delightful Tom Gathright; Gene Ramsey, for his wit, photographs, and archival newspapers; Trooper Ed Tinsley; Andrew Puttagio; and the staff of the Nelson County public library, for making available their impressive Hurricane Camille archive. Also, Paige Shoaf Simpson and Jerry H. Simpson Jr., for their 1970 book *Torn Land*, which told the story of what happened in Nelson County while that experience was still raw, and put on the record interviews with many people who are no longer living.

In Mississippi, I wish to thank Linda Van Zandt and the staff of the Mississippi Oral History Program at the University of Southern

Mississippi in Hattiesburg, who made available the more than forty interviews with Camille survivors on the Gulf Coast that were originally conducted by Mr. R. Wayne Pyle. I also wish to thank Janice Stegenga, Mary Ann Gerlach, Julia Guice, and Dr. David Schoen. For their competent and patient editing. I would like to thank the literary lion John Thompson and the literary lioness Lilly Bechtel, as well as my editor at Kensington, Gary Goldstein, for his unflagging enthusiasm for this project. Thanks to my agent, Ellen Levine, without whom this flower would have died on the vine. Thanks to the Virginia Center for the Creative Arts, which provided refuge and escape from the Internet during the writing of parts of this book. And thanks to my favorite Russian, Anya, and to Sam, for her creative inspiration.

PART ONE

~~~

A RIDER NAMED DEATH

"And I saw, and behold, a pale horse, and its rider's name was Death, and Hell followed him."
—Revelations 6:8

"Camille was like going to hell.
It was like Hiroshima."
—Janice Stegenga

From Frances Fitzgerald's house along the Tye River in the tiny town of Tyro, in Nelson County, Virginia, there is a soul-stirring view of the Priest. The bony, forested crest of this old knob rises to just over four thousand feet, making it one of the highest peaks in these parts. In the twilight, the Priest and its companion peaks, the Friar and Three Ridges, seem to march into infinity, and into a seemingly infinite color-series of blues and grays and blue-grays—an ever-shifting palette only faintly suggested by their name, the Blue Ridge Mountains.

Spread out below these towering mountains is a lovely, flower-spattered meadow, which in the autumn is scattered with great round hay bales that look like immense loaves of golden bread. The fields are borded by lazy, wandering hedgerows that follow the streambeds, marked by a meandering line of sycamores and oaks and willows and mountain ash. It's God's country: some of the prettiest, most pastoral landscapes on the East Coast.

The Priest is a thing that smites even the dullest of hearts with its sheer loveliness—yet to view this landscape simply with one's heart is to almost completely miss it. Because standing here in this pretty valley, overshadowed by mountains lifted off a scenic calendar, you are ringed by danger and by death, and the tangible record of catastrophe is everywhere. Above you are places where the mountainsides have been raked bare and now stand raw and exposed as open wounds. Scattered in the foothills below are immense boulders, some of them as big as boxcars. How did they get there? What cataclysm brought them down?

The Priest is beautiful, but looked at in a more ominous way it is also a great, broad blade almost a mile high that rakes water out of the sky. In scientific terms, its steepness and height create an "oro-graphic effect," lifting moisture-laden air masses up into higher elevations, where they cool, condense, and fall as rain—sometimes not gentle rain but fierce, relentless, murderous rain. The very height and drama of these mountains are the source of their danger. The towering crags and ridges form a steep watershed or catchment area, a gigantic basin or bowl, which gathers water from a vast area and sends it cascading down into narrow streambeds. And the meadow around you, it now becomes obvious, is actually a vast floodplain that has been repeatedly inundated by water and by mud. At times this lowland has become the valley of the shadow of death, and no birds have sung.

Then there is the nonobvious matter of Nelson County's location on the globe. Its particular latitude (about thirty-eight degrees north of the equator) maximizes the chance that disintegrating hurricanes coming up from the distant Gulf but still loaded with almost unimaginable cargoes of water will unburden them in these mountains. That's why the soporific Tye River, chuckling over its bed of round stones through this peaceful valley, is actually a ravenous beast—the mythological dragon of the human imagination, only temporarily asleep.

We may know these things rationally, but we don't really know them deep in our hearts, down in the fearful realm below thought.

Part of the reason all this danger is hidden is that we are trapped in human, psychological time. We're inclined to measure everything against the sixty or seventy or eighty years most of us will be given. Anything that occurs less frequently than this tends to be invisible to us—it vibrates on a slower pulse. Yet even the longest human life on record is so brief it's akin to a bird's shadow passing across a wall. Compared to geological time, compared to the rocks and hills around us, a human's lifespan is indistinguishable from that of a mayfly, which is born and dies in a single day.

But there are moments—extraordinary moments—when human time comes into direct conflict with geological time. When the implacable inhumanness and grandeur of these great processes rise up around us, like a sleeping monster, and eat us alive.

Such an event occurred here in the mountains of central Virginia on the night of August 19, 1969, when the remnants of Hurricane Camille collided with a complex system of water-laden air currents in the middle and upper atmosphere. Almost completely without warning, and within the space of eight hours, one of the heaviest rainfalls ever recorded on earth—billions of tons of rain—cascaded down these mountainsides, turning these lovely crags and streambeds into a terrifyingly effective drowning machine for all life below. Humans, animals, trees, boulders, houses, cars, barns, and everything else were swept away in a fast-moving slurry, a kind of deadly earth-lava that buried everything in its path. The bodies of many people, asleep in their beds when the avalanche smashed into their houses in the night, were never found. The next morning, when Frances Fitzgerald climbed down out of the hole in the ceiling where she and her husband had fled to escape the flood, she saw drowned, half-naked bodies hanging from fences and trees around her house.

"We were encircled by death," she said.

The rainfall was so cataclysmic, the Office of Hydrology of the Weather Bureau (now the National Weather Service) later estimated that it approached "the probable maximum rainfall which meterologists compute to be theoretically possible." People had to cover their mouths even to breathe. Birds perched in trees simply drowned. A team of geologists, after calculating how much soil would be stripped off the mountainsides due to normal wind, water, and weather, concluded that about two thousand years of erosion had taken place in a single night. Other scientists later attempted to calculate just how unusual an event this was. The hydrology office estimated that an event of this magnitude "occurs, on average, only once in more than one thousand years." Another researcher, at the University of Virginia, pointed out that such catastrophic events were so rare that one had to look beyond human history and instead study the geologic record of ancient "paleofloods" imprinted in the rocks and soil. Using radiocarbon dating of these ancient sediments, he calculated that the hardest-hit area (the Davis Creek basin) had probably not seen such an event in the previous three to six thousand years—since before the building of the pyramids at Giza.

But whatever metrics one uses, what occurred in Nelson County, Virginia, in the last days of August 1969—and a few days earlier along the Mississippi gulf coast—was an event out of the nether regions of mathematical probability, out of an entirely different scale of time than the one to which humans are accustomed. After it was over, when the mountainsides collapsed in a deafening, continuous roar, people marvelled at the smell that hung in the air—a pungent, earthy smell, the smell of rock and soil that may not have been exposed to air and light for thousands of years. It was the smell of deep time.

It was as though, on an ordinary day in August, in an ordinary place, time itself had been ripped open and laid bare.

This is the story of a collision between human and geological time.

It's the story of the fragility and unknowableness of everything we think is predictable and secure.

It's the story of what people do when the worst that could possibly happen, happens.

For many, it became the story of the end of the world.

CHAPTER ONE

5:30 A.M., Thursday, August 14, 1969
New Orleans

A SCATTER OF STARS still glittered through the moss-draped live oak trees along Saint Charles Avenue when Nash C. Roberts Jr. slipped out from between the sheets and slid his feet stealthily onto the bedroom floor. He was doing his best not to wake Lydia, his dear wife of twenty-nine years, who slept lightly as a cat. As for himself, he'd been wide awake and on edge for hours. He could never sleep when bad weather was brewing. As a professional courtesy to his clients, he probably *shouldn't* be able to sleep: He was a meteorologist providing site-specific weather reports to oil and gas companies with hundreds of millions of dollars invested in offshore drilling operations in the coastal marshes and the Gulf of Mexico. It was his job to be nervous—especially now, smack in the middle of hurricane season, when something fearful was afoot in the atmosphere.

He reset the alarm for 6:45 A.M., for Lydia and the boys, dressed quickly in a light cotton suit and tie appropriate for the sticky August heat of New Orleans, tiptoed downstairs and made himself a cup of coffee, and was out the door before six. It was only a twenty-minute drive from his modest brick home in Metarie to his office on Camp Street, just a couple of blocks outside the French Quarter.

The headquarters of Nash C. Roberts, Meteorological Consultants, in the downstairs lobby of the St. Charles Hotel, were as comfortable and unpretentious as an old shoe. There were butt-worn leather swivel chairs and metal filing cabinets and a couple of sad, neglected potted plants in the corner. Several inelegant teletype machines clattered out, in code, the weather conditions throughout North and South America. A gently murmuring voice box reported activities on

7

the world's commodity exchanges, many of which were weather-dependent businesses in need of meteorological advice. Drafting tables were strewn with synoptic weather maps and radar images, along with the compasses and protractors that Roberts's staff of five meteorologists used to draw, freehand, vast and detailed weather maps each day. Even in 1969, these were old-fashioned methods, but Nash Roberts was famous for his old-fashioned devotion to detail.

Nobody was in the office yet. Roberts flipped on the lights, hung his jacket up on the back of a chair, loosened his tie, and sat down to figure out what in the world was going on. For the past three days, he had had his eye on an infant storm system that was thrashing its way up the Caribbean through the Yucatan Channel, a path so favored by incoming storms it was almost like a hurricane highway. He'd started watching this thing back on Monday, August 11, as it passed over the island of Guadeloupe in the Lesser Antilles. The storm was now located about sixty miles west of Grand Cayman Island, a little less than five hundred miles south of Miami.

It was still fairly early in the hurricane season—as a general thing, the Caribbean basin didn't turn into a boiling cauldron of storm systems until the middle of September. Even so, the sea-surface temperature down there was eighty degrees or perhaps even warmer. Since sea-surface temperature was what stoked the engines of a hurricane, anything could happen, and happen quickly. It was as if, as the hurricane season progressed, the entire Caribbean Sea caught fire, with great flickering plumes of heat energy rising up into the atmosphere, seeking just the right conditions to tip over into that infernal rotation, creating a swirling chimney of air eight or ten miles high, or even higher. Once that happened, the towering vortex would begin hungrily vacuuming warm, soggy air upwards, feeding upon the heat-energy like a voracious animal, whirling faster and faster, higher and higher—a deadly, self-reinforcing spiral, expelling its exhaust up to the edge of the tropopause and unleashing forces that were practically unimaginable.

When *that* happened, everything came down to the elementals: shrieking wind, towering water, abject fear, and death.

Most of these systems were spawned on or near the coast of Africa, many on the Abyssinian Plateau of Ethiopia, where they'd begin life as bush-league atmospheric disturbances called tropical waves. This one was no exception, having been born in the African highlands where man himself was born, and drifted in a lazy parabola down across the South Atlantic. Carried by the prevailing easterlies around the great high-pressure system known to meteorologists as the Bermuda High—a kind of mountain of air that was a more-or-less permanent fixture of the atmosphere there—the system had moved into the steamy blue of the Caribbean Sea.

Last year, 1968, had been a particularly busy one: more than a hundred tropical waves had been detected and tracked across the South Atlantic into the Caribbean. Most of them would build up, rise, condense as rain, and expend their energies over the tropical sea, harmless as a dispersing cloud of butterflies; others would storm ashore with towering, torrential rains, causing massive flooding and mudslides in Caribbean countries. But for reasons that were still not entirely clear to anyone, a very few of these budding storm systems—in '68, there were only three—would begin to revolve into a "closed system," tighten down into a menacing vortex, and begin hurtling towards the Gulf coast like a death star. Once their winds accelerated to 74 miles an hour, they officially became hurricanes, and everyone and everything in their path was in peril.

For Nash Roberts this is when sleep would not come, and he'd simply move out of Lydia's bed and into his office on Camp Street. He'd work around the clock for days on end, snatching catnaps on an old sofa, never really taking his attention off the incoming storm. It was, he liked to tell people, part of his technique: He'd become so deeply and completely engrossed in the study of the storm that it was almost as if he were having a love affair with it. "It's like being married," he'd tell people. "Your wife or your husband can detect a change before anyone else can. I have to have that kind of relationship with a hurricane."

The critical thing everybody wanted to know about an incoming hurricane was where and when it would make landfall. And though he didn't like to admit this publicly—it sounded a little silly, really— Roberts had learned to understand and predict the storm track of hurricanes partly by thinking of them as humans. He "psyched them out"—got inside their skins. "Hurricanes are like people," he liked to say. "They're always trying to find the easy way to go." Like a spinning top, a hurricane would continue to move forward unless something blocked its progress. If it ran into a high-pressure area (really just a mountain of air, like the Bermuda High), it would find an easier way around. If it came upon a low-pressure trough (a kind of ditch in the air), the spinning top of the hurricane would slip into the ditch and follow it as far it could go, like a gutterball. The key thing was to figure out what was *steering* it, and to assume it would always choose the easier way if it could find one.

Like every other meterologist, Roberts diligently analyzed data: he studied the vortex reports, the ocean currents, the high-altitude winds, and all the rest of it. But "all that data that comes in only tells you what *has* happened. It doesn't tell you what's *going* to happen." How you used the information every other weatherman had in order to prophesy the future involved experience, intuition, and a deep personal relationship with the wind.

It was still too early for Roberts to have any real relationship, any real *feel,* for the as-yet-unnamed storm system churning up past the Caymans. So far, it was just a collection of muddy smudges on the radar reports, which had first been detected by satellite back on August 5, off the west coast of Africa—part of the season's steady parade of tropical waves marching west over the rim of the world. A Navy reconnaissance plane had flown into the center of the system and recorded a barometric pressure measurement of 29.50", and 55-mile-an-hour winds—a middling storm, frightful to be caught in at sea, but still far short of a hurricane. Officially, it was now a tropical storm (meaning that it had organized circulation and maximum sustained winds of over 39 miles an hour).

The system was still fairly small, but Roberts knew well enough how rapidly things could go from worrisome to dead scary out there in the Gulf. He also knew from more than thirty years of studying these great ocean storms that hurricanes differ dramatically. It really *did* make sense to give them names, because each seemed to have its own personality. Some were big and sloppy and lumbering; they were like old people, slow-moving, fat, and predictable. They'd overwhelm the entire Gulf, like 1961's Carla. Others were quick and nimble and erratic, like children (and dangerous in a child's unwitting way). Some storms would move right up to the Coast and then just stop there, as if they *knew* they'd die if they came ashore. It was eerie and probably entirely unscientific, but Roberts took it seriously: Some hurricanes even seemed to have an intelligence, a deliberateness, a *will*.

Though it was too early to say whether this infant storm would develop a will of its own, it was not too early to begin paying very close attention indeed. Because a full-blown hurricane is the most destructive force on earth, killing more people and causing more damage than floods, earthquakes, volcanoes, or anything else in nature's arsenal. According to the World Meteorological Organization, during the twentieth century hurricanes caused ten times as many deaths in the United States, and more than three times as much damage, as earthquakes.

Nash Roberts's knowledge of hurricanes and their dreadful power was something he could *feel*. And poring over the incoming data, he could feel it now, a combination of vast knowledge and experience shot through with plain old clammy human fear. Maybe wind shear in the upper atmosphere would break up the baby storm system and it would just go away, like most storms did. Or maybe atmospheric conditions would align like fateful stars, and something truly awful would come roaring in off the Gulf. It was too early to tell. It wasn't only the well-being of Shell, Mobil Oil, and his other offshore clients that he was concerned about. He was worried about the well-being of his own wife and family—which in a strange sort of way included the millions of people living along the Gulf coast from east Texas all the way to Pensacola, Florida.

Whenever a big hurricane began bearing down on this region and that clammy fear returned to his gut, Roberts became a man transformed. Not only was he a studious professional meteorologist and consultant to drilling companies, bent over his weather maps at the office on Camp Street, he also became a star, his voice and image broadcast up and down the coast on New Orleans's Channel 6, WDSU-TV. Roberts's eerily prescient ability to predict the path of incoming hurricanes, combined with a calm and amiable on-air personality, had made him the most trusted weather forecaster on the Gulf. He was the Walter Cronkite of hurricanes. If Walter Cronkite said something was so, by God, it was so. And if Nash Roberts said a hurricane was coming this way, then by God, it was coming this way.

Roberts's on-air career had started as a bit of a fluke, back in the

late 1940s, when Channel 6 asked him to go on the air to explain an
incoming hurricane to the station's listeners. He dragged his maps and
charts into the studio and gave a simple, folksy chalk talk, using a
grease pencil and a big washable plastic weather board. He just
wanted to tell the people, as simply and directly as possible, exactly
what he knew, precisely how bad he thought it was going to be,
where and when he thought the thing was going to come ashore,
and—most important—whether people should stay or leave. "There's
no reason to hype up a hurricane," he explained later. "There's already built-in hype."

Listeners loved his calm, gentlemanly manner, his patient explana-
tions, his air of courtly authority. They loved his enthusiasm, too: To
him, there was nothing more interesting, more challenging, or more
consequential than the complex, ever-changing atmospheric chess
game called "the weather." At fifty-one, he had a broad, open face;
sensuous, expressive lips; and a receding hairline. Somehow, he managed to convey the impression of being a country boy who'd come to
the city without becoming citified or fancied up (even though he had
been born and raised in New Orleans). He was credible, believable,
a straight shooter—a genuine expert in a world of television weather
"personalities" who had good hair and no real training at all.

AFTER THAT FIRST broadcast, a local company, Higgins Industries,
started trying to get Roberts to do a regular local weather report—at
the time, a genuine novelty, because only big markets like New York
or Los Angeles had local weathermen. For two years, he resisted,
telling Higgins that he had no training in television whatsoever, and
no particular interest in it either. Even so, when he finally agreed to
do a seven-and-a-half-minute weather segment on the six- and ten-
o'clock news starting in 1951, he turned out to be a natural in the new
medium. His on-air personality was entirely without artifice or preten-
sion. The only props he used were his signature grease pencils and
his plastic weatherboard, explaining the weather with circles and ar-
rows like an enthusiastic high school football coach explaining a favorite play. Even later, when fancy technologies like Doppler radar
became available, Roberts stuck with his humble, low-tech props.
People loved this.

And they loved the fact that he treated them with respect—so much respect, in fact, that he constantly enlisted their help. As a hurricane bore down on the Coast, he asked his listeners to keep track of barometric pressure, rainfall, windspeed, and other meteorological markers at their locations. These requests were not merely ruses to get ratings; they weren't secretly shredded the moment they arrived at the television station. Roberts really wanted to know. After the storm had passed, his mailbox at Channel 6 would fill up with letters from dentists in Pascagoula and old ladies in Hattiesburg, with long lists of barometric pressure readings and windspeeds and rainfall records, along with the times and locations where they were taken. One could imagine people leaning earnestly into this task, jotting down lengthy columns of figures in narrow, studious script, sometimes by flickering candlelight, as the wind screamed in the eaves, the surging sea drew closer to the door, and they wondered desperately whether it was already too late to flee.

In effect, Roberts was conscripting his entire listening audience into a meteorological observation team. They were all in the same boat, and he was just asking for their help with the bailing.

Nash Roberts's first big breakthrough came in 1957, when he correctly forecast that Hurricane Audrey, a Category Four, would hit southwest Louisiana. Audrey was a horror, with 12-foot tides and gusts up to 180 miles an hour. While most forecasters believed she would make landfall around 10:00 A.M., Roberts insisted to his listeners that the storm would come ashore six or seven hours earlier, in Cameron, Louisiana. He was right—and more than four hundred people, many of them asleep in bed, were killed that night.

"They should never have fallen asleep with that thing bearing down on them," he said afterwards.

After that prophetic call, when a hurricane began threatening the Gulf Coast, people asked, "What does Nash say?" and tuned in to Channel 6. His neighbors started watching his driveway to see if his car was there at night. No car meant he had started sleeping at his office down on Camp Street—and that meant trouble.

Eventually, Channel 6 outfitted a small room off Roberts's office as a makeshift studio, with a coaxial cable running down the street to the television station. That way, even in the teeth of a hurricane, he didn't even have to leave his office to make a broadcast. Usually he worked alone with a small minicam, but in August 1965, when Hurricane

Betsy started rampaging towards the Gulf coast, the station sent over two big cameras, a cameraman, and a floor director.

Betsy was a huge, ferocious storm, a Category Three that was more than six hundred miles wide from edge to edge, with an eye estimated to be forty miles wide at one point. She was not as bad as the great hurricane of 1947, which was the one many local people thought of as "the worst it could possibly get," but she was still an awful storm. Betsy was also an absolute nail-biter that kept Roberts and his audience on edge for days when she performed an astounding loop-the-loop and reversed course out in the South Atlantic. She'd formed east of the Windward Islands in late August, and had begun drifting northwest in the usual lazy parabola of hurricane travel, seemingly bound for landfall in the Carolinas. Then, on Saturday, September 4, she abruptly came to a halt about 350 miles off Daytona Beach, Florida. She stalled there overnight, and the next morning, when she started moving again, she was headed *south* and west, quite contrary to almost all known hurricane tracks. From the makeshift studio next to his office, Roberts kept the people of the Channel 6 listening area updated all day and all night long.

Betsy rampaged southwest into the Bahama islands chain, across Great Abaco Island, then down across the island city of Nassau, where she stalled for about three hours, pounding the place with relentless rain and winds gusting to over 140 miles an hour. Then she crossed the Florida Keys, nearly submerging Key Largo, regained strength as she passed over the Gulf, and seemed to be preparing to make a direct hit on the city of New Orleans. New Orleans is generally acknowledged to be the most flood-endangered city in the United States, and everybody who lives there knows it. The city is not just dangerously close to sea level; Much of it is actually eight or ten feet *below* sea level, protected only by a system of levees and pumps. The city is almost completely surrounded by water. In any direction you choose to leave, you run into water: either Lake Pontchartrain, the Mississippi River, the Gulf of Mexico, or the bayou. Choose your poison. Any rational person, looking at the site map of the Big Easy, would have to say that putting a city there at all is insane. No wonder then that New Orleans has always been a town with attitude, and revelers down on Bourbon Street favor a potent drink called the "hurricane," as if to throw a good, stiff drink smack in the face of fate.

As it turned out, Betsy came ashore a bit west of New Orleans, in the tiny town of Grand Isle, which hangs out over the Gulf on a narrow peninsula slender as a bending reed. Almost every building in Grand Isle was destroyed. In New Orleans, the storm surge raised the Mississippi River by ten feet, flooding into Lake Pontchartrain north of town, overrunning the levees that surrounded the lake. In some parts of the city, floodwaters reached the eaves of houses.

By 10:00 P.M. that night, the center of the storm was just a little west of New Orleans. Windows were blowing out of the St. Charles Hotel, venetian blinds were catapulting down the street. Roberts was broadcasting live in front of a plate glass window of the studio to give viewers a look at what was going on outside. Viewers could see behind him, the wind starting to rip things off the roof of the Whitney Bank building. The plate glass window bowed in the 120-mile-an-hour wind and then, suddenly, shattered. Something flew into the back of Roberts's neck, and though he was certain he'd been struck by a piece of flying glass, he just kept on talking to the camera, trying to appear calm for the benefit of those who were far more frightened, and in far more real danger, than he was. When they went off the air, he discovered he'd been hit by a rock that had flown through the window. Water was all over the floor and cables were everywhere, and even though he feared he might be electrocuted at any moment, Roberts continued to broadcast all night long, until the storm finally blew herself out.

Betsy cemented Nash Roberts's reputation. The New Orleans *Times-Picayune* took to calling him "the closest thing there is to a living legend on local television." People on the street would simply declare, "If Nash says it's gonna hit, you better git!" (Actually, he liked to tell people in his slow, self-effacing drawl, there was only one surefire method for detecting whether the Big One was finally about to hit New Orleans. That would be when his wife, Lydia, got ready to evacuate: "She's never left before. But the day anyone sees Lydia leaving, it's time to clear out!")

Some listeners became convinced that Roberts's ability to predict hurricanes went beyond anything that could be explained by science. Some thought he had "the shining" when it came to The Big Wind— some sort of prophetic second sight that enabled him to predict a hurricane's landfall more accurately even, at times, than the National

Hurricane Center. Scientists at the NHC tended to frame their forecasts in terms of probabilities, but Roberts always tried to give his listeners a flat-out prediction about where he thought the thing was going to come ashore, and when. It was amazing how often he was right.

When asked about his forecasting abilities, Roberts was fond of telling interviewers that "three-quarters of meteorology is science and twenty-five percent is art." The "art" part, he'd say, "is not teachable. It's an instinct or an intuition or whatever you want to say." Then he'd add with a sly wink, "I use everything everybody else uses, but I have a little extra thing that I do on my own."

It was that mysterious "little extra thing that I do on my own"—the twenty-five percent—that captured many people's attention. Along the Gulf Coast, hurricanes are not really defined by the realm of "meteorology" at all, like thundershowers or high-pressure systems. They are a force that seems to emerge out of the heart of The Mystery itself, nameless and horrifying, more akin to the pale horse of Revelation than to the dew on the grass. They are relentless, implacable. Nobody knows exactly where they come from, or exactly where they go. Nobody knows when they will appear, or exactly how bad they're going to be. All that's known is that they will come, and they will be bad—perhaps very, very bad.

So when it came to be known around New Orleans that Nash Roberts, uncanny prophet of God's tempests, had been born a "veil baby," all manner of dark stories began to circulate. Babies occasionally will be born with the translucent amniotic sac draped over their faces, a sign that since ancient times has been taken to mean that the child will have second sight: the ability to see things that others cannot. Superstitions involving these "veils" or "cauls" abound. Roman midwives sold cauls near the Forum as good luck charms. Cauls were thought to be protective against shipwrecks and drowning, perhaps because the baby survives even though its face seems to be "underwater." Even as late as the 1870s, cauls were advertised for sale in British newspapers, as charms for sailors going to sea. Charles Dickens's great hero David Copperfield was born with a caul, "which was advertised for sale, in the newspapers, at the low price of fifteen guineas."

For a hurricane forecaster, being born a veil baby was kind of a double dose of good luck—the gift of second sight, and, should the first gift fail, protection against drowning.

IN AUGUST 1969, Nash Roberts was not the only one keeping a weather eye on the storm system slowly chugging up the Yucatan Channel. Seven hundred miles to the east, at the National Hurricane Center in Miami, its director, Dr. Robert Simpson, was also carefully watching the storm system that was swirling off Grand Cayman.

Fifty-six at the time, Simpson, too, had been studying these demonic ocean storms for most of his professional life. He was a University of Chicago Ph.D. in meteorology, and one of the world's foremost experts on the great storms the Honduran Indians called *Kukulkan*—God of the terrible wind. But he was also a grown-up version of the six-year-old boy who had once been swept right out of his parents' oceanfront house in Corpus Christi, Texas, when a hurricane came ashore and very nearly killed him and his entire family. It happened on a Sunday afternoon, September 14, 1919. That day, the world as he knew it ended, and his lifelong obsession with hurricanes began. Like Nash Roberts, Robert Simpson did not need anyone to tell him what a hurricane *feels* like, or what it can do.

From his perch at the helm of the National Hurricane Center, Dr. Simpson was watching closely as the reports came in from Navy WR-121 hurricane hunter planes, which had been sent out to investigate this new storm system. In particular, they were looking for the first telltale signs that the system had begun to circulate. It was the deadly spin, however lazy and slow it might be at first, that he was afraid of. Throughout the morning, Simpson monitored the incoming reports as the reconnaissance aircraft flew out to two potential trouble spots: an area near the southwestern Bahamas, and another near Grand Cayman Island. The report from the Bahamas came back negative. No spin. The Navy plane flying back and forth across the tropical wave near the Caymans radioed in that maximum winds had been clocked at 50 knots, and a low-pressure center measured at 991 millibars. Then, a few minutes later, the pilot reported something else: The system was beginning to circulate. The firmament was slipping into a great, slow-turning wheel, like a mandala of clouds.

It was one o'clock that afternoon when Dr. Simpson sent out a weather bulletin that officially christened the new storm:

ADVISORY NO.1 1PM EDT THURSDAY AUGUST 14, 1969

A NAVY RECON PLANE RECONNOITERING A TROPICAL WAVE IN THE
CARIBBEAN THIS MORNING ENCOUNTERED A RAPIDLY DEVELOPING
DEPRESSION WHICH REACHED STORM INTENSITY WHILE THE AIRCRAFT
WAS STILL IN THE AREA. . . . THE NEW STORM, TO BE KNOWN AS
CAMILLE, IS MOVING WEST NORTHWESTWARD 12 TO 14 MPH WITH
STRONGEST WINDS ABOUT 60 MPH OVER A VERY SMALL AREA NEAR
THE CENTER. . . . CAMILLE IS EXPECTED TO MOVE ON A CURVING PATH
TO THE NORTHWEST REACHING THE VICINITY OF THE WEST TIP OF
CUBA EARLY FRIDAY MORNING . . . CONDITIONS FAVOR RAPID
INTENSIFICATION OF THIS YOUNG STORM.

Camille.

It was a French name, meaning "pure, virginal, unblemished." A
sweet, old-fashioned, lilac-scented name, something a maiden aunt
might be called.

A Latin form of the name also had another, more sinister meaning: "Child attendant at a sacrifice."

It wasn't a very big storm. But it was intense, and it was accelerating rapidly.

Studying the steady stream of incoming data, Robert Simpson in
Miami and Nash Roberts in New Orleans felt shivers of nervous antic-
ipation.

It was hard to tell what this thing was going to do.

One thing was sure, though: Only a fool would turn his back on
it now.

CHAPTER TWO

12:00 noon, Friday, August 15
Pass Christian, Mississippi

MARY ANN GERLACH had always had great legs and lousy luck.

Stylish and pretty, she was someone who could always seem to find a man, a job, or a party. When she got to laughing and cutting up, knocking back a few drinks or taking a turn on the dance floor, it was as if the whole world were young. Bobby Gentry's "I'll Never Fall in Love Again" and The Hollies' "He Ain't Heavy, He's My Brother" were big hits that year, and she loved slow-dancing to those tunes with her beau of the moment. She was always surrounded by people, because she was loads of fun to be around. And when she threw back her head and laughed, high-spirited as an unbroken colt, all the men's eyes turned towards her.

Gerlach worked as a cocktail waitress on the graveyard shift, midnight to 8 A.M., at a place called Caesar's Palace. Despite its ostentatious name, it was "just a regular little old nightclub" on the beach in Pass Christian, on the Mississippi Gulf Coast. It was her job to draw men's eyes, and she did it all night long, flirting, laughing, and collecting tips. And when she left work in the morning, she climbed into her brand-new Corvette—one of the sexiest cars on the beach—and continued drawing men's eyes all the way back home to her apartment.

But if God had given Mary Ann Gerlach good looks, He seemed to have taken away a few things in the bargain. A calm and happy relationship with her parents, for instance. Or contact with her children. Or the ability to stay married for very long. She was now thirty-one, and married—mostly happily—to her sixth husband, Fritz. Fritz was a thirty-year-old Navy Seabee who was sweet and funny and kind, and who looked wonderfully handsome in his uniform. They were about to celebrate their second wedding anniversary in four days, on Tuesday, August 19. For Mary Ann, that was a real accomplishment. She'd already given Fritz a diamond ring for the occasion, and he'd returned the favor by giving her a watch with a diamond-studded band. Mary Ann was a sucker for almost anything that glittered. She had a nice little box with a couple of diamond rings left over from past marriages, and some really nice dinner rings and other sparkling treasures. Fritz had also given her a mink, which she kept in a closet, wonderfully soft and shiny with status.

Still, as with many of her patrons at the bar where she worked, having a few laughs and gin-and-tonics at 2:00 A.M., there were plenty of things in Gerlach's past that she'd just as soon not talk about. All those marriages, for instance. She didn't mind getting married, but when the guy started getting jealous and dependent and whining a lot, she'd just bolt. She was a party girl, not really a wife or mother. She'd had three children along the way—two boys and a girl—whom she loved dearly. One of her ex-husbands had custody now, so she didn't get to see them very much.

Then there was her "family"—meaning her mother and her brother, who were the only ones still living. They had not spoken to her in five years. It was so unfair, really. But back when she was living in Jacksonville, Florida, her husband at the time, Denny, had called her mother in a state of complete (and probably drunken) despair. Mary Ann had run off on him, he said, and he couldn't find her, and he was coming completely unglued. He couldn't live without her, he said. Not long afterwards, to everyone's surprise, Denny actually killed himself. Mary Ann always knew he was weak, unstable, and crazy-jealous, and also that he drank too much—but none of that mattered to her mother. Her mom just blamed *her*. So not long after Denny committed suicide, her mom said she didn't want to have anything ever to do with Mary Ann as long as she lived. Fair world, huh? Denny kills himself and *she* gets blamed. But Mary Ann had always been tough and resilient, a survivor. The same high spirits that made her so popular at parties had also pulled her through the many disappointments and setbacks of her life.

Despite it all, Mary Ann and Fritz Gerlach had worked out a more-than-passably-happy life in Pass Christian. The only real problem was that they didn't get to see each other as often as they might have liked. Fritz worked from eight A.M. to four in the afternoon. He also moon-lighted as a bartender on weekends and tended bar one or two evenings a week at the officer's club. So, Mary Ann was often coming in the door at eight in the morning just as Fritz was leaving for work. As they passed in the doorway, they'd exchange a few fond little kisses—or, sometimes, much more. There were mornings when Fritz would wind up dragging her into the bedroom and just have to be late for work. To hell with it.

They had a pleasant one-bedroom apartment in a handsome brick building called the Richelieu Manor, a couple of hundred yards from the beach near the western edge of town. The apartment was on the second floor, with a wall of small-paned windows facing out towards the Gulf. It was a "shotgun" apartment, long and narrow, with a liv-ing room and dining room on the ocean side; a kitchen and bathroom in the middle; and a hall leading to the bedroom at the back of the building. It was modest but comfortable, and a big step up from many of the cheesy apartments Mary Ann had lived in over the years. The best thing about it was that she could sleep during the day. She'd lived in plenty of places where you could hear people talking right through the wall, or people walking around overhead, but the Richelieu was made of poured concrete and brick and was so solid it was almost soundproof.

Mary Ann Gerlach had been born Mary Ann Warwick in rural Georgia, in the town of Hazelhurst, in 1937. She told people she was the great-great-granddaughter of General Braxton Bragg, one of the legendary commanders of Confederate troops during the War of Northern Aggression. She was almost sure it was true, too. Anyhow, saying *that* in the South was like saying you had the blood of kings in your veins. It impressed people, especially the boys.

Her dad had been an enterprising farmer and rural entrepreneur. He owned two farms with sharecroppers, a fertilizer business, a gro-cery store, and a couple of rental properties. Mary Ann had zero in-terest in any of that. No way she was going to stay in that two-bit burg with its insufferable small-town gossip, suffocating heat, and farm news on the radio. She wanted to find the bright lights, the party, and the men. The summer after she graduated from Jeff Davis High School in Hazelhurst, she moved down to Jacksonville, where she had friends and had heard a girl could easily get work waiting tables or being a cocktail waitress. Thirteen years later, in 1967—after multiple marriages, Denny's death, and all the rest of the wreckage—she decided to put Jacksonville in her rear-view mirror and get a fresh start someplace new.

That's when she moved down to the little town of Pass Christian, on the Mississippi Gulf Coast about an hour east of New Orleans. (The name is pronounced "Pass Christi-*ann*," after Frenchman Christian L'Adnier, who discovered the place. Most locals simply call it "The Pass.") Since before the 1900s, The Pass had been a refuge for wealthy people from New Orleans, fleeing the sultry summer heat and (in earlier days) diseases like typhoid and yellow fever. Grand antebellum homes with fluted white columns and wide summer porches grew up along the coast. One two-and-a-half mile stretch of coastline in Pass Christian, called Scenic Drive, contained so many grand homes that in 1965 *U.S. News and World Report* said the concentratiuon of wealth there was comparable to Palm Beach, or to Newport, Rhode Island.

The other thing that immediately struck a visitor's eye were the moss-draped live oak trees, some more than three hundred years old, and ten or fifteen feet around at the base. A local Live Oak Society even named and registered the oldest and most noble specimens; and once in the 1950s, the good ladies of the Pass Christian Garden Club held a round-the-clock vigil to keep the highway department from chopping down a certain particularly notable tree. They succeeded.

The most significant building on the Gulf Coast was Beauvoir (meaning "beautiful view"), the last home of Jefferson Davis, president of the late, great Confederate States of America. Located about fifteen miles up the beach from Pass Christian, the house was genteel but not gaudy, with a grand porch facing the ocean. It was originally owned by a wealthy patroness named Sarah Dorsey, who invited Davis and his family to live there after the South had been defeated in the war. Davis had spent a couple of years in a northern prison and he was nearly broke. He accepted Dorsey's offer gratefully; she eventually sold him the house and he lived there until he died, tending a small vineyard, receiving visitors, and writing his memoirs. Today the house is maintained as a museum and shrine to a man whose birthday is still a school holiday in seven southern states. Pope Pius IX, one of Davis's many admirers, personally wove a crown of thorns and sent it to him in prison. This thorny crown, symbol of the southern sense of misunderstood martyrdom, is displayed in a glass case in the museum at Beauvoir.

But there was another part of the Mississippi Gulf Coast—one that seemed miles away from the grand mansions, the mint juleps, and the good ladies of the Live Oak Society. That was the world that Fritz and Mary Ann Gerlach tended to live in. It was a world filled with cheap motels called Sun-Kist and Lazy-Daze, with all-night bars, used-car lots, pawn shops, and thrift stores. "It was just really a tacky, tacky town and coast, period," Mary Ann said. The people who populated this other world were those who could not afford to live on the water and tended to inhabit the back streets and the bayous. Mary Ann's diamonds and her mink were proof that she wouldn't *always* live there—but for the time being, she did.

The back-street, bayou people were less-affluent whites, young transient males in the military, and blacks. For America's blacks, the 1960s had been been a hard-fought struggle to break through to racial equality, and on the Gulf Coast the battle was fought on the beaches. Blacks who were bold enough to venture onto the twenty-four-mile-long, man-made beach that stretched from St. Louis Bay in the west to Biloxi Bay in the east were setting themselves up for trouble, whether from white landowners or even the police. It was only in 1959 that an open confrontation between blacks and whites near the Biloxi Lighthouse first openly challenged the status quo. The next year, emboldened blacks staged "wade-ins" at Biloxi beach, which triggered a bloody race riot but eventually led to an awkward truce and the first integrated beaches in Mississippi memory.

Still, it was a nice place to live in many ways. There were plenty of clubs where Mary Ann could get work, and also lots of good-looking young men in uniform, because the Gulf Coast was crawling with military types. There was the Navy Seabee base in Gulfport, Keesler Air Force Base just up the beach in Biloxi, Tech-Taf (short for "Technical Training—Air Force"), and all kinds of NASA guys working on the moon shot and other space programs. She'd always loved cute boys in uniforms. And she was lucky enough to have married one of the cutest.

All things considered, she was happy. She had a job. She had a nice apartment and a nice car. She had diamonds and a mink. And she had Fritz.

Maybe Mary Ann Gerlach's luck had finally changed.

THAT FRIDAY, August 15, there were two big stories on the front page of *The Daily Herald,* the main newspaper serving Pass Christian and the rest of the Mississippi Gulf Coast. One was datelined Saigon: U.S. military spokesmen reported heavy fighting along the Cambodian border, where an estimated five thousand North Vietnamese troops were trying to seize control of one of the provincial capitals of Tay Ninh, An Loc or Song Be. The Viet Cong's Liberation Radio said the new offensive was designed to "show our iron will that the longer the Americans prolong their war of aggression, the more they will bleed and die." It had been a terribly bloody week, but no worse than many others. Field reports indicated at least two hundred Americans had been killed in the past four days, with the death toll for the week expected to hit three hundred.

On the doorsteps of America, daily newspapers arrived soggy with blood. In late spring, the Associated Press noted, the Vietnam War had officially claimed more American lives than the Korean War: a total of 33,641. It was even worse on the other side: One day in that summer of 1969, it was reported that 1,450 enemy soldiers had been killed in a twenty-four-hour period. If the war were measured in mountains of dead bodies, the Americans actually seemed to be winning. But it did not feel like victory to anyone.

At the beginning of August, President Nixon announced that the United States would withdraw twenty-five thousand soldiers, the equivalent of a combat division, by the end of the month. He described the withdrawal as a "significant step forward" toward peace in Vietnam. But still no real end was in sight, and the anti-war protests grew angrier and more widespread. When American B-52 bombers launched their biggest attack of the war, activists vowed to demonstrate against the war in more than forty cities and keep it up until the bombing stopped. Thousands marched up Sixth Avenue in New York, and in other cities coast to coast. *The Smothers Brothers Comedy Hour,* a popular television show, was canceled by CBS. The network claimed it was simply a business decision, but the comics countered it was because they routinely lampooned the Nixon Administration and the Vietnam War. The whole fabric of civil society felt as if it were being wrenched apart. Even the comedy shows weren't funny anymore.

The other story in the local paper that afternoon of August 15 had nothing to do with politics or the war at all. The headline read:

CAMILLE, PACKING 100 MPH WINDS, MOVING ON CUBA

According to the story, a small, intense hurricane named Camille was moving north out of the Caribbean towards the western tip of Cuba. Chugging along at about 12 miles an hour, it posed a threat to Florida and the Florida Keys, but seemed to be traveling so far to the east that it posed no direct danger to Pass Christian or the Gulf Coast.

"It's too early to tell what part of Florida or how many of the Keys will be affected, but some of the Keys will have to batten down," Dr. Robert Simpson, director of Miami's National Hurricane Center (NHC), told the Associated Press. Camille was shaping up to be the most dangerous Atlantic storm of 1969, he said.

"This is still a young, immature storm. In this state of development, it could go on to become one of the great storms, or it could rise and fall in intensity as Gladys did last year."

Gladys had moved ashore near Clearwater, on the west coast of Florida, but exactly where Camille was bound was still too early to say. "Somebody will get a pretty good beating," Simpson added.

Nash Roberts, in his private forecasts for offshore clients, pointed out that if by any chance the storm began to turn west towards the Louisiana coast, it would be about thirty-six hours before the gale winds reached the mouth of the Mississippi River. In other words, people in New Orleans would have plenty of warning if that happened. So far, though, the thing looked as if it was going to continue marching steadily north-northwest, towards the relatively unpopulated big bend in Florida's west coast.

At the moment, there seemed no doubt at all that Camille would hit the Isle of Pines, on Cuba's western coast—once the site of an infamous political prison now converted to a school where ten thousand Cuban youths were taught about communism and agriculture. That would be bad news for Fidel, since the harvest of the island's two big money crops, tobacco and sugar, was now in full swing. Ever since coming to power, Castro had been pushing for the great goal of a ten-million-ton sugar crop. The closest he'd ever come was 6.8 million tons, back in 1961. Now Camille was threatening to downsize his communist dreams once again. The Cuban Civil Defense Committee decreed a state of emergency in the Isle of Pines and Pinar del Rio, as wind and heavy rain began raking the area.

Elsewhere in *The Daily Herald* that day, the fashion page ran a spread on French couturier Pierre Cardin, who was introducing his fall and winter fashions with a special "moon collection" for "the world of tomorrow." A model was shown wearing a black cocktail dress ringed by strange protuberances that appeared to be either Hula-Hoops or a haut couture representation of the moon's orbits.

The whole world seemed mad about the moon landings, which had occurred less than a month earlier, on July 20. Two American astronauts, Neil Armstrong and Buzz Aldrin, had deftly landed a small lunar module, named Eagle, on the Sea of Tranquility shortly after four o'clock in the afternoon. "Houston, Tranquility Base here," Armstrong radioed back to earth. "The Eagle has landed." An estimated 600 million people—one-fifth of the world's population—witnessed this moment on television.

A few hours later, the astronauts took a comically bouncy walk out onto the powdery lunar surface, where the gravitational pull was only one-sixth that on earth. President Nixon called to congratulate the men in what he said, "certainly has to be the most historic telephone call ever made."

For days the astronauts had been touring the country, making speeches and accepting awards. Their wives, almost identical in their beehive hairdos, great tans, and relentless smiles, were also in the papers almost every day, dutifully waiting for their husbands to show up for some event or other.

The big news on the sports page was the upcoming pro debut of O.J. Simpson, the spectacular running back and Heisman trophy winner from Southern California. Said to be the most promising rookie since Joe Namath, Simpson had been paid an astounding $300,000 when he signed with the Buffalo Bills.

Elsewhere, J.C. Penney's was having a back-to-school sale on two-tone oxfords for girls—now only $4.88 a pair. On television, the big shows were "Bewitched," "The Flying Nun," "That Girl," and "The

Wackiest Ship in the Army." And in an ironic touch that only fate could have arranged, Pass Christian's Moonlight Drive-in announced that *Gone with the Wind* would begin showing Wednesday.

That Friday, *The Daily Herald* reported not a word about what was going on in upstate New York, where all roads leading to an alfalfa farm near a small Catskill Mountains resort town called White Lake were completely jammed. Troopers on the New York State Thruway had begun asking carloads of kids to turn around and go back home, but most of them refused. "No chance!" one ponytailed kid replied. "This is where it's at." The "it" was something called the Woodstock Aquarian Music and Art Fair, a massive outdoor rock festival featuring an amazing roster of stars: Janis Joplin; the Grateful Dead; Richie Havens; Jimi Hendrix; Crosby, Stills and Nash; Creedence Clearwater Revival; Jefferson Airplane; and The Who.

3:00 P.M., Friday, August 15

All that morning and afternoon, Dr. Robert Simpson monitored the storm from his big desk at the National Hurricane Center. For the past few days, as Camille had tracked north-northwest towards Cuba, deepening and strengthening by the hour, he'd been in communication with a Dr. Rodriguez, his counterpart at the Cuban weather service. He'd only met Dr. Rodriguez in person once, at a scientific conference, but he had enormous respect for his skills as a meterologist. Dr. Simpson also had a very warm and collegial professional relationship with the man. The two of them regularly exchanged weather data, especially in situations like the present, when a potentially dangerous hurricane was making for the coasts of both countries.

Strictly speaking, Dr. Simpson's professional relationship with Dr. Rodriguez was "under the radar." The U.S. government was in no mood to develop anything like official relations with the Cubans, since only seven years earlier, in 1962, the world had been brought to the brink of nuclear war in what came to be known as the Cuban Missile Crisis. But Robert Simpson was a weatherman. He only cared about providing accurate information to his countrymen. So when Dr. Rodriguez began relaying information from Havana radar directly to the NHC, Dr. Simpson was only too happy to accept it. At three o'clock that afternoon, he issued a weather bulletin based partly on Dr. Rodriguez's reports.

BULLETIN 3PM EDT FRIDAY AUGUST 15, 1969

CAMILLE GROWS STRONGER AS IT EDGES CLOSER TO CUBA . . . AN ESSA RESEARCH PLANE TRACKING HURRICANE CAMILLE DURING THE DAY REPORTED A STEADY INTENSIFICATION OF CAMILLE AND SOMEWHAT SLOWER MOVEMENT AS IT CONTINUES TO APPROACH THE SOUTHWEST COAST OF CUBA . . . THE EYE OF THE HURRICANE IS CLEARLY IN VIEW OF THE WEATHER RADAR IN HAVANA WHICH IS SUPPLYING REGULAR REPORTS TO THE NATIONAL HURRICANE CENTER . . . CAMILLE . . . WHILE STILL AN IMMATURE YOUNG HURRICANE WITH A VERY SMALL INTENSE CORE IS NEVERTHELESS THE MOST INTENSE HURRICANE SINCE BEULAH OF 1967. MAXIMUM WINDS ARE AT LEAST 115 MPH OVER WATER.

Mary Ann Gerlach knew about the hurricane from people at the club, who'd read about it in the paper or heard about it on the radio. Even though Camille was now at the Category Three level, nobody seemed particularly worried, since she seemed to be heading towards Florida. Still, for people living along the Gulf Coast, a developing hurricane—no matter how insignificant or far away—always created a buzz of skittish excitement. They were part of the fabric of coastal life, since almost every summer brought news of at least one coming ashore somewhere.

How people reacted to an approaching hurricane was a kind of Rorschach test of their whole outlook on life. The diligent, and those with lots to lose, boarded up their homes, like the industrious ants in the children's fable, then got ready to leave town. The pious, the fearful, and the experienced prayed. Other people—particularly kids or those who felt they had nothing much to lose—saw it as a chance to party.

Gerlach was one of those who saw it as an opportunity to cut loose and celebrate. The first thing that popped into her mind when she heard about the storm, she said later with a laugh, was *"Party!"* She'd been through a few hurricanes, and a few near-misses, down in Jacksonville. Her experience was that, when a hurricane blew through, "for three or four days the lines are down, and you cook out, and you play cards, just have a really good time." It was time off work, time to see friends, time to have a few more drinks than you normally would. It was like a crazy little unplanned vacation. People would go down to the beach and cavort in the great foam-whipped swells, or teeter along the seawalls, balancing in the monster wind. There was a special kind of excitement in the air, a tingle of mortality. In an odd way, the faint whiff of death made everything kind of fun.

News of the northbound hurricane was received quite differently by Wade Guice, the Harrison County director of civil defense. To him, the storm was an occasion to calmly and methodically get prepared for the worst—whether or not it came anywhere near the Gulf Coast. "Civil defense" simply meant helping the community act as one single, coordinated body in the face of disaster, whether it be war, floods, hurricanes, tornadoes, or anything else. Two or three times a summer, a hurricane would begin to develop somewhere in the Caribbean basin, and at that point Guice would jack things up to a state called "increased readiness." No panic, no real action, just gearing up, getting ready, just in case. He'd make sure the schools that he anticipated using as storm shelters were lined up. He'd check with the shelter managers. He'd check with the Red Cross. Top off the fuel tanks. Make sure food and water were available. Get the hurricane precaution sheet ready to take down to the local newspaper. It happened to be a Friday, so he had to hustle up a bit to catch everyone before they left or closed their businesses for the weekend.

Guice (pronounced like "rice") was a big, good-looking man, forty-two years old, who liked to smoke fat cigars and exuded an air of easygoing authority. He loved his job. He seemed born for the role of being shepherd and protector of a small coastal community. About ten years earlier, when he and his wife, Julia, were running a small real estate agency in Gulfport, they had become deeply convinced of the need for developing a defense posture for the community. In those days (the late 1950s) the real fear was nuclear or biological attack by the Soviet Union. Senator Joe McCarthy had succeeded in instilling fear across the nation that communists had infiltrated the highest levels of the US government. At the beach, kids would defiantly scratch in the sand, "Better dead than red!" as if to hold off the communist hordes at the shore.

But the threat of natural disaster, especially hurricanes, was never far away. Wade and Julia Guice had thrown themselves into the task of defending their community against any threat, manmade or natural, as unpaid and overworked volunteers for various agencies. Eventually, they realized they were devoting so much time to the job that they either had to get out of real estate or out of civil defense. So they sold the real estate business. Julia went to work for the city of Biloxi, as its director of civil defense, and Wade went to work for Harrison County, as its director.

"We had never worked harder, made less money, or enjoyed anything more in our lives," Guice said later. "It was simply a matter of setting our priorities, of reassessing our values. It was a tremendous change from that attitude of 'we will become millionaires' to that of 'we will become effective servants.'"

Born in Mississippi in 1927, one of six kids, Wade Guice grew up on the edge of poverty during the Depression. His father nicknamed him "Hardtimes." He remembers wearing cardboard in his shoes to protect his feet from the holes in winter. Grits and day-old bread were staples, supplemented by mullet, which could be caught so easily with a net cast out into the Mississippi Sound that they were known locally as "Biloxi bacon." Still, he says, "Hell, we didn't know we were poor, because everyone was poor!"

His father was restless, always seeking his fortune, and the family moved a lot. "He was always searching for that pot of gold and he tried many, many things," Guice recalls. His father tried farming, he tried the ice business, he tried real estate. The family lived on the Gulf Coast awhile, then when Wade was six years old, they moved to a hardscrabble inland farm up near Hattiesburg. Living there, he remembers, "was a grand way for a youngster to come up." Among his chores was the task of cutting kindling for the stove, and one morning, when he'd badly bungled the job, his mother sat down beside him and kindly gave him his first serious mother-son talk. She was "an extremely beautiful woman in every respect, inside and out," recounts Guice. "She looked deep down into my very soul as only a loving mother can and said, 'Now, I want to tell you something, and I want you to remember this the rest of your life. Whenever you take on a job, regardless of how great or small that job is, you give it the very best that you can."

Wade Guice never forgot those words.

A few years later, when he was eight, Wade, his brother, Charley, and his little sister, Cloe-Joe, were sitting in the kitchen of the farmhouse listening to their mother read the comic section of the newspaper. Suddenly, she looked up from the paper and he saw stark fear in her face. What she had seen was the reflection of a fire on a wall outside the house. They all scrambled out into the yard. Their woodshingle roof was ablaze, apparently from a spark from the fireplace. His mother started to scream frantically for help—a woman alone with three small children, far out in the country, with a house in flames. But there was no one within shouting distance of the farm.

Eight-year-old Wade noticed a ladder lying up against the house, left by repairmen who had been working on the roof. He scrambled up the ladder, looked at the fire, and shouted down:

"Mother, I think we can put this fire out!"

So one woman, two six-year-olds, and an eight-year-old, alone in the country, set about putting out the blaze. Wade organized a bucket brigade, using three gallon milk buckets set up in a relay. His mother filled the milk buckets halfway so the six-year-olds could handle them, Chloe-Joe dragged a bucket to the base of the ladder, and Charley humped the bucket up the ladder, rail by rail. Then Wade, at the top of the ladder, dragged the bucket across the roof to the fire and dumped it on. To save time, he'd just roll the empty bucket off the roof, warning those down below with a shout: "Here comes an empty one!"

Eventually, to Wade's amazement, they managed to put the fire out. Shortly after it was extinguished, a couple of men showed up and acclaimed the young boy a hero. It was "a heavy burden for an eight-year-old to have to carry," he remembers.

Still, he'd had his first taste of civil defense, the teamwork it took to fight back against disaster, and the satisfaction of a job well done. He liked the whole thing well enough that a few years later, he signed up for a wartime civil defense training program for kids, tooling around the neighborhood on his Schwinn bike, wearing a little arm band and a helmet, protecting his nation against the enemy.

Not long after, at the age of sixteen, Wade Guice went to war for real. He left tenth grade to fight in the Pacific, promising his mother that he'd come back and finish high school. He served on a T-2 Tanker, shuttling fuel oil between Okinawa and Saipan, operating a twenty-millimeter antiaircraft gun. He saw other ships get hit by kamikazes, but he and his vessel emerged unscathed. When he got home, he finished high school and went off to Mississippi Southern to begin studying for the priesthood in the Episcopal Church—something that was entirely his mother's idea. One night he saw two bullies beating up a fellow student and he waded into the fray and beat the living daylights out of them. The trouble was, he enjoyed every minute of it. That's when he decided, "a man that's cut out for the clergy shouldn't *enjoy* a fistfight, for heaven's sake!"

And that was the end of his brief and unsuccessful foray into the ministry.

Not long afterwards, he met Julia Marie Cook, "a petite, ninety-seven-pound girl, with dark hair and brown flashing eyes, a real beauty." She was a nice girl, but "quite frankly, I was not too interested in nice girls at that time." Still, they became very fond of each other until one day, rather abruptly, Julia asked him, "When are we going to get married?"

"Well, next weekend is okay with me," he told her.

So they did. And Julia Guice became the love of his life, a devoted wife, business partner, mother of his three children, and the best friend he ever had. She also became a professional ally in the world of civil defense, the profession for which Wade Guice had been born.

In the early days of his work in civil defense, Guice more or less had to make things up as he went along. His first office was in a converted van that he obtained through surplus property; he got electricity by running an extension cord out the window into the office of the president of the Board of Supervisors. In the winter, he heated the place with a kerosene stove. Eventually, he moved into the basement of the courthouse, closer to the centers of power.

Guice was what he liked to call a "shirt-sleeve professional," a guy who really knew how to take action. He favored the KISS system of planning: "Keep it simple, stupid!" He explains, "I have always been offended by these catalogue-size plans, that you have to turn to addendum four, attachment three, appendix fifteen, to find out what the hell we are talking about."

To him, the whole idea of a civil defense program was pretty simple: It was "the fire department, the police department, the ambulance organizations, or the waterworks, all of local government working together in one single coordinated effort to, number one, survive as a community; and then rebuild and restore the community to an effective purpose after a disaster, whatever the disaster may be."

The system that he'd helped develop was severely tested in 1965, when Hurricane Betsy roared ashore. Though the eye of the storm made landfall near New Orleans, an hour away, Harrison County was hit by the right front quadrant, generally the most destructive part of the system. The county sustained about a hundred million dollars' damage.

Even so, operationally speaking, the response of the Harrison County civil defense program to Hurricane Betsy was a huge success. Not a single life was lost, of which Wade Guice was enormously proud. And by putting the system through its paces, Guice and his staff were able to see holes that needed patching and fix them. They tightened up the emergency operations center, streamlined interdepartmental coordination, and just generally got more professional about the whole thing.

He felt reasonably confident that his community would survive, even in the unlikely event that The Big One—a real monster, maybe even a Category Five—came ashore on the Gulf Coast.

But that seemed quite unlikely to happen anytime soon.

CHAPTER THREE

5:00 P.M., Saturday, August 16
National Hurricane Center, Miami

IN THE FLICKERING, greenish glare of the satellite monitors, Dr. Robert Simpson's face gave almost no clue as to what he was actually feeling. To the rest of the staff at the National Hurricane Center, his craggy, bespectacled face was a mask of imperturbable authority. He was, after all, the Center's director and one of the most respected hurricane experts in the world. He was the one to whom millions of Coast-dwellers turned, when they wanted to know which way the Terrible Wind was blowing, and whether or not to flee.

But inside, as Dr. Simpson stared at what was unfolding on the bank of monitors, some small part of him was also a lonely, frightened, six-year-old child.

In a lifetime of studying these savage ocean storms, he had never seen anything quite like this. He'd lived through vast scientific breakthroughs in the human understanding of hurricanes—the birth of radar, and the development of computer modeling, dropsondes, and hurricane-hunter airplanes that could penetrate into the very eye itself—but he had never seen what he was seeing now.

The midsummer tropical wave that had turned into Hurricane Camille off the Cayman Islands a few days ago had passed over the western tip of Cuba shortly before midnight, seventeen hours earlier. His fellow meterologist Dr. Rodriguez, had sent him regular reports from the Cuban weather service in Havana, as Camille continued to gain strength and spin, and the great dark cloud-towers of her eyewall massed into the upper troposphere. By the time she clipped the west coast of Cuba, flattening tobacco and sugarcane fields, dropping ten inches of rain and killing three farmers, her winds had accelerated to 115 miles an hour, making her a Category Three storm.

Once Camille made landfall over Cuba, Dr. Rodriguez noted, her windspeeds decelerated to around 96 miles an hour. This was entirely expected, of course. Passage over land almost always puts the brakes on hurricanes, because they are like giant jet engines, sucking up vast amounts of warm wet air and using it as high-octane fuel. This warm wet air, supercharged with latent heat energy, is the gas that fuels the combustion chamber of the storm. Once its fuel supply is blocked, a hurricane almost invariably downshifts and begins to lose power.

Sometimes the shock of landfall will knock the stuffings out of a storm, causing it to get disorganized and simply rain itself out. What astonished Simpson was that the instant Camille passed back over into the Gulf, she revved up again, regaining her 115-mile-an-hour windspeed in a couple of hours. Then she just kept spinning faster—and faster, and faster. Camille wasn't a huge storm; in fact, she was relatively small, only about 80 miles across. Her eye was only about eight miles in diameter, but the *acceleration* of her windspeed was absolutely amazing. Now, tracking north-northwest across the sparkling Gulf and altering the atmosphere for hundreds of miles around her, Camille's windspeeds had hit an astonishing 150 miles an hour. On the radar monitors she was looking uglier by the minute.

IN 1969, meteorologists tended to rank hurricanes by their most menacing particulars, wind speed and minimum barometric pressure, the way boxers are ranked by their weight, reach, and record. It would be a couple of years later that Robert Simpson and an engineer from Dade County, Florida, Herb Saffir, devised a simple one-to-five scale to rank and categorize hurricanes by their potential destructiveness. As part of a report for the United Nations, Saffir, an expert in wind damage, came up with a table of the damage that could be expected from various wind speeds. Simpson added calculations for damage from storm surge—the mountain of water that sweeps ashore as the hurricane eye makes landfall—which is the deadliest, most destructive aspect of hurricanes. Nine out of ten people killed by hurricanes are killed by storm surge. Taken together, these calculations became

known as the Saffir-Simpson Hurricane Damage Potential Scale, and
are now used by meteorologists in most of the world. (The Saffir-
Simpson Scale will continue to be used throughout, though it came
into wide use a few years after Camille.)

A Category One hurricane, for instance, has maximum sustained
winds of between 74 and 95 miles an hour and causes storm surge of
3 to 5 feet. Since low barometric pressure is one of the most reliable
measures of a hurricane's deadliness and force, scientists also note
that Category Ones have a low-pressure center that drops as low as
980 millibars (normal atmospheric pressure at sea level being about
1,014 millibars). The damage caused by "cat-ones" is considered minimal—they knock down tree branches and flatten shrubs, damage mobile homes, flood low-lying coastal roads, but leave permanent
buildings intact.

A Category Three, by contrast, comes ashore with sustained winds
of up to 130 miles an hour and a 9- to 12-foot storm surge. Barometric
pressure drops to between 945 and 964 millibars. Cat-threes cause extensive damage, toppling big trees and completely destroying mobile
homes. All poorly constructed signs are obliterated. There is structural
damage to small buildings and to roofs and doors. Serious flooding
may occur at the coast and many smaller coastal structures are destroyed; larger structures are damaged by battering waves and debris.

But nothing compares to the abject fear and destruction wrought
by a Category Five hurricane. Category Five means the worst that
could possibly happen. Sheer terror. Cataclysmic damage. And, quite
possibly, death by drowning, asphyxiation, blunt trauma from flying
debris, or the various calamitous bodily reactions of fear: heart attack
or stroke.

Cat-fives have maximum sustained winds of at least 155 miles an
hour. They may cause storm surge of 18 feet or more. And barometric pressure drops below 920 millibars. (This astoundingly low pressure is a primary factor generating storm surge: Like air being sucked
through a drinking straw, low pressure in the hurricane's eye lifts up
the surface of the ocean into a dome-shaped mound of water 18 or
more feet high.) It's important to remember that the damage inflicted
by hurricanes increases *exponentially* as wind speed increases. That
is, if you increase wind speed from 50 to 100 miles an hour, that's a
mathematical increase of 50 percent. But the damage wrought by

these terrible winds is proportional to wind velocity *squared*—or more than four times the destructive force.

One of the eeriest calling cards of an approaching cat-five is also one of the quietest, and hence the most dangerous: Three to five hours before the arrival of the eye, low-lying escape routes from coastal areas may be cut off by rising water. Which means that, as the horror comes roaring ashore, escape is often impossible. Once the storm arrives, damage from Category Five hurricanes is considered catastrophic—something close to complete destruction. Most trees of any size are uprooted or even snapped in half. There is extensive damage to the lower floors of all structures less than 15 feet above sea level within five hundred yards of shore. Most roofs on houses and industrial buildings have collapsed or been ripped away. There is extensive shattering of glass, complete destruction of smaller buildings, and general desolation. Very likely, you are also looking at coastal ghost towns, because there has probably also been massive evacuation of residential areas on low ground within five to ten miles of shore.

Even so, mere enumeration of the damage caused by one of these great storms does not sufficiently convey their spectacular power, nor the dead panic of being trapped in the middle of one. To get some sense of the forces that are unleashed when a hurricane is formed, picture the almost unimaginable destruction wrought by the atomic bomb that leveled Hiroshima in 1945. This weapon was more than a thousand times more powerful than any previous conventional weapon; it represented the most awesome power ever unleashed by man. Its power was measured in kilotons (the equivalent of several tons of TNT). But "the atomic bomb was vastly overshadowed by the hydrogen bomb, whose explosive power is measured in megatons (millions of tons), making it thousands of times more powerful than the atomic bomb," according to Dr. David E. Fisher, professor of cosmochemistry at the University of Miami. Yet the energy released by a hurricane is measured in terms of *thousands* of megatons. "If you could harness the energy released by just one good-sized hurricane in one day, it would supply electricity to all of the United States for nearly an entire year," Dr. Fisher has pointed out.

Category Fives dwarf any other kind of storm on the planet. Cat-fives, in fact, are a cavalcade of wonders, so filled with marvels that they seem to come from some other world than our own. In fact, NOAA hurricane expert Dr. Hugh Willoughby has observed, "The eye-wall of a hurricane is as different from our normal atmosphere as our atmosphere is from that of Jupiter."

On Labor Day of 1935, a Category Five storm slammed into the Florida Keys and killed more than four hundred people, sweeping Matecumbe Key clean of every building and tree. The wind, weaponized with sand, stripped not only the clothing off bodies, but the skin as well, so that skinless corpses were found clad in nothing but leather shoes and belts. The few who survived described seeing an eerie illumination in the pitch-blackness of the storm—high winds had lifted sand granules aloft, generating static electricity that caused flashes in the sky "like millions of fireflies." Other such storms have rammed a two-by-four through the trunk of a palm tree; generated blue lightning flashing sideways in sheets; and swept enormous steel ships from one place to another as if by magic.

Category Five hurricanes are very rare. Since 1886, when record-keeping began, only twenty-three hurricanes have achieved Category Five status over the ocean (about one every five years). Rarer still are cat-fives that retain their astounding windspeeds until they make land-fall. In fact, up to that August day in 1969, in the entire twentieth cen-tury only one Category Five hurricane had made landfall in the US: the great Labor Day hurricane of 1935. In over a hundred years, the only other storm of such magnitude was now in Robert Simpson's radar monitor, taking dead aim not at a sparsely populated chain of islands at the country's nether edge, but heading directly for the heav-ily populated United States mainland.

Her name was Hurricane Camille.

THAT SATURDAY afternoon of August 16th, as Camille hurtled towards the Florida Panhandle, Robert Simpson was growing increasingly des-perate to get a good look at this monster. Almost from the beginning he'd had a very, very bad feeling about this storm. For one thing, there was her amazing rate of acceleration, her *vitality*. She had pro-gressed from 40-mile-an-hour winds to a full hurricane in less than a day, and she still showed no signs of slackening. "It was apparent al-most from the outset," Simpson was to write later, "that Camille would be an explosively deepening storm." For another, there were the satellite photos taken from space, which showed "the most wicked eyewall I have ever seen."

Still, a bad feeling was not the same thing as an informed forecast. What he urgently needed was *information*. Because very soon, it might be up to him to order the evacuation of hundreds of thousands of people—or to stand by while their lives were put in mortal danger.

Like every other forecaster in 1969, Simpson had three main weapons in his information-gathering arsenal. One was coastal radar, which provided a minute-by-minute look at the incoming storm. The second was pictures provided by weather satellites orbiting in space, which had their limitations: The images were fairly low resolution, and since the craft could not be stopped or navigated from the ground, observers had to be content with "fly-by" pictures taken as the satellite periodically flew over the storm. High-altitude cloud cover often obscured the storm's core, making analysis more difficult. In fact, the space data had already become central to an emerging dispute about Camille's potency and power: "Some satellite experts who were analyzing the images were sure the storm was losing intensity," Simpson said later. "I was sure the storm was getting stronger. I was convinced it was becoming close to a *record* storm just from the way the eye structure was changing. We could see the structure, but not what the central pressure was, or what the corresponding strongest winds were."

That's why it was so critical to unleash the third and best tool in the forecaster's arsenal: the hurricane-hunter airplane, which could bore directly into the center of the storm and send back richly detailed, first-hand information. Hurricane-hunter planes and their intrepid crews were the most reliable source of information about the interior workings of hurricanes, including their barometric pressure, windspeeds, and pressure gradients. Of course, flying directly into the eye of any hurricane—much less a Category Five—is not for the weak of heart, to say the least. Over the years, since these perilous missions first began in the late 1940s, four hurricane-hunter planes had been torn out of the sky. A Navy recon plane was lost in Hurricane Janet, over the Caribbean, in September 1955. Three U.S. Air Force planes had been lost in typhoons in the Pacific. Most had vanished without

a trace, and with no word from the lost crews about what those terrible last moments had been like, as the craft tore apart at altitude or
went into a horrific downward spiral into the sea.

The day earlier, Friday, Dr. Simpson had tried desperately to commandeer a plane to send into the oncoming storm. But the Navy,
which was responsible for reconnaissance flights over the Gulf of
Mexico, had ordered most of its airplanes to Puerto Rico in preparation for an experimental flight into another storm, Hurricane Debbie,
which was forming on the heels of Camille. Debbie seemed a perfect
target for one of the first full-scale trials of Project Stormfury, a government attempt to determine if it was possible to weaken hurricanes
by "seeding" them in the same way that clouds are seeded to trigger
rain. The meteorological theory behind the project was complex, and
its prospects were dubious, but there was enough hope that cloud-
seeding could weaken hurricanes that Stormfury had been given the
thumbs-up and the funding. The project director Cecil Gentry would
later be succeeded by none other than Simpson's wife, Dr. Joanne
Simpson, a leading tropical meteorologist and expert in the computer
modeling of clouds.

At this moment, though, all Robert Simpson really cared about
was getting a look inside Camille. Shortly before 1:00 A.M. that morning, he had finally succeeded in getting the Navy to dispatch one old,
decrepit Super Constellation, WR-121 known as a "Connie," to fly out
of Jacksonville, Florida, and into the storm. The pilot reached Camille
just off the tip of Cuba and made repeated attempts to penetrate the
tumultuous winds in the eyewall, but turned back without success.

"The turbulence got so bad the crew was concerned whether the
WR-121 would survive," Simpson said. "Connies are big, bulky planes,
and the eye was a small, tight place. They were entitled to be afraid."

As a general rule, it was thought that when a hurricane's eye is
less than ten miles wide, it's too dangerous to maneuver inside the
eye because there simply isn't enough room to make the tight turns
required to take the necessary measurements while avoiding the turbulent eyewalls.

Nobody could blame the pilot and crew for turning back from
what could have been a fatal mission, least of all Simpson himself. He
had been among the first researchers to fly directly into a hurricane,
back in the late 1940s. He knew about the fear and wonders that lay

up there. In 1947, he'd flown into a hurricane off Bermuda on an Air Force B-29, in an attempt to investigate the storm's structure and currents at high altitude. He expected the storm's top edge to be around thirty thousand feet, or roughly six miles high. But even after the plane climbed to forty thousand feet—nearly as high as the B-29 could fly—the cirrostratus clouds were still inclined steeply higher, like a phantasmal Everest built of ice and air.

As the plane turned toward the center of the storm, Simpson later wrote, "Through this fog in which we were traveling at 250 miles an hour there loomed from time to time ghostlike structures rising like huge white marble monuments . . . Actually, these were shafts of super-cooled water which rose vertically and passed out of sight overhead . . . Each time we passed through one of these shafts, the leading edge of the wing accumulated an amazing extra coating of rime ice . . . We were so close to the center of the storm by the time the icing was discovered that the shafts were too numerous to avoid . . ."

A WHOLE OTHER WORLD was up there, peculiar as Jupiter, a world filled with marble tombstones made of air, and supercooled moisture that looked like apparitions, and ferocious winds that could dismember a body or lift a million tons of water aloft as gently as a fistful of feathers. What other mysteries did these supernatural storms still withhold from human knowledge? Who knew what else lay up there?

But this was no time for airy speculation. What Simpson needed now was an airplane, and he needed it desperately. For almost a full day, as this frightening storm accelerated, he had been "flying blind," without any aircraft reconnaissance to tell him for certain what was unfolding at the core of the great, spiraling storm now spinning towards shore. Finally, after calling everyone else he could think of, he rang up the commander of the Air Weather Service at Scott Air Force Base, in Illinois.

"Look," he told the commander, a two-star general, "we're in a desperate situation here. I've got to get a plane into this storm! I've got to get a better handle on this thing. I may have to order an evacuation of something like a hundred and seventy-five thousand people, and millions of other people along the Coast could be in danger."

The general seemed to understand what was at stake.

"Most of my planes are on the West Coast," he said, "but within the hour, we'll have two planes heading into that storm."

Shortly afterwards, Simpson was in radio contact when an Air Force C-130 reconnaissance aircraft succeeded in breaking through Camille's eyewall, into the eerily clear, low-pressure tower at her core. But when the pilot radioed in the data, Robert Simpson wasn't sure he'd heard him correctly. The pilot reported that the barometric pressure inside the hurricane stood at 908 millibars, or 26.81 inches of mercury. If this was true, it would be the lowest barometric pressure ever measured by a reconnaissance aircraft in the Atlantic. In fact, Simpson wasn't even sure a pressure reading this low was *possible* at this latitude.

"Are you sure this is right? Over," Simpson radioed the pilot. *"Can you take that measurement again? Over."*

The pilot retook the pressure measurement, and the reading held. This creature was rapidly turning into one of the most intense hurricanes of all time. And it was still accelerating.

"This thing is on the make," Simpson remarked to a colleague. "It just won't quit."

What was even more worrisome was that the conditions in the Gulf seemed perfect for Camille to keep right on intensifying. Sea-surface temperatures were extremely warm, more than 82 degrees Farenheit—almost as if the gods were jacking up the octane level of the storm's fuel supply.

There was a remarkable absence of wind shear or other disturbance in the upper atmosphere, meaning that there was little to break up Camille's development into the great saucer-mouthed funnel that was the signature shape of the greatest storms. And, perhaps most worrisome of all, the extreme low pressure at her center now seemed to be drawing from massive moisture sources that were only rarely tapped by hurricanes this far north. Camille was voraciously vacuuming warm air heavily laden with moisture from as far south as the equator. Images from the still relatively primitive weather satellite photography showed Simpson that moisture was being pulled into Camille's rapidly accelerating vortex. Strong "feeder bands," sucking moisture into the storm, were pouring into the center. The satellite picture looked like an immense octopus, its many arms swarming down over the rim of the world.

Taken together, all of this meant that Camille had almost unlimited fuel to burn, and nothing at all to stop her rampage across the Gulf.

The prevailing upper-air profiles suggested that she'd keep tracking to the north-northwest, towards the Florida Panhandle between Fort Walton Beach and Saint Marks, directly south of Tallahassee. But if Camille began veering to the west of her projected track, her incredible storm surge might overwhelm the ring of levees and submerge New Orleans. The loss of life would be unimaginable. The civil defense folks in New Orleans kept tens of thousands of body bags on hand, just in case.

Simpson could not know for certain where Hurricane Camille was headed. He did know this much for sure: In the next six to eight hours, she had the potential to become one of the deadliest storms in American history—perhaps even *the* deadliest. She could be worse even than the great Galveston storm of 1900, which killed between six and ten thousand people—so many people that the bodies were simply stacked up in the harbor and burned like cordwood, so many that bodies were still being found five months after the storm. Galveston's highest winds had been measured at a bit more than 120 miles an hour; the recon aircraft reported that Camille's wind velocity had already accelerated to *one-hundred-and-fifty* miles an hour. The Galveston storm killed so many people primarily because the city, built on an offshore barrier island, was not evacuated. The Weather Bureau's man in Galveston, climatologist Isaac Cline, had dismissed as absurd the notion that a hurricane could devastate the city, and his stance had discouraged any evacuation, as well as the building of a seawall. It also had led to the deadliest natural disaster in US history.

Robert Simpson had no desire to go down in history as the next Isaac Cline.

Fear and loneliness: They weren't scientific emotions, and in the present circumstance they were anything but useful. They did nothing but interfere with Simpson's job. Nevertheless, he felt them, just as vividly as he'd felt them that day half a century earlier, when he was six years old and a hurricane put an end to the world as he knew it.

It was a Sunday afternoon in July—September 14, 1919. He was living in the family oceanside home in Corpus Christi, Texas, along with his parents, his uncle, grandmother, and an elderly boarder who always farted when he came creaking down the stairs. That day, the sky had turned an eerie greenish-gray kind of dark. A firetruck had come trundling slowly down the street, with somebody shouting warnings that a big 'cane was on the way. But big blows, even hurricanes, were not all that unusual on the Gulf Coast of Texas in the summertime. Only three years before, the fire department had sent trucks down his street, warning people to get to higher ground because a hurricane was coming—and people did, mad with fear, taking terrified kids wrapped in blankets, days' worth of food, and even pets, up to the bluffs above town. And then nothing much happened. It just rained hard overnight, and blew down a few trees. That was it. People returned to their houses the next morning, sheepish and wet.

This time, when the fire trucks came by, almost nobody made a move. The sky got darker and greener. A terrible wind began to shake the house. Bobby Simpson scanned his parents' faces, monitoring the fear level, and he felt comforted. They did not seem terribly upset or worried. The main thing he was interested in was Sunday dinner, already laid out on the dining room table: fried chicken, mashed potatoes and gravy, butter beans, hot rolls, and Yorkshire pudding.

That's when the first stage of the storm surge hit, rolling up the long gravel beach, flooding across the road, smashing into the house, rattling the rafters. He checked his mother's face and then he saw it: Fear. Fear and bewilderment that the security and safety and comfort of home could suddenly shudder in an onslaught of the sea.

A neighbor's house dislodged from its moorings and actually began to float. Then another house came loose. Then the second storm surge hit, the big one, sixteen feet high, flooding into the dining room and sweeping Sunday dinner right off the table, the shock of cold brine and seaweed in his face, his mother screaming, his father grabbing for him, loading him onto his back, swimming—impossibly, incredibly—out the kitchen window as the sea-surge swept his family home, with its tidy little pictures and china cabinet, into the bottom of the ocean.

No words could describe the shock of that moment. When the sea and the wind stole his Sunday dinner right off the table, it was the permanent end to the world as he knew it, the end of childhood and the beginning of a lifetime obsession with these great ocean storms, the most destructive force on earth.

Now, half a century later, Robert Simpson found himself sitting at the helm of the National Hurricane Center, studying the stream of incoming data in order to predict where this thing was apt to go, so all the other Bobby Simpsons and their families would know whether to stay or to flee. It was an agonizing place to be. Simpson knew as well as anyone how unpredictable hurricanes could be. They'd sometimes seem to stall out and come to a complete standstill (as Camille had already done a couple of times), then start to move in an entirely new direction. Other times they'd perform crazy loops or curves or even angle back on themselves, like a drunken figure skater. Most of the time—well over ninety percent of the time—they'd simply bear north after entering the Gulf of Mexico. But what hurricanes did "most of the time" was completely useless information; it was what the 'cane would do *this* time that mattered.

Projecting the storm-track of a potentially devastating hurricane was deadly serious business; it was Simpson's life's work, the most serious task he would ever have. He knew very well that his projections of the hurricane's path would be interpreted by civil defense people all across the Gulf Coast and Florida to determine whether or not to evacuate the populace. But evacuations were enormously disruptive and expensive—it was generally acknowledged that they could cost half a million dollars per mile of coastline. What if he got it wrong? You couldn't order evacuations too many times before people would claim you were "crying wolf" and stop listening. If The Big One did come ashore, however, and nobody evacuated, there would be massive loss of life—just as it had happened when he was six years old, in Corpus Christi. That day, about three hundred people were known to have died, though because large numbers of unaccounted-for tourists were not included, the total was probably much higher. Some washed out to sea and were never found. Others were crushed in the wreckage of collapsing buildings. Some were found but never identified, including a baby black girl in a yellow pinafore, called "Snookems" by workers at a local funeral home, who came to symbolize the heart-wrenching chaos of the storm.

Shortly before five o'clock on Saturday afternoon, the NHC sent out a weather bulletin encapsulating Simpson's best understanding of the storm, as well as all his fears:

ADVISORY NO.11 5PM CDT SATURDAY AUGUST 16, 1969

SMALL HURRICANE CAMILLE BECOMES VERY INTENSE . . .

PREPARATIONS AGAINST DANGEROUS WINDS AND 5 TO 12 FOOT TIDES
IN THE AREA FROM FORT WALTON TO ST. MARKS SHOULD BE COM-
PLETED TONIGHT. . . . HIGHEST WINDS ARE ESTIMATED 150 MPH NEAR
THE CENTER. HURRICANE WINDS EXTEND OUT ABOUT 50 MILES AND
GALES EXTEND OUT ABOUT 150 MILES FROM THE CENTER. RECONNAIS-
SANCE AIRCRAFT LOCATED THE CENTER OF CAMILLE NEAR LATITUDE
24.8 NORTH, LONGITUDE 86.7 WEST, OR ABOUT 380 MILES SOUTH OF
FORT WALTON FLORIDA. SMALL CRAFT FROM PENSACOLA TO CEDAR
KEY SHOULD SEEK HARBOR.

There was no longer any question that Camille had become an extremely intense and dangerous storm. The big question now was:
Where was she headed?

At this moment, Camille seemed to be aimed squarely toward the
point where Florida, Alabama, and Mississippi converge on the Gulf.
But the key to understanding where a hurricane will hit is to understand what's *steering* it. In this case, Simpson and his staff at the NHC
were confident that upper-wind profiles showing northwesterly flow
along the southern Gulf would deflect the northward-moving storm to
the east, driving Camille ashore on the relatively unpopulated coastal
bend of Florida.

"Camille is still not showing the northerly turn, but we are expecting that she will," Simpson told the Associated Press. In the meantime,
the NHC had issued a hurricane watch from Fort Walton Beach, on
the Florida Pandhandle, east to Saint Marks, Florida, directly south of
Tallahassee. It looked like the whole "armpit" of Florida was going to
take a hit. Just to be on the safe side, there was also a hurricane *warning* from Fort Walton all the way west to Biloxi, Mississippi.

(There is a good deal of difference between a hurricane "watch"
and a hurricane "warning." A watch means that a hurricane poses an
appreciable threat to a specific area, but there appears to be no immediate danger yet. Most sensible reaction: Don't panic, but keep
posted. A warning means that the storm is headed for you, complete
with winds in excess of 74 miles an hour, heavy rain, and rough seas.
These effects can occur two hundred to three hundred miles from the

hurricane's center. Most sensible reaction: Leave *now*, because it will quickly be too late to change your mind.)

In Pensacola, the Naval Air Station and the Coast Guard were ordered under a "Hurricane Condition Three." So was Eglin Air Force Base, near Fort Walton Beach. A Coast Guard spokesman said "Condition Three" meant "tie down everything you want to keep." The Navy announced it planned to fly its planes out to inland bases in Texas and Tennessee. Eglin also prepared to evacuate its fleet of Strategic Air Force bombers.

IN NEW ORLEANS, Nash Roberts had moved into his Camp Street office, near the French Quarter and was now watching Camille around the clock. He'd begun to develop an intense personal relationship with this girl. Like Simpson, he was amazed and frightened by her. She was a hard-headed woman—ferocious, driven, tempestuous. *Man,* she was tough!

Despite the fact that the NHC continued to predict—with good reason—that she'd soon turn north towards the Florida Panhandle, as the hours went by she just kept pounding along, north-northwest, willful and stubborn and unchanging. Roberts began to have doubts about the predicted northward turn. Camille didn't seem to want to budge; it did not seem to be in her nature. Besides, Roberts also knew that extremely powerful hurricanes can simply alter the atmosphere around them, so that instead of being deflected by a front they simply destroy it and barge on through. If she did that and continued on her current path, she wouldn't run into Florida at all, but hit far to the west, smack into the eastern edge of Louisiana, not too far from Bay St. Louis and Pass Christian, Mississippi.

At 4:00 P.M. that Saturday afternoon, Nash Roberts told his offshore clients that if Camille continued on her current track, "gales would reach the mouth of the Mississippi River around 1:00 A.M. Sunday and the center would reach the eastern coast of Louisiana by midnight Sunday. Evacuation of all locations from South Timbalier area [a coastal region well to the west of New Orleans] eastward by noon Sunday seems advisable based on current data."

THAT SAME Saturday afternoon, nineteen-year-old Pat Michaels and thirty other graduate students took the day off. They were all spending the summer doing field research in various scientific disciplines at a laboratory in Ocean Springs, across Biloxi Bay from the small city of Biloxi.

The grad students got a choice between spending the afternoon fishing or playing ball. Michaels chose fishing. Sitting at the end of the pier, looking out over the bay and idly dangling a line in the water, he couldn't get over the "absolute clarity of the air and blueness of the sky." Later on in life, when he became a professional meteorologist and the state climatologist of Virginia, he would learn that this is characteristic of powerful hurricanes: For hundreds of miles around, they leave the air shimmeringly clear.

The meterology of this phenomenon is elegantly simple. Almost all weather—and until the late twentieth century all human experience—occurs in the lowest part of the atmosphere, called the troposphere, which extends from the earth's surface up to a kind of "ceiling" or atmospheric boundary (called the tropopause) roughly eight to ten miles high. As warm air rises up the great vertical chimney of the hurricane's eye, it eventually reaches the tropopause and then begins to spread horizontally, like smoke rising and then spreading across the ceiling of a room. At these high altitudes, the air begins to cool, causing it to begin sinking in a vast ring around the storm. As the air sinks, it begins to compress and warm. The warmth evaporates moisture, and "sublimates" ice (turning it directly into vapor) so the clouds disappear and the air clears.

For the past few days, Michaels had been paying close attention to the forecasts from the National Hurricane Center in Miami—partly because he was a budding scientist and fascinated by the developing hurricane, partly because he was spending the summer housed in an antebellum mansion a couple of hundred feet from the Gulf of Mexico. Wisdom, as they say, is the better part of valor. So far, though, the NHC's hurricane warning area (the real danger zone) was about 125 miles to the east, in Fort Walton Beach. Ocean Springs was on the far western edge of the hurricane watch area (the nervous zone). At this point, it looked as though the lab wouldn't suffer much more than some rough seas, high wind, and rain. That was all right—in fact, that would be interesting to a youthful weatherman.

Sitting out on the pier that afternoon, Michaels noticed a patch of thickening cirrus clouds on the southeastern horizon. He recognized them as blowoff from the top of Camille—high-altitude exhaust, in the form of ice particles, as she drew moisture from the sea-surface into her spinning core, lifted it up eight or ten miles into the troposphere, then exhaled into the sky.

He noted this remarkable sight, and then went back to fishing.

THE HUSBAND-AND-WIFE team of Wade and Julia Guice, meanwhile, had activated the civil defense departments in Harrison County and the city of Biloxi. True, The National Hurricane Center's forecast put Biloxi (like Ocean Springs) only on the far western edge of the hurricane watch area, but that was just too close for comfort. And anybody who grew up on the Gulf Coast knew how quickly these predictions could change.

Wade Guice held an executive committee meeting at midday, just to touch base with the police and fire departments, shelter managers, and everybody else who might be involved in the event of a disastrous landfall. In an interview with the local paper, he emphasized that if Camille made landfall around Pensacola, Florida, in line with the NHC's predictions, the effects locally would be fairly minimal. If she moved farther west, however, Harrison County would be in genuine danger. He urged people to stay tuned to TV and radio, which in many households meant Nash Roberts, on WDSU-TV out of New Orleans. Roberts was not quite as comforting as the NHC: To hear him tell it, Camille might well come ashore farther west than predicted.

Guice told the newspaper he was asking grocery stores, lumber yards, and other retail stores to stay open Sunday, in case Camille turned and started coming their way, so people could buy food, batteries, candles, plywood, and other supplies. In the event of the storm's intensification, the county's hurricane shelters, all of them in schools, would be opened, Guice said. He also asked anyone who had sandbags to contact the civil defense office.

Just in case.

MEANWHILE, in upstate New York, at the Woodstock Aquarian Music and Art Fair, it had begun to rain. As Camille bore down on the Gulf Coast, the whole eastern seaboard was convulsed by a series of severe storm systems. The first big storm had come around ten-thirty the night before, forcing Indian sitar player Ravi Shankar to stop his performance and scramble for cover while a crew of shirtless hippies unrolled plastic tarps over the sound equipment. By that morning, the weather had cleared a bit, but then it clouded up again, and light rain fell intermittently all day. The festival site was turning into a sea of mud.

The two things Woodstock's producers did not foresee were the crowds and the weather. The original idea for the festival was "three days of peace and music," to be held in the bucolic little Catskill Mountains town of Woodstock, about a hundred miles north of New York City. The producers' expectation was that around fifty thousand people would show up, so that's how much water, food, and parking, and how many Porta-Potties they arranged for. Four weeks before the festival was set to begin, the city council of Wallkill, a town near Woodstock, got cold feet about the potential for crowds and chaos. It backed out on the permits allowing the show, and with only four weeks to go, Woodstock had to be moved to a whole new location—a six-hundred-acre alfalfa farm owned by Max Yasgur, near the small town of White Lake. (Correct: Woodstock didn't happen in Woodstock.) Yasgur's farm had a thirty-five-acre field that formed a kind of natural amphitheater, and it was here that carpenters hastily hammered together what was then the largest performing stage ever constructed, along with eighty-foot scaffolds on either side to hold massive banks of speakers.

Nobody was prepared for what happened next. Instead of fifty thousand, more than four hundred thousand people showed up—a biblical migration that created a fifteen-mile traffic jam streaming into the festival site. On Friday night, folk-rocker Arlo Guthrie yelled out to the rain-soaked crowd, "The New York State Freeway's closed, man. Far out!" Almost overnight, Woodstock had become the third-largest city in the state of New York—but without running water, food, shelter, adequate parking, or medical facilities. The crowd was so vast that many could barely even see the world's largest performing stage. The ticket situation was completely out of control. "Anybody can get in—tickets don't matter," one observer said. The producers had no choice but to call the festival free. It was the first impromptu gathering of what later came to be called Woodstock Nation, and it was riotous, disorganized, and uncomfortable. There were two births, three deaths, and thousands of minor injuries (mostly cuts to bare feet).

Then it began to rain. Over that weekend, the heavens opened repeatedly on the concertgoers at Woodstock. The indelible visuals of that watershed event invariably include images of people huddling in a sea of mud, or stark-naked girls deliriously throwing up their arms in the rain. State police reported that fifty or sixty people had been arrested for various drug violations, including LSD, mescaline, and hashish. Elsewhere in the state, troopers reported arresting another hundred people bound for Woodstock after spot-checks of cars. One car contained a suitcase half filled with marijuana and peyote. At the concert itself, the police, overwhelmed, simply turned a blind eye on kids smoking pot.

"As far as I know, the narcotics guys are not arresting anybody for grass," one state police sergeant said. "If we did, there isn't enough space in Sullivan or the next three counties to put them in."

Before the rain sent everyone scrambling for cover on Friday, Richie Havens and John Sebastian got up on the sound stage and gave solo performances. Then Country Joe and the Fish wound up the crowd with their famous "I-Feel-Like-I'm-Fixin'-to-Die Rag."

On Saturday afternoon, Santana got the crowd rocking with its driving, Latin-rock percussion sound. Filmmakers shooting a movie called *Woodstock* captured a magnificent dark thunderhead blossoming in the sky above the sound stage. A stiff wind picked up, the sky darkened, and on both sides of the stage, the eighty-foot-high speaker towers began to shudder and sway. They seemed in danger of toppling over onto the crowds.

"Get away from the towers! Get away from the towers!" somebody started yelling over the PA system. People scurried to cover the sound equipment with tarps, but they just flapped wildly in the wind, like spinnaker sails at sea. A couple of kids glanced fearfully at the massing thunderhead above them.

"The fascist pigs are seeding those clouds!" one muttered darkly.

As the evening wore on, stoked by the delirium of the crowd, the rain, and controlled substances of all kinds, the great banks of speakers reverberated with performances by Canned Heat, Creedence Clearwater Revival, a drunk and depressed Janis Joplin, Sly and the Family Stone, The Who, and Jefferson Airplane. The Hog Farm, a commune from Taos, New Mexico, took over security. That evening it distributed a mimeographed newsletter to the crowd:

SURVIVE—SURVIVE—BE HIP—SURVIVE
BULLETIN. . . . 8 PM SATURDAY

Welcome to Hip City, USA. We are now the third largest city in New York, and like New York City basic services are breaking down. Gov. Rockefeller has declared us a disaster area. The situation now: limited food, a great scarcity of water, crowded but improving medical facilities. . . . Meanwhile everyone is cooperating and our spirits are good. With the mud, traffic and breakdowns we could be here a couple of days. The festival promoters have been overwhelmed by their own creation. They've created a great free festival, but we can't remain passive music consumers; we must take care of ourselves. If you're hip to the facts below, pull together in the spirit of the Catskill guerilla, and share—everything will be cool. We've had virtually no cops, and there's been no violence. We can take care of ourselves. Dig it!

About the same time, the Air Force C-130 reconnaissance plane and crew that had penetrated Camille's thundering eyewall earlier in the day succeeded in penetrating it a second time. The pilot radioed back the new barometric pressure reading inside the eye, where it was so eerily clear and still that a spangle of stars could be seen overhead. At the NHC in Miami, Robert Simpson could hardly believe what he was hearing. The measurement, 905 millibars, or 26.73 inches of mercury, was even *lower* than the pressure measurement taken earlier in the day—the one that had broken all previous records for Atlantic tropical cyclones.

Camille was turning into a genuine weather phenomenon.

At 10:00 P.M., Nash Roberts sent out another bulletin to his offshore clients. His tone was more strident, and less ambiguous than it had been a few hours earlier: "If present course and speed are continued, the hurricane center would reach the east Louisiana coast between midnight Sunday and 4:00 A.M. Monday. All offshore locations from the South Marsh Island area [southwest of New Orleans] eastward should begin evacuation at daybreak Sunday."

Even so, the National Hurricane Center continued to predict a landfall in Florida, far to the east.

ADVISORY NO.12 11PM CDT AUGUST 16

CAMILLE . . . EXTREMELY DANGEROUS . . . THREATENS THE NORTHWEST FLORIDA COAST . . . LOCATED NEAR LATITUDE 25.8 NORTH . . . LONGITUDE 87.4 WEST, OR ABOUT 325 MILES SOUTH OF PENSACOLA FLORIDA . . . TIDES UP TO 15 FEET EXPECTED IN THE AREA WHERE THE CENTER CROSSES THE COAST . . . HIGHEST WINDS ARE ESTIMATED 160 MPH NEAR THE CENTER.

Only time—a matter of hours, in fact—would tell whose prediction was right.

All that was certain was that Hurricane Camille was now a full-fledged Category Five, a bona fide screaming terror. Wade Guice, monitoring the incoming weather reports, grimly received the latest updates. He knew very well that 15-foot tides and 160-mile-an-hour winds were comparable to the great hurricane of 1947, the Big One, the worst anyone in these parts could remember. It was worse than Betsy, which had caused a hundred million dollars' damage in his county alone.

There was nothing to do now but wait to see which way the wind blew.

PART OF Pat Michaels's job that summer was as a laboratory and field technician in a project studying circadian (daily) activity rhythms of the five species of fiddler crab that populated the coastline. He enjoyed the intellectual challenge of the project, and the fact that it got him out on the beach, day and night. One of the prevailing theories was that—because they all lived so close together—each of the crab species had developed a different niche. Some would make their living down in the tidal zone, tracking the tides, while others farther up the beach would track the sun.

"My lab studies verified this, and I was quite a happy fellow to be experiencing scientific success at the age of nineteen," he remembers.

Part of the study involved field observation, so when the moon was bright Michaels would light up a Coleman lantern, go down to the beach, find a place to sit, and start counting crabs. That Saturday, sometime after midnight, he went out onto the moonlit beach with his trusty lantern to do real field science, and also, if possible, to have a good time. It was a gorgeous night on the Gulf, balmy as velvet, and the sky was filled with stars even though the moon was bright. The celestial tableau was so majestic, in fact, that his attention drifted away from the fiddler crabs scuttling around him in the sand.

He noticed, clearly visible in the bright moonlight, a small thunderstorm forming perhaps twenty miles north of the lab. He watched as the thunderhead slowly unfolded in the moonlight, like a giant cauliflower blossom. He realized that the upper-atmosphere winds that were steering the thunderstorm had to be the same winds that were steering Hurricane Camille, somewhere to the south, out over the Gulf. If the National Hurricane Center's predictions were right, and Camille was moving to the northeast, towards the Florida Panhandle, then this little thunderstorm should be moving in the same direction. It should be moving somewhere to the right of due north.

Suddenly, his breath seemed to stop in his throat.

The thunderstorm was *not* moving northeast.

He watched as ever so gradually, almost lazily, it seemed to come about, like a ghostly ship in the moonlight, and begin drifting to the west. Directly toward Ocean Springs, the lab, and *him*.

He grabbed his Coleman lantern, abandoned the fiddler crabs, and headed for the dorms at a dead run. He had to warn people that Camille was headed this way.

By tomorrow, this place could be gone.

CHAPTER FOUR

5 A.M., Sunday, August 17
250 miles south of Mobile, Alabama,
Latitude 26.9 North, longitude 87.9 West

TEN MILES ABOVE the Gulf of Mexico, at the rim of the great horn-shaped vortex, there was only a deafening darkness and the roar of molecules. Sheets of lightning, electric-blue and glittering, arced across Camille's moonlit maw. For a moment the vast slope-sided throat was visible in metallic light, and down inside, great ragged shrouds of moisture shape-shifting from ice to vapor and back spun furiously up the roaring eyewalls, like ten-mile-high ghosts. As the storm sucked these phantasmal vapors up into the eyewall, they cooled and began condensing, and gray veils of rain cascaded down the interior walls of the tower, releasing great blasts of heat energy, further stoking the inexorable engine of the storm.

The creature was like a malignant organism, sprawling across the curvature of the earth. Its great spiraling arms trailed phalanxes of thunderstorms fifty miles wide and hundreds of miles long. It spun off eddies of cyclonic wind that turned into tornadoes over land, waterspouts over water. It was a kind of gigantic atmospheric machine, feeding hungrily on warm, wet air off the tropical oceans and from as far south as the Brazilian rain forests, down across the equator. This frenzy seemed to feed upon itself: The furiously spinning vortex created a low-pressure center, almost a void, which vaccuumed up heated water vapor from unimaginable distances, convulsing the atmosphere up to the edge of the stratosphere more than ten miles high. The inrushing, heated air fueled the spin, which deepened the void, further accelerating the storm. The result was a colossal convection cell—actually, hundreds of cells organized into a great ring by the spinning vortex—so powerful that it swallowed up a quarter-million tons of water vapor every second, a total cargo of over two billion tons of water drawn up into the air and held there as if it weighed no more than a hummingbird.

Strangely, pouring down the center of the storm's eye was a warm, gentle channel of downrushing air. Nature's little joke: At the very heart of this savage storm, there was a downdraft, an exhaled breath, soft as a summer day. But an unearthly stillness surrounded this descending plume so that straight up through the eye, the velvety, moonlit heavens were clearly visible, glittering with faraway stars— the distant crucibles of matter where atoms, riven to their core, released the power that fuels the universe. This storm bore more kinship to those distant star-forges than to the tiny, wretched humans far below, most huddled fearfully in their darkened houses or storm shelters, listening uneasily to the tempest outside their doors.

The storm's sound was entirely inhuman. People who have heard the noise and lived to tell of it said it reminded them of things they knew—the roar of freight trains, jet engines revving on the runway. Sometimes the wind's scream accelerated up above human hearing, a piercing shriek that simply disappeared somewhere above sixteen thousand cycles per second. In truth, it was a sound that came from the crucibles of heaven, from the anvils of the stars. The result was chaos, a numinous darkness, and rain beyond reckoning.

PAT MICHAELS raced up the beach toward the dormitories at the lab in Ocean Springs, his Coleman lantern swinging wildly in his hand. When he got there, he pounded on the doors and started yelling.

"The hurricane has changed direction—it's heading *here*! You gotta get up! We gotta get out of here!"

But the sleeping grad students reacted only with groans. They all knew that, before they went to bed the night before, the NHC had said the storm was not headed this way. Besides, it was barely four o'clock in the morning. If they were going to get out of bed, they needed an authoritative reason to do so, not just the hysteria of some nineteen-year-old fiddler crab technician.

About the same time, on the incoming radar images at the NHC in Miami, Robert Simpson saw Camille begin her ominous turn to the

west. Within the hour, his office sent out an updated advisory, filled
with truly worrisome news for the people of Pass Christian, Bay St.
Louis, and Gulfport, Mississippi:

ADVISORY NO. 13 5AM CDT SUNDAY AUGUST 17, 1969

CAMILLE . . . EXTREMELY DANGEROUS . . . SHIFTS A LITTLE WESTWARD . . .
THREATENS MISSISSIPPI, ALABAMA AND NORTHWEST FLORIDA
COASTS . . . HURRICANE WARNINGS HAVE BEEN EXTENDED WESTWARD
TO NEW ORLEANS AND GRAND ISLE LOUISIANA. . . . PREPARATIONS
AGAINST THIS DANGEROUS HURRICANE SHOULD BE COMPLETED AS
EARLY AS POSSIBLE TODAY . . .

HIGHEST WINDS ARE ESTIMATED 160 MPH NEAR THE CENTER . . . TIDES
UP TO 15 FEET ARE EXPECTED IN THE AREA WHERE THE CENTER
CROSSES THE COAST. THE CENTER IS EXPECTED TO MOVE INLAND NEAR
MOBILE TONIGHT . . .

GALES WILL BEGIN IN THE WARNING AREA TODAY AND REACH HURRI-
CANE FORCE FROM BILOXI EASTWARD ACROSS COASTAL ALABAMA AND
EXTREME NORTHWEST FLORIDA BY LATE THIS AFTERNOON OR EARLY
TONIGHT. EVACUATION OF THE LOW LYING AREAS THAT WOULD BE
AFFECTED BY THESE TIDES SHOULD BE DONE AS EARLY AS POSSIBLE
TODAY BEFORE ESCAPE ROUTES ARE CLOSED.

Within half an hour after the NHC's newly revised advisory had
been sent out, the administrative director of Ocean Springs Laboratory
was the one pounding on every dormitory door he could find.

"NHC has changed their forecast! They say she's headed *here!*"

By first light, the shimmering blue skies of the day before had disappeared completely. Now, south into the Gulf, the sky was frighteningly dark. Traffic was already streaming north out of town. The local
stores were filling up with people buying batteries, food, jugs of water, flashlights, and plywood.

Pat Michaels and twenty of his fellow students decided they'd try
to ride the storm out in the lab's new dormitory, a building that had
been designed specifically to withstand a hurricane's storm surge. The
roof was held up by immense steel girders secured by heavy-duty

wire cable and anchored in a concrete slab. The students took up a collection, went to town, and bought batteries, canned food, and every bottle of Jax beer they could find.

Stores were so swamped with people buying hurricane supplies that many places were sold out by noon. Store owners started criss-crossing plate glass windows with duct tape, or boarding them up completely with plywood. Old hands pulled out precut pieces that they'd stored from previous storms. The 9:45 A.M. Mass at Nativity BVM Church in Biloxi was interrupted by hammering, as carpenters nailed plywood over the stained glass windows. The fourteen stations of the cross slipped into the dark.

There was a crazy, edgy excitement in the air. The winds were picking up, but it wasn't even raining yet. Kids romped in the great, oily swells rolling in off Mississippi Sound, as if this were a big, un-expected surf party. The animals sensed something more menacing. Rosemary Tully, a social worker in Gulfport, noticed that her cat was extremely agitated that day. The animal wanted to go out; he wanted to come back in; he wanted to go out. He jumped madly from seat-back to seat-back, eyes wild, hair on end. She also noticed that the flocks of seabirds that normally populated the coast—pelicans and seagulls and terns—seemed to have completely disappeared.

Johnny Longo, an alderman for the city of Waveland, also noticed the absence of seabirds that day. It was eerie, how silent the Coast had become. As the storm drew closer, he also noticed that breathing was becoming more difficult. The barometric pressure was dropping so rapidly that it made you feel out-of-breath just standing still. The air felt muggy, still, and oppressive. An old-timer who lived next door told him, "That means it's a bad one coming."

Gerald Peralta, police chief for the city of Pass Christian, had driven over to Gulfport the night before, and he too had sensed some-thing spooky in the air. Because he'd lived in the Pass his whole life, "you could tell something was going to happen. It was—I just can't describe it to you—it was a quiet, still, 'something's coming' night."

GLIMPSED from high above—from an orbiting weather satellite, for ex-ample—the most arresting feature of the incoming hurricane was its graceful, multi-armed spiral. At the center of the spiral was the eye, clear and eerily still; and revolving around the eye was the roaring, ten-mile-high vortex of the eyewall, a kind of immense smokestack formed by a closed ring of intense tropical thunderstorms. Spinning out from the center of the spiral were the great, trailing arms known to meteorologists as rainbands—a hundred or more smaller thunderstorms, veiled with rain and savagely turbulent, embedded within the spinning vortex now bearing down on the little town of Pass Christian.

The spiral is one of nature's favorite geometric forms—imagine the whorls of the nautilus shell or the petaled face of a giant sunflower—yet it remains a mystery why hurricanes are structured as gracefully curving, logarithmic spirals. DNA, the instruction book of all life, is a microscopic double spiral. The same pattern is repeated, on an unimaginably grander scale, in deep space: Many galaxies observed through a telescope manifest themselves as great, curving reams of stars interleaved with cosmic dust—flickering spirals spinning about the galactic core. The "whirlpool galaxy," known to astronomers as M51, is a spiral that looks almost precisely like a hurricane—except that it is sixty-five thousand light years across. Yet after decades of observing hurricanes with satellites and reconnaissance aircraft, and after countless mathematical simulations on supercomputers, this most basic property of the hurricane vortex—the sheer beauty of its spiral—still remains to be unequivocally explained by theorists.

The basic mechanics of the hurricane "heat engine" are better-understood. Hurricanes are born over balmy tropical oceans in the midlatitudes, in the late summer and fall, when the sea's surface temperature has warmed to at least 80 degrees Fahrenheit. All hurricanes derive their energies from the great, ghostly evaporation of water from these warm tropical oceans. Once it is formed, a hurricane is basically a colossal heat engine that feeds off this superwarm sea surface, ingesting, processing, and exhausting massive amounts of moisture. In the process, key energy transformations occur, as vapor shape-shifts into water, water turns to ice, and each of these transformations further stokes the engine of the storm. The engine is governed by the rules of thermodynamic efficiency, which lay down a couple of simple laws: The warmer the underlying ocean surface and the colder the tops of the clouds, the more rapidly the engine will run. To the benefit of all mortals, there is an upper limit on both of these boundaries, so that only in extremely rare instances does the hurricane tachometer blow past the 180-mile-an-hour mark.

Hurricane Camille was one of those extremely rare instances.

The hurricane gathers the sun's heat from an enormous expanse of sea surface and pumps it into a low-pressure center, where the air begins to spiral and rise, drawing in more warm, wet air to fill the void, forcing it to rotate faster and faster. As air rushes inward toward the center of low pressure at ever-increasing speeds, that air expands because atmospheric pressure decreases. This process is fed continuously by the warm sea surface, which releases enormous amounts of water vapor through evaporation, a process that is accelerated by inrushing hurricane winds fanning the foamy whipped surface of the sea. As wind speeds increase, ocean spray is ripped from the crests of waves and churned into the air, creating a kind of flying froth. Once the wind accelerates to around 75 miles an hour, so much air and water are whipped together that there is no longer a clear distinction between the firmament of sea and the firmament of sky. Up has become down and down has become up.

All this warm, soggy, rapidly evaporating air—hurricane fuel—rises in ascending spirals inside the tower formed by the circulating thunderstorms of the eyewall. As the air rises, it begins to condense and fall as rain. This releases heat energy, which warms the inside of the eyewall clouds, increasing their bouyancy and causing the storm clouds to ascend to enormous heights, ten miles or more, high into the frigid upper troposphere.

Eventually, though, these ascending spirals of buoyant air collide with the tropopause, the "ceiling" of the troposphere. This atmospheric boundary is a layer of air in which, rather suddenly, air temperature stops growing cooler with height and instead begins growing warmer. This abrupt temperature reversal—akin to the sudden layer of warm water that swimmers sometimes encounter when diving into a cold lake—acts like a lid on a pot of boiling water. The rising air, its upward progress impeded, begins to spread laterally, forming an anvil-shaped overhang at the stormclouds' summit. Some of the air loses energy by radiating its warmth to space, cooling like the embers of a dying fire. Some of the air spreads inward, converging over the center of the eye and then, as it cools, gently descending down the hurricane's throat. The rest of the air spreads outward, forming a high-altitude ring around the hurricane's eyewall; when this air cools, it descends around the towering eyewall like a kind of down-going sleeve. By virtue of the earth's rotation, this sleeve acquires a slow, counterclockwise spiral as it descends. In effect, the hurricane becomes a series of interlocked, ascending and descending spirals—its savagery and power matched by an elegance akin to that of the nautilus shell or the double helix of DNA.

At the center of the mature hurricane, in the mid- to upper altitudes, air temperature begins to rise because as air descends into the core it becomes increasingly compressed. Ultimately, air temperature in the vortex core can rise as much as 25 degrees Fahrenheit above the surrounding air temperature—meteorologists refer to this as the hurricane's "warm core." In fact, in satellite images that use thermal sensors, the hurricane stands out as a hot spot in a cold sea of tropical air, and the hot spot expands and glows brighter as the storm intensifies. It's tempting to compare the storm's warm core to the body heat of a living organism.

The warm core "is the heart of the hurricane engine," according to NASA meteorologist and hurricane expert Dr. Jeffrey B. Halverson. Because the air in the core of the hurricane is so much warmer than the surrounding air in the eyewall, it is less dense and thus weighs less. (In other words, there are fewer molecules occupying a given space and thus less atmospheric mass pressing against the ocean surface.) So as the air in the core warms, central pressure falls. As the difference in air pressure between the core and the eyewall, known as the "pressure gradient," increases, the inflow of air to the low-pressure center accelerates. (This is why the lower the central pressure, the higher the wind speed.) As more moisture-laden air is vacuumed into the core, it ascends in a counterclockwise spiral, rising to an altitude where it condenses into rain, which releases heat energy, which impells warm updrafts higher into the troposphere, which draws more air into the machine, which starts the whole process over again.

A hurricane is not a "perpetual motion machine"—even the greatest of all hurricanes spin themselves out in a matter of days—but once the process is set in motion, nothing on earth matches its fearful power. And nothing in man's power can stop it or even slow it down.

ROBERT TAYLOR was up before sunrise that Sunday morning. He was
a forty-year-old lawyer from Gulfport, a Korean War veteran and an
avid, lifelong sailor. The morning's mission was to take his beloved
thirty-four-foot ocean-racing sloop, the *Morgan 34*, from the small-
craft harbor in Gulfport around to the shelter of Back Bay, behind
Biloxi, a distance of ten or twelve miles up the coast. There he could
moor her and hope she'd be safe from the incoming storm, which
seemed to get worse with every new weather update.

So far, 1969 had been a terrible year for Bob Taylor, and losing his
boat was a blow he wasn't sure he could take. Earlier that year, his
house had caught fire. Then he'd badly blown out one knee. But by
far the worst that had happened was the death of his beloved wife,
Beverly, after a prolonged, ugly fight with cancer. He'd met the rav-
ishing Beverly Ann Glass not long after graduating from Tulane
University Law School in New Orleans. She was a statuesque blonde,
a graduate of Duke University—an uptown girl from New Orleans,
who'd agreed to move to the small town of Gulfport and be a lawyer's
wife shortly after they married in 1957. When Bev died in May, Taylor
had been beside himself with grief. He was bereft in every way, emotionally, mentally, physically, and financially. In the months after her
death, he struggled to "reestablish myself as a person and establish my
law practice," but every step was like slogging through deep mud. His
father had taken him fly-fishing for salmon in Newfoundland that
summer, and that seemed to help a little. What seemed to help more
than anything, though, was racing his sailboat, the new love of his life,
Morgan 34. That summer, he really didn't remember anything of consequence except for returning to work, trying to live with his grief,
and getting out in the boat.

Taylor arrived at Gulfport Harbor before first light that Sunday,
around five in the morning. A good-natured, generous man, he was
an experienced seaman, and rather than tend to his own boat, he
quickly became involved in helping other people get theirs moved to
safety. Some couldn't get their engines started; some lacked man-
power or were having other problems. So Robert Taylor helped those
guys get going. As a consequence, the *Morgan 34* was one of the last
three boats to leave the harbor and head up the coast for the Back
Bay of Biloxi. Taylor's friend Billy Barrett, a young bachelor, showed

up at the harbor and decided to help him motor up to the bay. The two of them had almost made it into the lee of Deer Island, close to the mouth of the bay (and safety) when the first morning line of squalls from Camille started slamming the boat relentlessly inshore. They fought to get the storm sails up, but the wind was too stiff; they were just driven back against the shore, like a fallen leaf. They struggled to get into the lee of Deer Island, out of the wind, but they couldn't manage to do it. Finally, they decided to give up and return to Gulfport harbor.

By now, the seas and the wind had grown so wild that the two men began to have trouble even bringing the sloop into the harbor, because of the narrow channel leading into the marina. As they were attempting to come in the channel, a powerboat was—somewhat inexplicably—on its way out to sea. Despite his deft seamanship, Taylor worried that he might collide with the other boat, because he had so little control in the high wind and smoking seas. Moments after the powerboat made it clear of the jetties at the mouth of the channel, its engine died. Powerless and adrift, the boat immediately blew back onto the rocks on East Pier, and the two crewmen jumped off onto the shore. Within seconds, the boat began disintegrating against the rocks. Camille was simply pulverizing it, breaking it into splinters in moments.

And she was still more than two hundred miles offshore.

Bob Taylor had been living on the Gulf Coast during the great storm of '47. He'd seen that monster turn Highway 90, the coast road, into nothing but a jumble of concrete. He'd seen it completely destroy the yacht harbor, lifting off roofs like paper party hats, but he'd never seen anything like this.

He and Barrett managed to get the sloop into the harbor and secure her as well as possible in the teeth of the wind. They took out all the electronic gear—radios, sonar, depth-finders—and stowed them in the trunk of Taylor's car to keep them dry. They stopped briefly at the yacht club to help manhandle bulky canvas sails and rigging upstairs for storage, and to take pictures down from the walls so they wouldn't blow off in the storm. Afterwards Barrett went home and Taylor stopped by the store to buy batteries, candles, and some canned goods.

Then he headed home.

He had to decide—quickly—whether to ride this thing out, or to bolt.

JANICE STEGENGA slept late that morning. For her, "late" meant nine o'clock—she was a young mother with a three-and-a-half-year-old child and a three-month-old baby, and just being able to sleep through the night was an unexpected gift that her husband, Harry, had given her. Today was Harry's twenty-eight birthday. She was supposed to be giving *him* the gifts! He brought her the baby in bed and she lay there dozing, with the infant's warm little musty-smelling head next to hers. She was almost entirely unaware of what was occurring outside their little house in Pass Christian, a couple of streets back from the beach. With two small children to take care of, she really didn't have time to read the papers or even listen to the radio much— and two weeks earlier, lightning had zapped the television set. She was living in a media-free cocoon of young motherhood, consumed with nursing and changing diapers.

Just then she heard a fire whistle down the street. In the Pass, they had a whistle system to activate the local volunteer fire department. The town was divided into "wards," and if there was a fire, a whistle would call up the volunteers in that ward to supplement the regular, full-time firefighters. Janice lay there in bed, counting the whistles to figure out where the fire was.

One, two, three, four, five, six, seven, eight . . .

Wait a second, she thought. There weren't eight wards in Pass Christian. What was going on? She went to the radio and flipped on the Gulfport station.

"Repeat, as of five o'clock this morning, we are advised by the National Hurricane Center that Hurricane Camille has turned to the west and is now bearing down on the Gulf Coast. Hundred-and-sixty-mile-an-hour winds, folks, maybe higher! That's very, very serious. That's Category Five. We're now in the center of the hurricane warning area, and Harrison County Civil Defense Director Wade Guice has advised all residents of the county to seriously consider evacuation, or moving to a shelter, before it's too late to change your mind."

Janice and Harry quickly went into a scared, hasty huddle. What should they do? This house they lived in was owned by Harry's Dutch parents, Piet and Valena Stegenga. The house was old, and Janice worried that it might not withstand the wind. She didn't worry about the water—Piet and Valena had told her that during the great hurricane of '47, this property was like an island. Water came up around it, but the lot stayed completely dry. The Stegengas liked to tell the story of the old man who lived next door, who always said that anybody who owned their property would never have to worry about hurricanes.

"When the water touches that land, half of Pass Christian is going to be gone!" the old man had said.

For a while, Harry and Janice considered going to his grandmother's house, where they'd stayed during Hurricane Betsy, four years earlier. Then the worst that had happened was they'd heard wind whistling in the antenna and a few tree limbs had fallen. But Grandma and Grandpa were old, and they'd be upset by a little crying baby. Finally, the young couple decided to stay at Harry's cousin's home, over in Long Beach, the neighboring town up the coast. The cousin had a brick veneer house that would at least be safer than their own.

Harry, who'd lived on the Gulf Coast his whole life, quickly made hurricane preparations, readying the house for their departure. He turned off the butane tank in the yard, to prevent explosions. He unplugged everything. He stacked rugs and radios and furniture up off the floor. He cracked the windows to equalize pressure, if the eye came through. He filled their little Volkswagen Beetle with family heirlooms and pictures. Then he and Janice loaded the kids into the car, along with Harry's half-sister Loretta, who'd shown up at the last minute and decided to come with them. They stopped at a gas station to top off the tank, knowing that if the hurricane knocked out the electricity, gas pumps wouldn't work.

When they arrived at his house, they were dismayed to find that Harry's cousin didn't want them staying there. He didn't think the house would stand—even though Janice and Harry felt sure that his house was stronger than theirs.

"Well, if it gets really bad, we'll just go sit in the hall," Janice suggested gently. But Harry's cousin wouldn't go for it. He was taking his family somewhere else, farther back from the beach and at a higher elevation. Janice, Harry, Loretta, and the kids decided the best thing to do was to go to the hurricane shelter at Quarles Elementary School, in Long Beach, about two miles inland. Staying at a shelter would probably be crowded, noisy, and uncomfortable, but it would also be safer than staying home.

At this point, they really had no choice.

"GOOD MORNING! What I have in mind is breakfast in bed for four hundred thousand!" It was almost noon that Sunday when Hugh Romney, better known as Wavy Gravy, founder of the Hog Farm commune, lifted his voice out over the muddy wreckage and the disheveled masses at Woodstock. "Now it's gonna be *good* food and we're going to get it to you. It's not just the Hog Farm, either. It's everybody! We're all feedin' each other. We must be in heaven, man! There's always a little bit of heaven in a disaster area!"

Woodstock had, indeed, turned into a disaster area—with round-the-clock entertainment. Shortages of food, water, and medical supplies were acute. In an eerie echo of Vietnam, military helicopters were flying in food, and flying out the most serious medical cases. "We have reached as close to the critical point as possible," Dr. William Abruzzi, chief medical officer of the festival, told the Associated Press. A chartered plane brought in seven doctors, nurses, and related personnel from New York City to man the hastily erected medical tents, but many more staffers were still needed. There were acute shortages of hypodermic needles and tetanus serum, which was especially important because so many festival fans were barefoot and getting cut walking around in the mud. A "freak-out tent" was set up for kids having bad reactions to the cornucopia of illegal substances that were freely available. One security guard remarked acidly, "This isn't a music festival—it's a drug convention."

Still, almost everyone, police included, was struck by how peaceful, polite, and well mannered the crowd was. "There has been no violence whatsoever," one medical officer said. "These people are really beautiful."

The music had gone on all night. Grace Slick and Jefferson Airplane's set had only ended around 8:00 A.M. this morning. Their performance was weak and dispirited, though, because they'd been up all night, waiting to go on, and the band seemed overwhelmed by the size of the crowd. More rain was expected today. After the feeding of the four hundred thousand, British rocker Joe Cocker got up and started doing his weird, epileptic gyrations for the crowd. He was just ending his set around three when a pounding thunderstorm broke, complete with atmospheric pyrotechnics. People scrambled for what little cover there was. It rained, hard, for an hour and a half, until finally some people just gave up on the whole idea of clothes and started walking around naked. There was so much rain, and so much mud, that afterwards it was discovered that the giant Woodstock sound stage had actually slipped six inches downhill.

The crowd began chanting between claps of thunder:

"No rain! No rain! No rain! No rain!"

ABOUT THE SAME TIME, early that Sunday afternoon, an Air Force WC-130 reconnaissance plane piloted by Marvin A. Little once again penetrated the roaring eyewall of Hurricane Camille, out over the Gulf. By now, she was less than a hundred miles from the mouth of the Mississippi River and bearing north-northwest at about fifteen miles an hour. The copilot, Robert Lee Clark, later wrote a description of what it looked like up there:

"Just as we were nearing the [eye]wall cloud we suddenly broke into a clear area and could see the sea surface below. What a sight! Although everyone on the crew was experienced except me, no one had seen the wind whip the sea like that before . . . Instead of the green and white splotches normally found in a storm, the sea surface was in deep furrows running along the wind direction . . . The velocity was beyond the descriptions used in our training and far beyond anything we had ever seen."

The descriptions of sea-surface turbulence Clark had learned about in training were based on 150-mile-an-hour winds. Dr. Robert Simpson, monitoring the crew's radio report back to the NHC, decided to jack up the estimates of Camille's wind speed to an almost-unprecedented 190 miles an hour. But what really floored him were the central pressure readings. Clark, Little, and the intrepid crew radioed in a central barometric pressure reading of 901 millibars, or 26.62 inches of mercury. That would make Camille second only to the great Labor Day hurricane of 1935, which developed a central pressure of 26.35 inches, at the time the lowest ever recorded in the western hemisphere.

If she kept this up, Camille would be only the second Category Five hurricane to make landfall in the United States in the twentieth century—and the only one to hit the mainland. She was turning into the "landmark storm of the century," Simpson would later say. And she just kept getting scarier. This time, she very nearly took down the Air Force pilot and crew. During the course of penetrating the eye, the plane lost one of its four engines and made a hair-raising escape from the storm area, only narrowly succeeding in making it back to Ellington Air Force Base near Houston. It was the last flight anyone was to make into Camille.

In his laconic way, Simpson later noted the crew's heroism in a written report: "This flight had performed an outstanding service in establishing the fact that Camille unquestionably was a storm of record-breaking proportions. This permitted the ESSA [Environmental Sciences Service Administration] Weather Bureau to advise all interests that Camille would bring wind violence and high tides greater than had been experienced by any previous storm."

At the same, a newly developed forecasting tool called the SPLASH model was providing Simpson with even more dire predictions. The SPLASH model (short for Special Program to List Amplitudes of Surges from Hurricanes) was a way of using computers to predict the height of the storm surge from an incoming hurricane. When Weather Bureau technicians ran the SPLASH model on Camille, they came up with something truly terrifying: a storm surge of more than twenty feet.

Most forecasters thought a twenty-foot storm surge was ridiculous, according to Bob Sheets, a later director of the NHC, who in 2001 wrote about Camille's hair-raising approach to land in a book called *Hurricane Watch: Forecasting the Deadliest Storms on Earth*. But Simpson took the new information seriously. Though forecasters at that time were advised to keep their predictions fairly general—such as "strong winds and dangerously high water are expected"—Simpson took the bold step of predicting that Camille's storm surge could be higher than fifteen feet.

Shortly after the recon flight returned, the NHC sent out a new, updated bulletin:

BULLETIN 5PM CDT SUNDAY AUGUST 17, 1969

CAMILLE . . . EXTREMELY DANGEROUS . . . HURRICANE FORCE WINDS
EXTEND OUTWARD 60 MILES AND GALES EXTEND OUTWARD 180 MILES
FROM THE CENTER . . . HURRICANE WARNINGS ARE IN EFFECT FROM
NEW ORLEANS AND GRAND ISLE LOUISIANA EASTWARD ACROSS THE
MISSISSIPPI, ALABAMA AND NORTHWEST FLORIDA COAST TO
APALACHICOLA . . . PREPARATIONS AGAINST THIS EXTREMELY
DANGEROUS HURRICANE SHOULD BE COMPLETED BEFORE DARK . . .

THE FOLLOWING TIDES ARE EXPECTED TONIGHT AS CAMILLE MOVES
INLAND . . . MISSISSIPPI COAST GULFPORT TO PASCAGOULA 15 TO 20
FEET . . . PASCAGOULA TO MOBILE 10 TO 15 FEET . . . IMMEDIATE EVACU-
ATION OF AREAS THAT WILL BE AFFECTED BY THESE TIDES IS ADVISED.

Mary Ann Gerlach got off work at the club that morning at the
usual time, 8:00 A.M., having worked all night. Her husband, Fritz, had
worked part of the night at the officer's club, and both of them were
beat when they got back to their apartment at the Richelieu. They'd
heard about the hurricane at work, of course, and interpreted it as a
chance to live it up a little. Mary Ann went out and bought "all kinds
of stuff to fix, you know, sandwiches and hors d'oeuvres and got a
bunch of stuff to drink. We were all going to get together and have a
nice big party." Since she'd just gotten off the night shift, she and Fritz
decided to lie down and get some sleep before going upstairs to the
party that was developing up on the third floor.

The apartment manager, Merwin Jones, told the Gerlachs that the
Richelieu was the safest place to be on the beach. In 1965, when
Hurricane Betsy came through, water had gotten up to about seven
feet deep in the first-floor apartments, but the building came through
just fine, he said. It was structurally sound, with a framework made of
steel beams. Mary Ann knew very well how soundproof the concrete-
slab floors in the building were. Besides, there were even black and
yellow signs downstairs in the building, designating it as a civil defense shelter! It seemed as safe a place as any to ride out the storm
and have a little hurricane party.

Meanwhile, others residents of the Richelieu began pitching in to
help manager Jones prepare the building for the storm. Ben
Duckworth Jr. was a twenty-four-year-old business school graduate of

Mississippi State University who was working a construction job in Gulfport. He shared a ground-floor apartment with Buddy Jones, a medical technician for the Navy. Buddy was called up for duty at the Seabee base in Gulfport that morning, but Duckworth and a couple of other residents helped Merwin Jones start boarding the first-floor windows with plywood, and carrying furniture up to the third floor. Richard Keller, a NASA engineer, cleared the pool area of patio furniture. Then they moved some of the residents' cars to higher ground. In the early afternoon, Ben's dad called from Jackson, up in the northern part of the state.

"Look, they're saying this thing is a Category Five, Ben. They're talking about a fifteen- or twenty-foot storm surge down there. Two-hundred-mile-an-hour winds! You've got to get out of there, son! Why don't you just come up and stay with us in Jackson?"

"Dad, I think it's too late. I heard on the radio all the roads leading out of here are completely jammed already. I think I'm better off just staying put."

"Please."

"Dad, I'll be okay. This apartment building is a civil defense shelter! It's got steel beams. I'll be all right."

Keller and his wife, Luane, also decided to stay. "Luane said she had seen Atlantic storms but had never seen a Gulf Coast storm," Duckworth later told a reporter. "She decided to stay and cook a roast."

Police chief Gerald Peralta spent much of that day trying to convince people to evacuate. Sunday morning, when the news came that Camille was aiming straight for Bay Saint Louis and Pass Christian, he and his three officers drove around town, ward to ward, urging people to head inland, for higher, safer ground. He stopped by the Richelieu apartments two or three times that day, trying to convince the manager and the twenty-six residents of the building to get out. Peralta later remembered encountering manager Jones in the patio area by the pool. Jones had a drink in his hand and seemed nonchalant.

"Mr. Jones, if this water gets over this first story, what are you going to do?" Peralta asked.

"Well, I'm going up to the third floor, because it's three stories."

"Well, if you get up to that third floor, and that floor washes out from underneath you, what are you going to do?"

"I guarantee—" Jones began, then paused. "Well, I don't think it will get there. I don't think it will get that bad."

Peralta gave up and left.

Meanwhile, the residents of the Richelieu who had chosen to stay either huddled in front of the television, watching Nash Roberts until the power gave out, or peering over the seaside balconies to stare in amazement as the storm surge rose over the narrow sand beach, then crossed US 90, the coast road, then came swarming towards the apartment building. Duckworth and the Kellers were joined in apartment 316, on the third floor, by a couple of others—Mike Gannon, a Navy Seabee recently returned from Vietnam, and a NASA engineer named Mike Bielan. The atmosphere in the room was far from the jolly hurricane party Mary Ann Gerlach had had in mind. They drank a few beers, but nobody danced. And everybody prayed.

The Gerlachs, meanwhile, had been awakened by all the hammering down on the first floor, and by the thumping and bumping of furniture being moved up to the third.

They got up, had something to eat, and then went to the living room windows, which faced the sea. They watched as the gray water, now well over the road, began engulfing the pool, the patio, and then the first floor of the Richelieu Manor apartments. And it just kept rising. Mary Ann could feel the building begin to shudder and pitch, almost as if it were a ship at sea. Wind-driven rain hammered the windowpanes like machine-gun fire. The wind was screeching in the eaves, as if the whole building were flying through the air at high speed.

"Fritz—we've got to get in the back! These windows are going to break any second, and it'll cut us all to pieces!"

Suddenly, she was genuinely scared, and so was he. The windows could blow out because of high-velocity wind, or because of sinking barometric pressure. Either way was scary and dangerous. The Gerlachs grabbed all the food and the drinks that she'd prepared, moved them from the dining room to the back bedroom, and closed the door, in the slightly ludicrous hope that they would be safe there. Then the lights went out. But the wind and water kept rising. Suddenly—

They heard the small panes in the ocean-facing windows in the living room begin to explode, one after the other. Moments later, to

Mary Ann's astonishment, briny water started rushing underneath the bedroom door. Their second-floor apartment was perhaps ten or twelve feet above the ground, yet the ocean was quickly submerging the rug.

"*Fritz, come help me!*" she screamed, and then both of them wedged their backs against the door to try to keep the Gulf of Mexico from forcing its way inside their bedroom. They succeeded in keeping the door closed, but within minutes, the bedroom windowpane exploded, by either being smashed in by the wind, or sucked out by extreme barometric pressure differences. Water rushed into the room. It rose around their knees, around their waists. The bed began floating up towards the ceiling, like a dream. The building pitched deleriously.

She reached over and grabbed the watch with the diamond-studded band that Fritz had given her for their second anniversary and put it on. If the watch got ruined, at least the band could be saved, she thought.

Then she wondered what it was going to be like to die.

CHAPTER FIVE

8:00 P.M., Sunday, August 17
Gulfport, Mississippi

AFTER SECURING his pretty little racing sloop *Morgan 34* at the Gulfport harbor, Bob Taylor had gone home and filled the bathtubs with water. If the water pressure went out during the storm, he wanted to make sure he could flush the commodes by pouring water in the toilet tank. He made sure he had some good bourbon in the house. He took a short nap.

Now, when he got up and flipped on the TV for the latest weather report, he discovered that the news had grown considerably grimmer over a couple of hours. In the late afternoon, the reports were of 160 mile-an-hour winds—a bona fide Category Five. A recording anemometer (wind-measuring device) on an oil rig out in the Gulf had hit 173 miles an hour before it jammed and the rig crew fled. And this was an hour *before* her center, with the highest winds, even arrived in the area. Now the winds were reported to be approaching 200 miles an hour. Was it possible to have a hurricane that was *worse* than a Category Five?

Was there a Category Six?

New Orleans weatherman Nash Roberts was reporting on WDSU that Camille was a growing and very dangerous storm, the worst ever. Still—perhaps because she was not headed for New Orleans but straight for Pass Christian, a hundred miles to the east—Roberts's tone was not strident or even particularly worried. He was his usual calm, courtly self, painstakingly providing listeners with the meteorological particulars. By contrast, local commentators on stations in Biloxi and Gulfport were basically warning, in something short of a scream: *"Get out!"*

Bob Taylor never really seriously entertained the idea of leaving his home. He'd been here during the hurricane of '47, and the water had not even covered his yard. He didn't even worry too much when, around twilight, a National Guard vehicle came cruising slowly through the neighborhood announcing through a loudspeaker: "Immediate evacuation is advised from this area! This is a very dangerous area!" Taylor realized he knew the guy operating the loudspeaker, so they chatted briefly and the man waved and drove off down the street.

Taylor couldn't think of any safer place to be than his own home. Besides, it was only three months since his beloved Bev's death and he was still terribly despondent. He felt sluggish and slow, as if he had sand in his blood. He just couldn't quite get himself going. Figuring out how to "reestablish himself as a person," how to climb up out of the dark hole of grief—it had to do with figuring out a reason to live. And if the truth be told, Taylor had not quite figured out how to do that. Life's precious gift did not seem quite so dear as it once had, so in a devil-may-care sort of way, he thought he'd just stick around to see what would happen.

It was about 8:30 P.M., just at the edge of summer dark, when a young woman he'd once represented in court, a schoolteacher from Arkansas named Mary Evelyn Wallace, came to the door. She looked wan and frightened.

"What do I do?" she asked him.

"I don't know—do you have any friends north of here?"

"No. I don't."

He suggested she go stay with a family that both of them knew, and she told him that she was thinking of going there anyway. Just then, Taylor's friend and crewmate Billy Barrett stopped by.

"Come on," Barrett said, "let's get out of here!"

"No, let's just stay here," Taylor insisted. "This house is well built. We'll be safe. Mary Evelyn, why don't you just stay here with us, and we'll all stick it out together?"

So, thrown together by the storm and the Fates, the three of them decided to ride it out: Wallace, the scared schoolteacher; Barrett, a young bachelor who had no family of his own; and Taylor, who had loved a woman but lost her.

Taylor's house was only one lot back from the Gulf, so the three of them got flashlights and walked down to the beach to look at the water. The narrow beach was already submerged and the tide was flooding over the coast road. The water looked ominous, muddy, and dark. The air was oppressively muggy, almost breathlessly warm, and the wind was starting to shriek in the powerlines. They walked back to the house and fixed sandwiches, and as they were eating at the kitchen table, the power went out. Around the neighborhood, electrical transformers began exploding, but they hardly heard them, because by then the wind had risen to a full-throated roar.

AT LEAST one Gulf Coast resident had more than a passing acquaintance with that sound. Albert Easterling Jr. was a lawyer and a former naval aviator who lived in the neighboring town of Long Beach. He'd attended the Naval Air Academy and seen action in the Atlantic theater in World War II. He'd been trained in smoke-evacuation procedures in the Navy's Constellation airplane (ironically, the same aircraft that is often retrofitted as a hurricane hunter). If you got smoke in the aircraft, you opened the front window of the cockpit on the pilot's side, then you went back and opened a window back in the cabin, all the while maintaining your flaps at an attitude that kept the aircraft straight and level. That cleared the cabin of smoke—and also sent the wind screaming right by your head. "That was exactly the way the wind sounded out there" as Hurricane Camille neared shore that night, Easterling later testified in a court case. Based on his experience as a naval aviator, he estimated the wind speed was 160 knots, or about 185 miles per hour. He added, though, that this was not the full force of the wind because he wasn't in the center of the storm, and his home was partially blocked by a neighbor's house across the street. That was a blessing: "I frankly think that [my] house would not have stood if it hadn't been for the house across the street."

Two meteorologists from the NASA Mississippi Testing Facility estimated the sound level at 100 decibels, and reported that it was continuous for two hours or more. That noise level is equivalent to the wall of sound produced by several low-flying jet aircraft or by rocket engines. People rather casually use the word "deafening" to describe loud noises, but the sound of Camille nearing landfall was, quite literally, deafening.

BY NOW, Harrison County Civil Defense Director Wade Guice was seriously worried. He'd been worried enough when the weather reports indicated that Camille was going to be as bad as the great hurricane of 1947. But now, the reports had kicked over into a whole new level of high anxiety. Earlier, the NHC was talking about 150-mile-an-hour winds and a 15-foot storm surge. That was bad enough—awful, really. But now it was talking about winds of 200 miles an hour, and a storm surge of 20 feet or more. There was one hell of a difference between those two. One *hell* of a difference!

One result was sheer terror. The other was—at least potentially—absolute devastation.

For meterologists, the critical measurement of a hurricane's intensity is its barometric pressure, which is a more reliable measure of the storm's power than is its wind speed. For civil defense people, the critical number is the height of the storm surge. It's the storm surge that kills, obliterates buildings, and zeroes out whole coastlines. And a twenty-foot storm surge—with a high tide and heavy surf on *top* of it—was practically unimaginable. Rolling in over the low, level coast, a surge like that could drive floodwaters so far inland it was impossible to anticipate the level of damage and destruction. Nothing like this had ever happened before.

The fluid mechanics of storm surge are complex, but the short story is that storm surge is the mound or dome of water that sweeps ashore as the hurricane makes landfall. Many things affect the height of the surge: the hurricane's wind speed and direction, its central pressure, the depth of the water offshore, the shape of the shoreline, the tides, and the topography of the ocean floor. Of all these variables, the most important factors are the storm's minimum pressure; the "bathymetry" or depth of the water near shore and the contour of the shoreline; and the hurricane's angle of approach to the coast. Though Camille was motoring toward shore at about fifteen miles per hour (a relatively leisurely pace), her central pressure was extraordinarily low, her wind speeds were almost unprecedented, and both the bathymetry and angle of approach were ominous—so her capacity for generating a devastating storm surge were truly terrifying.

Storm surge begins forming at sea when the revolving eyewall of the hurricane, drawing air inward from all directions into the storm's core, begins "piling up" water in the center, heaving it up like a fluid mountain. This accumulation of water in the hurricane's eye is magnified by the fact that air pressure in the center is extremely low, which helps to lift the sea surface in the center of the storm. The lower the central pressure in the eye, the faster the wind speeds, the higher the storm surge. At the same time, the hurricane's rotating air column, making contact with the sea surface, transmits this spinning wind energy downward through the fluid. A great column of water begins to rotate, moving toward shore at the same speed as the hurricane. Due to the complex physics of fluids and the vast, revolving forces of the storm, this spinning column of water takes a shape known as an Ekman spiral—eerily echoing the cosmic spiral shapes created by the hurricane high in the atmosphere. As above, so below.

(It's important to understand what storm surge is not. It's not a "tidal wave"—that is, it's not a wave caused by the planetary interactions of moon, earth, and sun that normally create the tides. The tides can add or subtract some height to the storm surge, but the surge itself is caused by a hurricane, not by tidal action. And a surge is not a tsunami, like the terrible wave that came ashore in Indonesia the day after Christmas 2004, killing over two hundred thousand people. Tsunamis are generated when a sea-floor event like a shifting tectonic plate, a landslide, or an earthquake displaces massive amounts of water, sending a great wave ashore, often at a great distance from the triggering, subsurface event.)

In the deep, open ocean, the upward doming of water—even at the center of an intense hurricane—may be barely noticeable, no more than a few feet high. That's because water piling up in the center of the storm is free to simply flow downward beneath the surface of the sea and spread outward, as if one were pouring water into a bucket with no bottom. (Though the fluid mechanics are not precisely the same, something similar occurs in tsunamis. The word "tsunami" means "harbor wave" in Japanese, and was coined by Japanese fishermen who returned to port and were astonished to find massive devastation from an ocean wave that, far out at sea, had passed harmlessly beneath their boats. It only turned into a catastrophe when it made contact with shore.)

As this great rotating column of water underneath the hurricane's rotating column of air begins to approach shore, the fluid mechanics start to change. Bottom friction increases. The flow of water moving downward and out of the water column from below is now impeded; it begins seeping away more slowly than the hurricane winds and the low-pressure center are piling up water at the surface. With outflow restricted at the bottom of the water column, water mass begins to accumulate at the top. An enormous dome or mound of water—the storm surge—smokes toward shore like the dark riders of the apocalypse.

And the only safe place to be is somewhere far, far away.

Storm surge, in short, is a phenomenon of shallow or shoaling water. Certain locations on earth are extremely vulnerable for this reason. These are places were ocean depth changes very gradually, or where densely populated coastal regions rise only a few inches or feet above sea level for miles inland. Along the crowded, low-lying coasts of India, Bangladesh, and Pakistan, for instance, hundreds of thousands of souls have perished in just a few hours during a single storm. Galveston, Texas—essentially a heavily urbanized sandbar—is another perilous location, which is why it became the scene of the deadliest hurricanes in US history one tragic day in 1900. And in New Orleans, and on the narrow crook of beachfront spanning Long Branch, New Jersey, to Long Beach, New York, the stage is set for unprecedented loss of life from storm surge due to the topography of the coastline and the sea bottom directly offshore.

Another such location, Wade Guice knew only too well, was the low-lying Mississippi Gulf Coast.

When a storm surge comes ashore, it is not a towering "wall of water," as some people imagine it. Since the elevated sea surface is shaped like a mound or a dome, often thirty to fifty miles across, it comes ashore as a thunderous, sudden rising of the waters. On top of the surge, hurricane winds and the tides pile up frothing whitecaps, which add more height, turbulence, and danger to the incoming mountain of water.

When storm surge makes landfall, its destructiveness is not evenly distributed, like one single battering ram of wind-driven force. Instead, as the storm rampages ashore, the mound of water is highest on the right side of the storm track. That's because (in the northern hemisphere, anyway) hurricanes spin counterclockwise, so the winds on the storm's right side are rushing ashore at maximum speed. On the storm's left side—the opposite side of the great spinning whirlwind—the winds are rushing away from shore. That's why sea level is often actually depressed on the left side of an incoming hurricane, as sea water is forced to flow away from shore.

The reason why storm surge is so dangerous and destructive can be understood by anyone who has ever carried a pail of water. Water is amazingly heavy. A cubic yard of it—imagine a block of water three feet by three feet by three feet—weighs sixteen-hundred pounds, or almost a ton. Storm surge from a single hurricane can easily surpass a million cubic yards of water. And when this much water—a million or more tons—is set in motion by hurricane-force winds, wave action, and the tides, it will devastate almost everything in its path, and drown anyone in its way. An incoming storm surge can result in pressures of up to five tons per square foot, and almost nothing can stand up to this. Forces of this magnitude have the power to virtually obliterate a coastline and everything on it—like the humble towns of Pass Christian and Bay Saint Louis that now lay in Camille's path.

For Wade Guice, the only good news in all of this was that, at least operationally, Sunday was an ideal time to have an evacuation. Everybody was where they were supposed to be—at home. Of course, though it was nice to be able to find people, he did not have legal authority to *force* anybody to evacuate. He and his staff would just have to get out there, warning—*beseeching*—people to get out. He'd have to get on the radio, get on TV, telling as many people as possible to leave or get to storm shelters. The media, especially the electronic media, was the central tool he had now. It didn't matter how much sophisticated scientific weather data was streaming in from the NHC and elsewhere. What mattered now was delivering that information to the people, and convincing them to take action on it.

Guice's job now was to be the man in charge of the Harrison County Civil Defense Emergency Operations Center, overseeing the entire evacuation, being the shepherd for the whole community. He couldn't get involved in any one of the many individual dramas that would unfold in the next few hours, even those involving his own family. He'd learned that lesson early in his career, when a big hurricane blew in and he stopped to help a woman dangling out of an overturned car. He'd been working to free her for over an hour when he suddenly realized that he shouldn't be there at all. His duty was not to *her*—others could take of her. His duty was to the tens of thousands of other people in the community whose lives were in mortal danger.

Guice knew very well that now there was only a narrow window of opportunity—a matter of hours—during which people could leave or get to shelters. After that, it was too late. Wherever they happened to be, they were trapped. Even if the civil defense department *wanted* to save somebody during the height of the storm—an extraordinarily dangerous operation for everyone involved—it only had a limited capacity to do so. His department did have access to a few amphibious vehicles that could be used for rescues, but he dearly hoped he wouldn't have to use them. It was simply too dangerous.

The best solution was to convince people to get off the beach, get out of town, go somewhere inland, and do it *now*. Guice and other local officials got on the radio and TV to hammer the point home, and to say that shelters had been opened in Harrison, Hancock, and Jackson counties. Red Cross personnel were prepared to receive a massive influx of refugees from the storm—if people chose to heed the warning.

Guice wondered: Did people out there have any idea, any idea at all, what was about to happen?

Everybody on the Gulf Coast knew about hurricanes, had grown up with them, had lived through them. But nobody had ever lived through anything like this.

Two-hundred-mile-an-hour winds.

Twenty-foot storm surge.

Wade Guice had never even remotely *heard* of anything like this.

PAUL WILLIAMS SR. was just a couple of days shy of his fiftieth birthday. He was a soft-spoken black man who worked as the caretaker or sexton at Trinity Episcopal Church in Pass Christian, a complex of white-clapboard buildings set one block back from the beach near Henderson Point. Trinity Episcopal was one of the prettiest churches on the entire Gulf Coast. Completed in 1849, it stood amid a grove of live oak trees bearded with Spanish moss. In its 120 years of seaside existence, the church was said to have weathered eighteen hurricanes. John and Louisa Henderson, who had donated the land for the church, also gave some adjoining land for a graveyard called Live Oak Cemetery. Part of the cemetery was designated "free ground," to be used for the burial of both blacks and whites—a startlingly magnani-mous gesture for its day.

Williams, his wife, Myrtle, and his family lived in a small house near the church. He'd grown up during the Depression in rural Mississippi, where his father chipped pine trees to make turpentine, cut wood, worked for the WPA, and did whatever else he could to get by. "He never had nothing steady, or no trade or nothing," Williams says of his father. What he *did* have was a huge family—"I think that all together, Mama had about seventeen children." Williams dropped out of school in the fourth grade and worked awhile helping his daddy make turpentine, toiled on a sugarcane farm or in a laundry in Houma, Louisiana. At the beginning of World War II he enlisted in the military, but was discharged because of a severe stomach disorder. Eventually he settled down in Pass Christian, got married, started working at the church and began having children—*lots* of children. Ultimately he and his wife had fifteen.

"Like I say," he told an interviewer years later, "I've never been a lazy man. I always did try to do and provide for my family, and that I did. That was a desire that I always had. I wanted in life to have a home, because Daddy, he never put us in a home. He moved us around like little kittens from one place to another. I wanted a home for my children, and that I got."

That Sunday, when the news started coming in about Camille's impending landfall, Williams and his wife discussed where they should take their family. He'd been through three hurricanes in his lifetime on the Gulf, and he knew how scary they could be. One time, when a big one was blowing in and water had flooded knee-deep into his home in the Pass, he gathered up his family and headed out the door towards his grandmother's house. "I had a baby in my arms, and one by the hand, and my oldest daughter, her name was Dorothy, she was very, very small, and the water like to took her away. If it wouldn't been for her first cousin Nook grabbed her by the hand, I mean *grabbed* her, the water would have swim her away."

He'd heard about Camille's twenty-foot tides and the monster winds, but he wasn't sure what to do or where to go. Once before, the Williams family had ridden out a hurricane in a shelter in DeLisle, a small town across the bayou behind Pass Christian, three or four miles back from the beach.

"Honey, let's go out to DeLisle," Williams told his wife. "I'd like to be where it's quiet, where there's not too much of a big crowd, because I can't rest."

"No," Myrtle said, "I don't want to go out there, because they cut up and cuss too much."

"Well, why don't we just stay in the auditorium over yonder?"

The auditorium attached to Trinity church was a handsome room with twelve-foot ceilings and an attic upstairs, where Christmas decorations and other supplies were stored. It had a concrete foundation, and seemed soundly built. Williams went to ask the Reverend Durrie Hardin, rector of the church, if he and his family could spend the storm in the auditorium.

"He didn't say no, he didn't say go, so I presumed it was okay, you see."

So Paul Williams, his wife, and family got ready to move in as Camille bore down on the coast that afternoon. The oldest children—Dorothy, Paul Jr. and Pamela—were married and no longer lived at home. But twelve other children were home that night, ranging in age from two to twenty-two: Floyd, Eddie, Esther, Charles, Clara, Jeremiah, Anna, Sylvester, Deborah, Otis, Myrtle Mae, and Malcolm. A couple of grandchildren were also present. The extended Williams family walked over to the auditorium, carrying food, water, a TV and a radio, to keep posted on the storm. The auditorium had a kitchen with a stove and Williams admonished the children that if they used the facilities, they needed to leave things as clean as they found them. "This is like y'all found the kitchen, this is the way I want y'all to leave it," he said. They made a little supper. Outside, the wind was picking up in the eaves. But "the little children—oh, they was having so much fun!" Finally he and his wife and the older children got the little ones bedded down. First, though, he told them all, "If the water starts coming in here, we're going upstairs, to the attic."

Not long after Williams lay down himself, his son-in-law, Nick, burst in.

"Papa, the water's coming in!"

When he got up, Williams saw that water was pouring in under the door, and rapidly spreading across the floor. He roused everybody, pulled down the attic's folding ladder, and started pushing them upstairs—his wife and the little girls first, followed by the boys and fi-

nally himself. For a second time, Williams tried to get the kids all bedded and settled down, but by now the wind was screaming in the
windows. Something—a downed tree or a boat, perhaps—kept
thumping up against the side of the auditorium.

The building shuddered, but held. When he peered down out of
the opening from the attic and shone his flashlight into the flooded
auditorium, Williams could see seawater rapidly rising in the room. It
was already almost to the top of the twelve-foot ceiling.

"Daddy, Daddy, what are we going to do?" the kids wailed.

"Well, I'm going to put some boards up there, and put y'all up
there a little higher," he told them.

Williams grabbed some old boards and rope stored in the attic.
Tying them horizontally across the rafters of the peaked attic roof, he
formed a small, jury-rigged hiding-place about five feet above the
floor. Then he shoved more boards across the horizontal pieces to
make a flat floor, and started lifting the kids up to what he hoped was
safety. While doing this, he was also doing something else: He was
praying. He prayed, hard, twice. All of them had gotten in. The water
was beginning to seep up through the square opening in the floor
where the ladder came through. He put his hand on the wooden
cross-member, preparing to lift himself up with the kids. Suddenly,
something broke, and that's the last thing he remembered.

He was flying through the air, or something like air, holding on to
what seemed like the linoleum platform of a kitchen, or perhaps a
hall. Then all that slipped out from under him, and he went down into
the water, twice, and came up kicking and gasping. Some kind of tree
was floating by, so he grabbed it and for some reason closed his eyes.
He thought desperately, "I can't swim!" If the water swept him back
across the bayou, and then receded, he'd either drown or would have
to walk out of the swamp. Just then the log he was clinging to collided with something with a jolt. He opened his eyes. It was the fork
of a standing live oak tree. He grabbed hold of the tree and hung on
for dear life.

Around him, the whole world was gone. There was nothing left
but him and the wind and the rain, battering his face and body. It
"whipped the fire out of me," he said later. He was freezing, shaking
worse than "one of these paint shakers." Above him, he could see the
sky glowing red. It was as if the world were on fire, and maybe it was.

Paul Williams had no way of knowing what was happening, where he was—or where any of his family might be.

If they were alive at all.

AS THE WIND rose to a high-pitched scream, Bob Taylor began to worry about his neighbors across the street—Vincent and Nathan Alfonzo, two brothers who had taught him how to sail as a young man. He decided to walk over to see if he could get them to come stay at his house, which he felt was safer than theirs. But shortly after he got outdoors, the wind knocked him flat on the ground, ripped the shirt right off his back, and rolled him fifteen or twenty feet down the street. He crawled back home, shirtless, on all fours.

He found Billy and Mary Evelyn huddled in the darkened house, listening to Nash Roberts on the transistor radio.

"Camille is now about twenty miles south of the mouth of Bay Saint Louis, Mississippi, moving north-northwest at about fifteen miles an hour. Highest winds are estimated around 190 miles an hour near the center, with some estimates up to two hundred or even higher. Hurricane winds extend outward sixty miles from the center, and gales 180 miles from the center. Let me say again: This is an extraordinarily dangerous storm, the worst on record in the Gulf Coast. At this rate, she should make landfall near Bay Saint Louis sometime between 11:00 P.M. and 1:00 A.M. tonight."

Bay Saint Louis was only two miles west of Pass Christian. The two small coastal cities were separated by the mouth of Saint Louis Bay, which was spanned by a highway bridge. The eye of the most intense hurricane in Gulf Coast history was headed almost directly for the mouth of the bay, a couple of miles from where they were sitting.

Sitting in the kitchen by candlelight, straining to hear Nash Roberts above the deafening shriek of the wind, Taylor, Barrett, and Wallace started talking about the construction of the house. Suddenly, such things were not idle chatter; they were matters of mortal consequence. Taylor said that it was an extremely well-built house, made of solid brick, not just brick veneer. It had been built by a friend of his. He'd watched it go up. Unfortunately, it was also a contemporary house with one solid wall of sliding-glass doors.

Barrett got up to mix a drink. "My feet are getting wet," he announced suddenly.

Taylor looked down and saw water gurgling under the kitchen door. "Oh, my God," he said—not because he felt they were in danger, but because he had an expensive Kerman rug in the living room of which he was very proud. He ran in there, grabbed the rug and hoisted it onto a sofa so it wouldn't get wet. Then he shone a flashlight through the glass doors and out on to the patio. Water was already a foot deep against the glass, and beginning to gurgle in under the doors.

"That's when I realized we were in trouble," he said later.

Within a minute, the water was knee-deep in the house and rising. Another minute later there was a tremendous crash and every glass panel in the house blew out. Not in, but *out*. Briny ocean water began pouring into the house. (In the chaos of the moment it was difficult to tell what had actually happened, but tornado studies have shown that it is unlikely—as is commonly believed—that the extremely low barometric pressure near the hurricane's eye sucks windows out of their frames. In this instance, more likely, wind, water, and debris broke weak parts of the walls, the wind lifted the roof, and the walls—at least, the windows—collapsed outward without the support of the roof.) The water rose waist-high, submerging the prized Kerman carpet on the sofa. Taylor noticed his new set of *Encyclopaedia Britannica*s floating into the hall. He'd just finished paying for them. He heard a crash in the kitchen. He waded in there and in the glare of the flashlight saw that the refrigerator-freezer had pitched over onto its side and was now afloat, like a white porcelain coffin.

Then the whole house seemed to shudder.

"What in the world was *that?*" Wallace asked.

They thrashed their way through now chest-deep water into the front room and found Taylor's new Delta 88 Oldsmobile floating in the living room. It had smashed through the double doors at the front of the house, ripping both off their hinges. In the trunk of the car, he suddenly realized, was all the electronic gear he'd taken off his boat to keep it dry. He and Billy pushed open a side door, trying to get water out of the house so the car would sink a little and not batter the house down. The vehicle began sinking, right in front of them. Then, suddenly, an enormous storm surge swept through the house. The water rose to their necks, lifting them almost to the ceiling. The car, the sofa, the encyclopedias, and everything else began battering the three of them, as they desperately tried to keep their heads above water and find something to hold on to. Taylor knew there was a steel beam across the double front doors—or at least, the opening where the doors used to be.

"Grab on to the door frame!" he yelled to the others. "It'll hold!"

All three managed to find their way to the frame of the door and then hang on to it while the Gulf of Mexico, swollen by Camille's low-pressure eye, surged in and out of the house like a deep-breathing sea monster. Everything was in slow motion. Out through the doorway, Taylor could see that the low-hanging clouds overhead had turned bright red, apparently the reflection of fires in the neighborhood. He recognized his neighbor's kitchen floating down Alfonzo drive, one he'd been in countless times. Looking up toward the beach, he noticed a neighbor's two-story house had become a one-story. Then it was simply disintegrating, like the powerboat had disintegrated against the rocks in Gulfport Harbor earlier in the day.

Something kept gently wrapping around Taylor's leg underwater. He kept trying to kick his foot free, a little panicked because in previous hurricanes, the wind and water had brought up enormous numbers of snakes out of the coastal bayous. Finally he lifted his foot out of the water to discover that a bit of fishline from a fly rod, left over from his trip to Newfoundland with his father, had wrapped around his leg.

Masses of debris were washing in and out of the house and the yard, and Taylor grabbed a ladder-back chair floating by. He used it to fend off the floating piles of wreckage, like a matador fending off a bull. Around him, he could see the interior walls of his solid-brick house beginning to break up.

The three of them hung there in the doorframe, watching the fire-lit waves surging in and out of the flooded house.

"Here comes a big one!" somebody would shout. "Get ready!"

And they'd hang on to the hinges and on to each other, so as not to be swept away by the next surge. A boat came floating down the street, and briefly the three considered trying to swim out to it and climb aboard. But the air was filled with flying debris, slashing into the water like a rain of machine-gun bullets. Even a flying pecan leaf or a pinecone felt like a hammer blow on flesh. A piece of corrugated tin or a traffic sign could cut off your arm. They decided it would be foolish to attempt commandeering the boat. They were better off just staying where they were, and trying to hang on as long as they could.

It was strange, but Taylor wasn't really afraid. He was too busy trying to keep from dying. Finding a reason to live had come down to the absolute elementals: Just breathe. Just keep from drowning. Just survive.

CHAPTER SIX

10:30 P.M., Sunday, August 17
Pass Christian

MARY ANN GERLACH thrashed around in the dark, flooded bedroom until she found a flashlight and flipped it on. The back windows had been completely blown out by the storm surge. The bed was now floating almost to the ceiling. The building heaved and pitched drunkenly. In the surreal glare of the flashlight, she could see enormous cracks opening up on the wall. It was apparent that the third floor— and the whole building—was about to come down.

"I know we're going to die, but I'm not going to die in here with that floor coming down on us!" she yelled to Fritz. The thought of being squashed by the collapsing ceiling terrified her even more than the prospect of drowning. Fritz, who did not know how to swim, was terrified by the thought of being left alone to drown in the dark bedroom.

"Please, baby, don't go out!" he begged her. "Stay here with me!" But she was determined. She half-thrashed, half-swam to a closet, fished out an air mattress she used in the pool, blew it up, and shoved it towards him.

"You take that and hold on to that, because I can swim pretty good," she told him. "I don't know if I'm going to make it, but I'm going to try."

Then she grabbed a foam-rubber pillow from a chair floating nearby.

"You know how scared of the dark I am, Fritz—I'm going to take the flashlight with me."

"Baby, don't go! Stay here with me!" He was grabbing on to her arm, trying to keep her from leaving him there in what was quickly becoming an airless grave.

"No! I'm going to swim out!"

Then she swam out the window. Within moments, she'd become tangled in what appeared to be a mass of telephone or electrical wires, and for a minute or two she just froze. She was too scared to move. All she could think of was what she'd heard about electrical wires in water: "I'm going to get electrocuted!" Then it dawned on her that the electricity had been off for over an hour. This building was going down, like a sinking ship and she had to get away from it, so she wouldn't be sucked underwater by the undertow. But she was still tangled in the mass of loose wires. Struggling to get free, she heard Fritz screaming.

"Help me! Save me!"

In the flashlight's glare, she could see that the roiling sea had washed him out the window of the bedroom. He was thrashing desperately to stay afloat.

"Save me!"

Then he went under and did not come back up.

Somehow, Mary Ann managed to break free of the tangle of wires and started paddling frantically away from the collapsing building. In her haste, she dropped the flashlight, and everything around her descended into darkness. She could see the lights from apartments on the third floor of her building, and make out the vague shapes of people. Then the structure began pitching forward—not a sudden, dramatic collapse, but a long, slow sinking into the sea, like the *Titanic*'s, until all the lights winked out and she was in complete darkness.

Hanging on to the small foam pillow like life itself, she thrashed hard to escape being crushed by the building. Around her the water was jammed by floating debris—broken furniture, pieces of wood, boards with nails sticking out. She kept gasping for breath, but couldn't quite seem to catch it, like when she had bronchial asthma as a child. The hurricane wind, or the barometric pressure, or something, seemed to have stolen her breath away.

She prayed without ceasing.

"Oh, Lord, if you'll just let me live, I'll try to be such a better person!"

She thought about how, when the water was roaring into the bedroom, she'd reached out to grab her diamond watch, but not to grab Fritz. She'd abandoned him to the water and to his deepest fears. Why had she only saved herself?

Once or twice, she saw people floating by with flashlights, clinging to debris, a short distance away. She'd hear them screaming and yelling, and then she'd see the lights go under and the voices fade away.

She lost her grip on the foam pillow, then struggled to grab on to something else. The water was so filled with floating detritus and garbage, it wasn't difficult to find something to grab. Finally, a tree came floating by and she crawled aboard it, sticking her face under some branches to get some breathing space and shelter from the stinging rain. But around her debris accumulated, in immense floating piles, until the tree seemed to be driven down under the water, under the wreckage, and her along with it. She dove underwater, trying to escape the piles, trying to swim out beyond them.

The dark water brought back all her fears of suffocating, fears that had plagued her ever since her asthmatic childhood. She was exhausted. She couldn't breathe. A couple of times, she nearly gave in to the darkness and the suffocation and just let herself go down. Then something would kick in and she would fight her way back up again. Finally she tipped herself upside down and frantically used her legs to thrash open a hole in the debris and force her face through. She took huge gasps of night air and just held on for dear life, praying.

"Oh Lord, just let me live! I'll try to be such a better person!"

10:45 P.M., Sunday, August 17
Long Beach, Mississippi

Janice Stegenga, Harry, and their two little children cowered in the storm shelter at Quarles Elementary School, in Long Beach. The shelter was full, and the atmosphere was edgy with fear and excitement. Families made little nests in the classrooms or in the halls. They had blankets and pillows and coolers full of food and drinks. Many had radios and even television sets. Children saw it as a special event, like a birthday party or a school outing, and they ran around wildly, laughing and playing.

Janice wandered down the hall and peered out the glass slit in a doorway of the school. She could see a telephone pole with two transformers on top swaying crazily in the wind. Boy, she thought, the wind out there is *unbelievable!* At that moment, she saw the telephone pole snap in two, like a matchstick, and the lights in the school went out. Little shrieks of fear and excitement rippled through the shelter, like a disturbance of birds. Feeling her way along the walls of the hallway, she crept back to where Harry and the children were huddled together. They all crowded there holding each other and listening to the screeching wind outside. Rocks started lifting off a flat tarred roof nearby and pelting against a window. It sounded like gunfire. Then, almost on cue, the windows exploded, showering the little family with rocks from the roof and tiny slivers of glass. One got in the baby's eye, and she began to wail.

Frightened as they were, they were all alive, mostly dry, and relatively safe. Janice somehow got the glass sliver out of the baby's eye. All they had to do was wait out the dawn, and pray that the Gulf did not rise any higher.

At that same moment, Harry's parents, Piet and Valena Stegenga, were in much more desperate straits. When they got news of the storm, they had gone to stay with Piet's mother and stepfather, both of whom were invalids and unable to care for themselves. Piet's mother, Anna Dambrink, was seventy-eight and had been wheelchair bound for two years. His stepfather, John Dambrink, affectionately known as "Pops," was eighty-four and suffering from dementia. Valena had to come take care of the old couple every day, and so did Piet's stepsister Elizabeth, known as "Sis." The elderly invalids were helpless on their own and now, without a truck or an ambulance, there was simply no way to get them out of the house to safety.

"I'm going to have to stay with them or drown with them," Piet had told his boss, when he'd asked what Piet was going to do about the incoming hurricane earlier in the day. "You can't save crippled people in a storm."

When Piet and Valena went down to the Dambrink home, Sis was there, along with her brother, Joey. That brought the total number of

people in the little house to six: Piet and Valena, Anna and Pops
Dambrink, and Sis and Joey.

Piet was a direct and practical-minded man who had quit school
in the seventh grade and spent his life working as a gardener at one
of the grand oceanside estates, selling vegetables door-to-door, doing
construction work at Keesler Air Force Base, and raising his family of
three. He had very serious doubts about whether the Dambrinks'
house would withstand the storm. He'd been listening to the radio,
and had heard about the 200-mile-an-hour winds.

"Y'all are in a low place over here," he told everybody. "There is
not going to be no house left."

"You're nuts," Joey said.

"There ain't going to be no house left," Piet repeated. "We're all
going to drown in this house."

Joey was unconvinced, so Piet asked him to drive down to the
beach to take a look at the water. It was only a couple of blocks away,
and when they got there, both were alarmed by the look of it.

"You see how high that water is," Piet told Joey. "You see how
rough that water is. I can't get out there in that water and save no people out there, as bad as this storm is. Everybody is going to be on their
own in this storm. Because there is no way of us helping nobody."

But Joey was adamant. He insisted that they were all going to
weather the storm in the Dambrink house. A short while later, when
a truck full of men from Keesler Air Force Base came by to warn them
to evacuate, Joey and the rest of the family still resisted. Like many
others along the coast, they were convinced that the safest place for
them to stay was at home.

They were still at home when the storm surge slammed into the
house, and Piet and Sis wedged their backs against the kitchen door
to keep the water out. But it was too late. Water exploded up under
the door. It burst through the windows and poured in over the sills.
It seemed to be coming from everywhere. Desperate, Piet pulled Pops
out of his wheelchair and attempted to shove him up on top of Sis's
car, out in the garage, to get him out of the flood. But Pops was heavy
and unresponsive as a rag doll. If Piet got one leg up on the car, it
would flop down. He was struggling to find some way to push Pops
up to safety when something knocked him down and the next thing

Piet knew, he was swimming, frantically trying to push piles of floating debris away so he could breathe.

He had no idea what had happened to Pops, to the house, or to anybody else.

"This is my own dear life now!" he thought.

And then he was alone in the darkness, in a world where everything was afloat and the wind shrieked in his ears like a sea witch. Around him, were great masses of debris, and he pulled himself up onto what was an enormous floating nest, mounds of rubbish piled up along each side. He lay down flat within it and huddled there for perhaps half an hour, trying feebly to shelter himself from the wind and rain. Once he drifted past an upright telephone pole, then he saw it snap in two like a matchstick. He wondered what had happened to everyone. He knew Valena couldn't swim a lick, so unless there had been some miracle, his wife had almost certainly drowned. He'd lost her: the woman to whom he'd been married for thirty-four years, the mother of his three children.

Suddenly he heard someone calling.

"Save me! Save me!"

"Where you at?" he shouted back.

"Over here! *Save me!*"

"Wait, I'm coming to get you! I'll come pull you out!"

He recognized his stepsister's voice. At least someone was alive.

"Sis, I'm coming! Just keep hollering so I'll know where you're at!"

"Over here! I'm over here!"

He struggled to make his way towards her.

"I'm coming, Sis! It'll take me some time to get across this trash and stuff, but I'm coming!"

Finally he scrabbled his way to the edge of the debris and there, to his utter amazement, he saw Valena, not Sis, clinging to a piece of plywood.

"Man, I tell you," he remembered later, "when I seen it was my wife, I just didn't know. I just didn't know. Boy, I'll tell you, I was stunned or something. I was just that happy!"

Valena, struggling for her own life, had been praying—indeed, bargaining—with God.

"Oh, God, please forgive me for telling my daughter-in-law that I would give anything not to have to come every day to my in-laws' to do!" she later remembered saying. "God, I didn't mean it like that!"

She prayed so hard, she said, that "it seemed like I could see Jesus."

Now her prayers were answered. Piet pulled his wife up out of the water, and the two of them huddled under the old piece of plywood on top of the rubbish pile, trying to keep out of the wind and the rain, holding on to each other to keep warm.

11:15 P.M., Sunday, August 17
Bay Saint Louis, Mississippi

Charles Breath Jr. was a boat dealer and longtime local resident in Bay Saint Louis who religiously kept up with the weather. He kept three barometers in the house, although only two were working that Sunday night as Camille bore down on the Coast. Breath, an old hand at Gulf hurricanes, had opened the back windows and doors of his house near the beach, in order to equalize the pressure inside and outside of the building. (In fact, this bit of hurricane preparation is almost always unnecessary, since most houses are so porous that pressure differentials equalize automatically.)

As the eye of the hurricane closed in on Bay Saint Louis shortly after eleven o'clock, Breath could feel his ears getting ready to pop as the atmospheric pressure plunged. He could barely catch a breath as he, his wife, Mary, and their three daughters prepared to move from the house on the beach to another they owned about five hundred feet back from the shore. In the turmoil of the family evacuation, Breath stopped to glance at a decorative, aneroid-type barometer he had hanging on the wall. When the weather is calm at sea level, the column of mercury in a barometer will stay just a touch below 30.00 inches on the glass tube. (Aneroid barometers indicate this reading with a needle.) Because one of the predominant characteristics of a hurricane is an extreme low-pressure center, the needle on a barometer often begins to twitch restlessly, inching down (or sometimes even up) by a few hundredths of an inch when the hurricane is still as much as five hundred miles away. Then, as the storm approaches, the needle begins to drop slowly but steadily, indicating a drop in barometric pressure. For most hurricanes, the reading never sinks too far below 29 inches. When it does drop significantly below that, you've got serious trouble on your hands. Hurricane Andrew, which would devastate South Florida in 1992—the third-most-powerful hurricane ever to strike the United States—had a barometric pressure reading of 27.13 inches.

But now the needle on Charles Breath's wall barometer was visibly dropping, down below the 28-inch mark, down to 27.50, all the way down to 27.00. Then it kept dropping. "I just couldn't believe what I was seeing," Breath said later. He rushed into the next room to check a second, Marine-type barometer, and that needle was dropping just as rapidly. In the brief period of time when the eye passed over and he was still in the house—not more than ten minutes— Breath noted a barometric pressure reading of 26.84 inches of mercury. He later said it might have been even lower, but he couldn't swear to it due to the panic and confusion of the moment. Measurements taken at altitude by the recon plane were slightly lower, at 26.61 inches. (When Nash Roberts found out about Breath's record-low barometric pressure reading, he sent a man over to borrow the barometers and have them checked in New Orleans. Roberts reported that they were within a tenth of a point of being right on the money; the slight difference could be accounted for by the difference in sea level between Bay Saint Louis and New Orleans.)

Charles Breath's reading was to stand for decades as the lowest barometric pressure reading ever taken at ground level in the continental United States, according to the National Weather Service. It was exceeded only by the Labor Day storm of 1935—down in the Florida Keys and thus outside the continental United States—which dropped to 26.35 inches. (In 1988, Hurricane Gilbert became the low-pressure record-holder in the Western Hemisphere with a reading of 26.22. Even so, Gilbert's maximum sustained winds topped out at 185 miles an hour, well below Camille's.)

IT WAS close to 11:30 P.M. on Sunday, August 17, 1969, when Hurricane Camille—the only Category Five hurricane to strike the continental United States in the twentieth century—made landfall near the town of Bay Saint Louis, Mississippi. Nash Roberts had made the call almost perfectly. The pattern of absolute devastation later indicated that the eye, about eight miles wide, stretched from Clermont Harbor in the west, to Bay Saint Louis and the western edge of Pass Christian, at Henderson Point, in the east. Because of her extreme intensity at landfall, exact measurements were impossible to obtain. But NHC Director Robert Simpson, later reported that "from an appraisal of the character of splintering of structures within a few hundred yards of the Coast, velocities probably approached 175 knots [201 miles per hour]." Gusts were thought to have gone as high as 210 miles per hour or more.

Social worker Rosemary Tully was peering out a window in the door of a school that had been turned into a storm shelter in Pass Christian. As the screaming eyewall passed overhead, the entire building began to rumble and shake. Classroom windows started to blow out, explosively, one after the other. Then it got dead calm.

"When the eye went over, the sky was blood red," Tully remembered later. "You could see the energy. It wasn't like sparks, but the air just seemed to be continually moving with energy, and the color was something you cannot imagine if you've never seen that. That the sky was blood red was what was so frightening. It was just like the whole world was on fire."

Much of the Gulf Coast *was* on fire, as electrical transformers exploded in a shower of blue sparks, houses collapsed, and propane tanks fell over, ignited, and blew up. Firelight danced off the bellies of fast-moving clouds. The hurricane spun off tornadoes in every direction—smaller, tighter vortices with even higher windspeeds than Camille's, which rampaged through neighborhoods, lifting houses off their foundations, ripping trees out by the roots. Over water, the tornadoes turned into waterspouts. The air and the water had become one.

Although the eye made landfall close to Bay Saint Louis, the storm surge peaked a couple of miles to the east, in Pass Christian. The Richelieu Manor apartment building was smack in the center of the highest hurricane storm surge ever measured in the United States: 24.6 feet. The wind-driven waves and high tide on *top* of the storm surge took the total to over 30 feet in some places—a wall of water three stories high.

In short, when she came ashore that night, Hurricane Camille was the most intense storm of any kind to ever strike mainland America in modern history. She was a force that no human being could withstand, except those blessed by God's purpose or saved by sheer luck.

At the moment she came ashore, it was far too late to know whether you would be one of those who were lucky or blessed. There was nothing to do but keep your head above water, hold on for dear life, and pray.

Sometime before dawn, Monday August 18
Mississippi Gulf Coast

Bob Taylor, Billy Barrett, and Mary Evelyn Wallace clung to the frame of the blown-out doors in Taylor's house in Gulfport, as the sea surged in and out of the flooded house. The water was up to his shoulders, and looking out the front door in the eerie, apocalyptic light, Taylor could see almost nothing but a couple of wildly thrashing trees—nearly all the other houses were gone. It was almost as if he were hanging off the rail of a ship at sea, with a foaming wake surging wildly around him. Across the street, where his friends Vincent and Nathan Alfonzo lived, there were no signs of life. He could see no evidence of a house there at all.

From time to time, when the storm surge slackened, Taylor loosed his grip on the door frame and paddled through the darkened house to the back door, by the kitchen. He was worried about the big house next door, which sat directly on the beach and had come completely unmoored from its foundations. In the reddish light from the sky, he could see that it was rolling around in the storm surge like a child's rubber ducky. If it came across his backyard, it would crush his home. For now, at least, the only thing that was preventing it from floating through the yard and crushing Taylor's house was a big live oak tree. Taylor prayed that the tree would hold.

Gradually, the wind seemed to shift direction, and pretty quickly the three survivors began to feel cold. Taylor thrashed his way into the bedroom, got some sweaters and blankets, and brought them back. Everything was sopping wet, but at least they kept the wind off. Wrapping themselves in the soaking clothes and blankets the three huddled in the doorway, not talking much. Gradually, the wind seemed to die down a bit. They watched as the water seemed to recede ever so slightly.

"It's leaving!" Barrett declared, jubilantly.

Then it started to edge back up again. Their hearts sank.

Finally, after a couple of hours, once more the water started receding, and this time it *kept* receding.

"It's really leaving this time! It's going down!"

They were soaking wet, freezing cold, and exhilarated beyond words. They'd survived.

About that time, a whiskey bottle came floating by and Barrett snagged it. The label had soaked off, so they couldn't tell what brand it was. When Taylor opened it, he found himself holding not quite half a bottle of Courvoisier cognac.

"That was the shortest-lived bottle of Courvoisier you've ever seen," Taylor said later.

When the water began to recede, it did so with a vengeance. It flooded out of the house so rapidly that Taylor, Barrett, and Wallace had to hang on to keep from being sucked out. As the water poured out of the ruined living room, Taylor started to worry about a new danger: The big live oak trees in his yard, unmoored by the waterlogged soil, might come crashing down on the house. He instructed the others to get underneath the steel beam where the blown-out sliding glass doors had been. He knew this was the strongest part of the house and the safest place to be. There they huddled in the mud and the wet and the slime, in their soggy clothes and blankets, trying to rest until dawn.

By now the transistor radio batteries had run out; Nash Roberts was long gone. They had no contact with the outside world at all. They had no idea how much damage had been done, or how many people had been killed. There was no evidence of any other living person. As a pallid, gray-green dawn came up in the eastern sky, they all grew silent. The devastation they saw around them was almost total. It was much worse than Taylor had even imagined during the night. He'd always loved and been proud of the beauty of his community—the stately live oak trees, the beach, the grand and gracious antebellum homes. As far as he was concerned, the Gulf Coast of Mississippi was the most beautiful stretch of oceanfront in America.

But what he saw now "reminded me of bombed cities I had seen in Korea," he said later. "The beach in the Second Street area where I live is a very pretty area, and here was my beautiful Gulf Coast and neighborhood all just demolished."

"I just couldn't help but believe that thousands of people had been killed."

A RAINY DAWN was breaking when Mary Ann Gerlach finally felt the mountain of debris she'd been riding had come to rest. She peered down over the edge of her mound of broken boards and trees, furniture and roofs, perhaps fifteen or twenty feet high—like a wet, frightened little bird peering down over the edge of its nest. She could see trees and what looked like the edge of the bayou. She could see a railroad track, apparently the one that ran behind Pass Christian, between the town and the swamp. Other than that, she had no real idea where she was.

A hard, gray rain was falling, and Gerlach was terribly cold. She couldn't stop shivering. All she was wearing were some cute little short-shorts and a little short-sleeved sweatshirt. She dug a small piece of plywood out of the rubble and tried to huddle under it out of the rain. One of her knees had been been badly gashed, and it wouldn't stop bleeding. She took off her bra and tried to use it as a tourniquet, to stop the flow of blood. Then she seemed to pass out, or fall asleep, or just go away someplace warm and safe in her mind.

She was awakened by shouts.

"Shirley! *Shirley!* Where are you?"

She saw a man stumbling down the railroad tracks in the rain.

"Help me!" Gerlach called.

The man walked down off the tracks into the ditch and waded towards her.

"Help me," she repeated.

"Have you seen Shirley?"

The man's eyes were glazed and staring.

"No," she said. "Please help me. I've been bleeding. I'm hurt real bad. Can you help me get to a doctor?"

She recognized the man: He was a doctor himself, a doctor in town. But he did not even seem to hear her. He turned around like a zombie, waded out of the water, and staggered off down the tracks.

A little while later a couple of boys came down the track. One of them she knew—a guy named Frank, who used to work at the post office in Pass Christian.

"Frank! It's me, Mary Ann! I'm over here!"

"*Mary Ann,* is that you?"

"What's left of me it is."

Frank had never seen her when she wasn't all dolled up for work—wearing a wig and makeup. Now she was bleeding, cut up, soaking wet, and shivering. Frank told her that rescue crews were out searching the Coast and the swamps, trying to find people. He sent the other boy off to try to commandeer a helicopter or an airboat to get her. But after an hour, nobody had come.

"We've got to get help to you," Frank said finally. He found a door in the rubble, loaded Gerlach onto it and floated her across the ditch to the railroad track. Then, though he was a diminutive man not much bigger than she, he loaded her onto his shoulder and started carrying her down the railroad tracks. He had to keep putting her down, to catch his breath. Eventually they ran into an enormous black man, big as a bear, whom Frank knew from the post office.

"Would you mind if this colored man carried you up the road where we could get an ambulance or something?" Frank asked her.

"I surely don't," she said. She was in no position to be anything but grateful. The black man picked her up in his arms like a little baby and carried her out of the swamp.

PAUL WILLIAMS, the caretaker of Trinity Episcopal Church, crawled down out of the live oak tree where he'd spent the night. Around him was an immense pile of debris, a piece of linoleum floor, broken rafters, and chairs. As things began to materialize in the dawn, he could see that he was in a cemetery, maybe the Live Oak Cemetery right behind Trinity Church. Tombstones were scattered among the mangled trees, and heaps of wreckage piled up ten or fifteen feet high. He could even see what looked like unearthed coffins lying out on the ground.

"Help!" he shouted. "Is anybody there?"

At first there was no sound except the wind in the live oak trees. *"Help!"*

Everyone in Pass Christian must be dead, he thought. His whole family must have drowned. Then he heard voices calling back.

"Hey, who's there? Is that you, Papa?"

He recognized the voices of his sixteen-year-old son, Malcolm, and his son-in-law, Nick.

"Malcolm! Nick! It's me, Papa! You alive!"

The three began hollering back and forth, as the dawning light came up over the devastated cemetery. The shouting was heard by people in the school across the street, which had been turned into a storm shelter. People came towards them, shining flashlights into the cemetery in the half-darkness, trying to locate the shouts. It took the search party half an hour to find Paul Williams and get him safely down out of the mountain of rubble, filled as it was with jagged boards and rusty nails. They helped him across the street to the school shelter, where he saw the Reverend Durrie Hardin, rector of Trinity Church.

"The rectory is gone," Hardin told him, sobbing. "I lost Helen. I lost my wife."

"I think I lost my wife too," Williams replied.

Trinity Church, which had stood for 120 years and survived 18 hurricanes, was completely gone. There was nothing left of the sanctuary, the auditorium, or the rectory. Live Oak Cemetery looked like a battlefield, heaped with uprooted trees, piles of debris and flotsam that had drifted up against the gravestones. With Nick, Malcolm, and a search party from the shelter, Williams picked his way through the cemetery, looking for bodies. They found his twenty-two-year-old married daughter, Myrtle Mae, and her five-year-old daughter, Bridget, lying lifeless together, like the Madonna and Child. Then they started finding the little ones, sprawled in the debris: Floyd and Eddie and Esther, all under seven. Then they found Charles, Clara, Jeremiah, Anna, Sylvester, and Deborah. The last one they found was Otis. Williams discovered his son pinned down under debris, in a serene little semi-circle of camellias, azaleas, and water oak trees. One by one, he and others laid the bodies of his children out on the sidewalk, all their heads in a line. The only one missing was Myrtle, Williams' wife of almost thirty years.

"Daddy," Malcom told his father, "Mama got her neck broke. We don't want you to see her."

Paul Williams had lost Myrtle, eleven of his fifteen children, and one grandchild, that night—thirteen family members in all, more than any other family on the Gulf Coast.

Police Chief Gerald Peralta stood nearby watching as rescuers helped Williams with his heart-rending chore.

"The thing that hurt me the most was watching that man carrying out the bodies of his family and laying them right there on the sidewalk," he recalled later.

For Paul Williams, no words could describe what had happened. In an interview many years later, he could only say, "Oh, Lordy mercy, nobody knows. Nobody knows how I miss them! It hurts. It hurts. It hurts."

IT SEEMED LIKE "a jillion years" that Janice and Harry Stegenga and their two small children waited in the storm shelter over in Long Beach. After the eyewall passed through, the wind began to die down. The torrential rains—eleven inches overnight—gradually slackened off and died. Then a pale dawn showed through the shattered windows of the school. The Stegengas ventured outside, into the Daughtery Park area near the school.

"Gee, that wasn't so bad!" Janice said out loud. "It wasn't as bad as I thought it was during the night!" A few trees were down, some telephone poles had been snapped off, the streets were strewn with wind-blown debris—but almost all the houses and buildings were intact. It looked like their home community had come through.

They loaded their things back into the Volkswagen and drove over to Harry's cousin's house. On their way, as the scenes of devastation grew more severe, the two adults grew increasingly quiet. When they got to the house, they discovered that three-quarters of it was simply gone. Rafters jutted into thin air; a crumbling, unsupported brick wall looked so fragile it appeared ready to collapse in the first breath of wind. Huge timbers had fallen into the hallway where Janice had suggested they could all hide if things got really bad.

If they had, they would all be dead now.

They continued driving down Second Street towards their home in Pass Christian, but the streets were completely blocked by downed trees and mountains of rubble. They started following a guy in a small civil defense jeep; he was inching his way along through people's backyards, sometimes stopping to get out and cut away tree limbs and branches with a chainsaw. Except for all the downed trees and rubble, though, Second Street seemed to be fine. It was amazing, really. Maybe it wasn't so bad after all—but the closer they got to the middle of town, the more they realized what had happened. Five blocks from the center of downtown, they drove into total and absolute destruction. The post office was gone; the bank was gone; Ringer's Grocery was gone. Almost every other shop and house was gone. In fact, everything west of Market Street had simply disappeared.

"Camille was like Hiroshima," Janice said later. "It was like going to hell."

When they got to the corner of Church Street, where the lovely white roofs of Trinity Episcopal Church and the rectory had stood, all that remained were a few storm-battered trees and some concrete steps leading up into thin air. They stopped the car and Harry got out. He had been born and raised in a house one block from this corner. But he stood there now, utterly stunned. He did not recognize where he was.

The church where he'd been an altar boy, gone. The school where he'd played basketball as a kid, gone. The house where he was born, gone. There were no landmarks, no points of reference. The world had been turned upside down. Trees were upended, their roots now reaching for the sky. The church roof was on the ground. Bits of clothing hung in the treetops. Even the dead had been thrown back out of their graves into the light of day.

A big live oak tree was down across Saint Louis Street, so they couldn't drive down to Harry's grandparents' house, which was only about a block away—if it was still there at all. Janice, Harry's sister Loretta, and the two children waited in the parked Volkswagen while Harry galloped down the street towards the home of Pops and Anna Dambrink. When he came back a short while later, he was crying. Janice had known this man for eight years and been married to him for five. In all that time, she'd never seen him shed a single tear. Now they were streaming down his face.

"The house is gone," he sobbed. "They're all dead. Somebody told me that Grandma and Grandpa and Aunt Sis are dead. I guess Mama and Daddy are dead, too, because I can't find them."

"Wait a second, Harry," Janice said, stepping out of the car and seizing his arm. "You don't know that for sure! Let's go see if we can find them."

They threaded their way through the wreckage to the storm shelter in the school across the street. In its west wing, sitting together at a table, were Harry's parents: Piet and Valena Stegenga. They looked wan and wretchedly tired. But they were alive.

Piet told them that he and Valena had spent the night, freezing cold and wet, on a floating pile of debris. The next morning, when it got light, they could see that Pass Christian had been laid to waste—where they were, only three or four houses were left standing. They walked up to one house that had been completely inundated by mud and water, after the owner, a woman, had opened both the front and back doors to let the storm surge sweep straight through. She had survived the night by cowering in the attic. She offered Piet a glass of whiskey and Valena a cigarette—which was the only thing on God's green Earth she wanted at that moment. Later, they walked back towards town and were stopped on the street by a television reporter from Channel 6, a local station.

"You'll never overcome this," the reporter told Piet.

Piet was fiercely defiant: "Yeah—I'll overcome it." When Piet thought about this encounter later, he added, "I knew in my heart that I'd have more than I ever had in my life. Listen, when I lost my clothes and everything, I was barefooted, I lost my shoes, my eyeglasses, I lost everything. And I knew in my heart and soul that I was going to bounce back and have more than I ever had in my life. I knew that. I knew that."

AT 8:30 that Monday morning, amid the muddy, rain-sodden wreckage of Woodstock, Jimi Hendrix mounted the world's largest sound stage to close out the festival's "three days of peace and music." He was wearing blue jeans, a beaded white leather vest with fringe dangling to his knees, and a red scarf wrapped around his enormous Afro—a resplendent prince of rock. By now, most of the four hundred thousand people who'd come to the Aquarian Music and Art Fair were on their way home, back to the real world or anywhere they could get a decent meal, a shower, and some dry clothes. The concert site looked like a Civil War battlefield. Max Yasgur had been paid fifty thousand dollars for the use of his alfalfa field, and at this moment it appeared to have been utterly trashed. It was a vast sea of mud-puddles, garbage, smoky fires, discarded cardboard boxes and hand-lettered signs, clothes and blankets, knocked-down tents, soggy sleeping bags, and sleeping bodies. For some reason, an awful stench was in the air. But when Jimi Hendrix stepped onto the stage and lit into a wailing, free-form electric guitar version of "The Star-Spangled Banner," everything seemed to come to a complete standstill.

"There were moments when the event overwhelmed anything the music could say," Rona Elliot, who worked in public relations for Woodstock Ventures, recalled later. "The morning of the end of the show, I was up in the operations trailer, and I can remember hearing this unbelievable guitar lick. I came out to a deserted sea of mud with maybe ten or twenty or thirty thousand people left—a sea of mud which had been turned over because of the rain. You put your foot in it and you went down six inches, eight inches, you know. And it was Jimi Hendrix playing 'The Star-Spangled Banner.' It is burned into my memory. I mean, it was a remarkable experience."

Another person who was there that day, John Binder, observed, "I think it sort of put that patriotic irony at the end of Woodstock and made it a very different event than it really would have been. Hendrix was saying, 'This is the left-handed version of patriotism.' "

Hendrix's over-the-top, electrified soliloquy later became a kind of anthem of the Woodstock Nation. And, for that matter, a left-handed celebration of the *whole* nation, a tribute to its love of freedom, its genius for innovation, and its ability to pick up the pieces and start over when the world ends.

THAT MONDAY AFTERNOON, the Gulf Coast newspaper *The Daily Herald* was unable to run the presses at its devastated plant on the coast. Still, the publishers managed to put out an abbreviated version by relaying stories to a printer in Columbia, South Carolina, and having the paper flown back to the Gulf.

The information was still very incomplete and not entirely accurate. It was as if the newspaper itself were in shock.

A warehouse in Gulfport that was being used as a shelter had collapsed in the storm, injuring forty to fifty people, some critically, the paper reported. Fires were still burning out of control in both Gulfport and Biloxi, but with almost all roads blocked by downed trees and wreckage, firefighters had been unable to reach them. Biloxi police said flooding due to heavy rain or raging high tides was ten feet deep in parts of the city, and the bridge between Biloxi and Ocean Springs was knocked out. The Red Cross reported that more than 44,500 people took refuge in 394 emergency shelters it set up in the hurricane warning area, from Grand Isle, Louisiana, to Apalachicola, Florida.

On her western edge, Camille had lashed New Orleans with 100-mile-an-hour winds. Violent tides had surged up the Mississippi River and, south of the city in the small town of Buras, Louisiana, now nearly deserted, a wall of water had crashed over the 15-foot levee and put the town under 14 feet of water. On her eastern edge, Camille struck Mobile, Alabama, with 75-mile-an-hour winds and a rash of tornadoes.

Still, the paper conveyed only a vague and uncertain sense of the size and ferocity of the storm. There was no information at all about fatalities. There were no reports from the hardest-hit areas: Bay St. Louis and Pass Christian. The *Herald* pointed out that the greatest storm on record on the Gulf Coast had been the hurricane of 1947, but that "some longtime residents guessed Camille would far exceed the wrath of the '47 devastation."

Still, even on the morning after the storm, nobody quite grasped the magnitude of the devastation.

CHAPTER SEVEN

12:00 noon, Monday, August 18
Biloxi, Mississippi

WADE GUICE was almost afraid to do it—not because he was apprehensive about flying, but because of what he might see. But around noon that Monday, the Harrison County civil defense director went up in a helicopter to look at what Hurricane Camille had done to his beloved Mississippi Gulf Coast.

It was a remarkably clear day. The departing hurricane, now moving north towards Jackson and the Tennessee border, had wiped the atmosphere clean. The Gulf glittered beneath a hot August sun.

What Guice saw below him almost beggared belief. From the Bay Saint Louis bridge eastward to a point just west of Jeff Davis Avenue in Long Beach—a distance of about ten miles—the area from the shoreline to two blocks back was virtually obliterated. There were almost no landmarks left at all. It looked as if a bomb had gone off. The beachfront was simply gone.

Camille's landfall on the Gulf Coast, it would later be determined, was replete with dark superlatives. Her storm surge was the highest ever recorded, 24.6 feet, "with some evidences that water levels may have been a few feet higher in locations where reliable water marks were no longer available when survey teams arrived in the area," Robert Simpson later wrote.

Camille's sustained wind velocities were unpredented for a landfalling hurricane in the continental US. Her central pressure was a near record. And now, Wade Guice could see unfolding below the stark evidence of what would turn out to be the most destructive Atlantic hurricane on record at that time.

The harbor front of Gulfport, normally a bustling, prosperous port

city, was a barren wasteland. Three enormous steel-hulled oceango-
ing tankers, more than six stories high from waterline to deck, were
hard aground at the north end of the harbor basin. An ultra-modern
banana-loading terminal had been ripped to pieces and scattered in
every direction. Mountains of downed trees, splintered houses, and
boats blocked all the streets, if the streets were there at all. Thousands
of houses and businesses had been destroyed. A huge steel barge
rested on dry land between the lanes of Highway 90. Immense oil
tanks had been lifted up like corks and dropped in incongruous
places. A twenty-six-foot sloop had been washed two and a half
blocks inland and rested on the lawn at the First Baptist Church. In
West Gulfport, immense rolls of paper used for printing newspapers,
big as rolled hay bales, were strewn in the streets. Elsewhere, a cat-
food canning plant had been demolished and acres of ground around
it were covered with cat food cans. An overturned yacht had been
rammed through the front wall of a house. A tugboat rested on top of
the rubble of another house. In fashionable East Beach, where 114 expensive homes had stood before the storm, there were only six with
less than major damage that Monday morning. Ninety-nine were gutted or torn from their foundations, and nine were completely gone.

All that remained of the three-story Richelieu luxury apartment
complex was a cement slab littered with debris. The building had
been removed from the face of the earth—roof, walls, windows, joists,
rafters, even the plumbing had been ripped out of the ground and
washed away. (It turned out, too late, that the story about the steel
beams was untrue. They were made of wood.)

By Guice's calculation, beneath him lay about sixty-eight square
miles of complete devastation. At this point, there was no telling how
many people had been killed, but clearly, untold horror was down
there. Meterologists would later say that "no Pacific Coast tidal wave
or Atlantic storm (hurricane or winter storm) has ever submerged so
much land to such a depth." In some places houses as much as two
miles back from the beach were submerged. Pass Christian, which
took the hurricane's blow head-on when she came in off the Gulf,
was overrun from the rear when the water in Saint Louis Bay crested,
rushed into the bayou behind the town, and trapped people with
flood tides coming from two directions. For those unfortunate enough
to have stayed, there was no place to run or hide. The wall of wind

and water had even reconfigured the offshore islands out in the Mississippi Sound. Ship Island, off Biloxi, was now *three* islands.

Looking down on it all from the chopper, Guice struggled mightily to keep his personal worries in check. He was the shepherd and guardian of this *entire* community, not just any individual member of it, including those in his own family. Still, when the helicopter flew over what was left of Biloxi, he couldn't help but look down to see if he could spot his own house. There it was: completely surrounded by mountains of debris, and with water coming directly up to the edge of it. The roof looked badly damaged, but the frame appeared intact.

Far more worrisome was the condition of the house where he'd sent his teenage daughter, Judy, to spend the night. On Friday afternoon, he and his wife, Julia, had sent Judy over to stay with a friend who lived on the north side of the Bay of Biloxi, the side farthest away from the ocean. It was at a reasonably high elevation—about sixteen feet above sea level. This was the sort of number a civil defense director in a hurricane-prone area would know as well as his own phone number—especially in a place he was sending his own daughter. But when he looked down at the north side of the bay now, he could see that the whole area had been inundated by water and ravaged by wind. His heart stopped for a moment when he spotted the house where Judy had been staying. It had been almost completely destroyed. If Judy had not gotten out, there was a good chance she'd been badly injured or perhaps even killed.

He stifled the thought, which seized his heart like a clammy hand. Self-discipline. Focus. He needed to center on these now. He was responsible to the thousands of other fathers, to the mothers, brothers, sisters, and children who were also, at this moment, terrified that they might have lost a loved one down there.

It was too early to tell how well he'd done with the first phase of his job: convincing people to evacuate. Now he was facing the second phase: digging out and rebuilding the community. It was obvious, especially from up here, that the logistical problems confronting him were staggering. The sheer magnitude of the damage was almost impossible to grasp. There was an undetermined number of dead bodies, human and animal, in the wreckage down there. Vermin control would become a problem quickly, as things began to rot in the hot August sun. There was no drinkable water. There was no food.

No electricity. No telephones. No transportation. Many people had no shelter, and some did not even have clothes.

The most crucial task was rescuing those who were still alive but trapped in the wreckage. The second was providing drinking water. People could become badly dehydrated in a matter of hours. If they started drinking contaminated water, a whole new wave of medical problems would develop. Generators: He'd have to set up priorities for the distribution of generators to restore power—a very serious and emotionally charged task in a disaster area where thousands of people were in extreme situations.

There would be a hundred decisions to make an hour, many of them critical. In the next few hours and days he would be at the center of the storm after the storm, manning the Emergency Operations Center. He and everyone else working on recovery would have to co-ordinate with every other agency that would be involved, a sometimes mind-bogglingly complex task. The Red Cross. The National Guard. The Salvation Army. The Seabees. And all the thousands of well-meaning but disorganized volunteers.

It would be five days before Wade Guice was able to lie down and get a night's sleep.

ROSEMARY TULLY emerged from the shelter in Pass Christian where she'd watched the blood-red eye come over. Her car had survived the night, so she tried to drive back home through the devastated town.

"It was just unbelievable that such destruction could come from wind, rain, and water," she said. "There were houses blown off from one side of the street clear across the street and piled up against two or three other houses on the other side."

Tully worked for the welfare department, so she knew many of the elderly people in town. As she wove her car in and out of the downed trees and wreckage, she thought, "Oh, my goodness, there's Mrs. So-and-so's house over there—it's just demolished. What in the world will she do?" She passed people on the street walking with their eyes open, glazed and unseeing. They were in shock, and so was she. She didn't know how she managed to drive. Some of these people, she knew, were strong enough to take it. Others were not. They would never recover,—emotionally, physically, or financially—as long as they lived.

Finally, Tully pulled her car over, laid her head down on the wheel, and just began to sob.

Dr. Marion Dodson, chief of staff at Hancock General Hospital in Gulfport, began transferring patients by helicopter to a hospital in New Orleans that morning, because the power had gone out in the storm and clearly might need days or weeks to be restored. Two patients, frightened and upset by what they had experienced, did not live through the ordeal of the transfer. A resident who was also a national guardsman helped Dr. Dodson gather up an enormous stockpile of wound dressings, antibiotics, and medications for tetanus and typhoid, and the two of them walked down to Waveland to set up a makeshift emergency care unit in the elementary school. All the roads were blocked by debris, so they went slowly, climbing over fallen trees and mounds of rubble. Without power, water, shelter, phone service, streets, or cars, it was almost as if human progress had been set back a thousand years.

Along the way, Dodson came across a young man splashing water on a porpoise that had become stranded on his front lawn. Its shining sides were heaving, so he took out a stethoscope and checked the animal's vitals. Its heart rate was normal, though elevated, and its airways were clear. It was just desperate to get back into the water. Several other people came along, including another doctor that Dodson knew. Kneeling down around the porpoise they all linked hands to form a kind of rescue stretcher underneath it, then they walked a short way out into the shallow Gulf and let it go. Dazed and frightened, the animal shook its bottle-shaped head and swam off, taking its own amazing story of the storm along with it.

DICK MERRITT, a real estate developer in Pass Christian, had weathered the worst of the storm on the roof of his house with his sixteen-year-old son Jonathan and the two family dogs: a French poodle and a little red miniature dachshund named Heidi. The dogs seemed to have weathered the storm fairly well—until the next morning when all the fur around Heidi's face turned completely white.

As the first light came up, Jonathan climbed down and walked out into the neighborhood, but all that morning he kept getting lost. "There were no landmarks, no highway, nothing. It took us almost four hours to get up to town. The only way we could do it was walk along the beach line because there were no streets, just big holes everywhere."

Alma Anderson, a beautician with a salon in Biloxi, had married into one of the oldest families in town and lived in a handsome home on the beach. She weathered the storm in the beach house with eight other people, but by morning the place was ripped to pieces and two people who'd stayed there were dead. When Anderson and her mother-in-law were taken to the hospital that morning, their shoes had been ripped off their feet. Her mother-in-law had had the clothes ripped right off her body.

"You know," Anderson recalled later, "even a newborn baby has more than we have. I couldn't explain to you the feeling when you don't have anything. You don't have any clothes, you don't have a home, you don't have any food. We had just spent money remodeling the house, but you didn't even have a dime to get a soft drink with. And it's a horrible feeling. From the time you're born you have something, even if it's rags. We didn't even have rags."

Older people had no eyeglasses, no dentures, no medication, no favorite pillow, no family Bible—much less a house, car, or boat. They didn't even have identification to prove who they were.

"I had furs, I had diamonds, I had closets full of clothes; but when it comes to your life, those things don't mean one thing," said Anderson.

Not everybody took away the same spiritual lesson from the devastation of the storm. Though looting did not appear to be widespread, at least a few people prowled around the ruined neighborhoods with gunny sacks and pillowcases, like kids at Halloween, picking up whatever they could find.

ROBERT TAYLOR and Billy Barrett were making their way over to check on Barrett's house when they heard a couple of rifle shots not too far off. Taylor's first thought was that somebody was shooting a looter. At that point, he realized he'd better check on his mother's house. She lived alone in a beautiful home of which she was justly proud, but when he got there he discovered the first floor had been completely inundated by mud and water. The Gulf of Mexico had swept right through it, end to end. The house next door was completely gone. Taylor walked around behind his house and spotted two women with a gunny sack picking up all his mother's silver out of the muddy yard. It was the only time in his life that he had ever slapped a woman, and he smacked her hard. Then he snatched the sack out of her hand. He walked into the desolate house, slip-sliding through the mud.

"Mother! Are you there?"

No answer. The staircase to the second floor was completely gone, so Taylor flung the sack of silver up on to the second floor landing. Then he went to see if anybody else in the neighborhood needed help. He found the next-door neighbors, Dr. and Mrs. Elkemer, trapped in their bedroom. It had once been on the second floor, but Camille had collapsed the two-story house into a one-story, so now he could get to them while still standing on the ground. He pried open the bedroom window and the Elkemers crawled out, still in their bedclothes, clutching a small dog. They were badly shaken, but appeared to be physically unharmed.

Then Taylor crawled through the wreckage surrounding what was left of the house belonging to his neighbors Vince and Nathan Alfonzo. The building had slipped off its foundation and was crazily tilted. Taylor tried to yank open a door or a window, but none would come free. Finally he started pounding on the side of the house.

"Hey, Vince! Are you there? Nathan!"

A few minutes later, the two elderly brothers crawled out the back window. After hanging off the edge of the roof all night as the storm surged through their house, they'd waited until the water finally receded and had lain down and fallen asleep on a soggy couch. Vince's hand had been severely cut from hanging on the roof, and Nathan had lost his dentures. They both looked about twenty years older than they had the day before, but they were alive.

Taylor remembered a poor little old widow who lived nearby, Mrs. McInnis, so he went to her house to check on her.

"Mrs. McInnis? Ma'am? Are you there?" Taylor shouted into the empty house, which had become an indoor beach in the storm.

Nobody seemed to be home. Just then he heard a small noise at the top of the stairwell and looked up to see the old lady peering furtively over the balcony. The stairway to the second floor was gone, so Taylor found a table, climbed up on it, and opened his arms.

"Jump, Mrs. McInnis!"

The old lady, well into her eighties, leapt into his arms. He put her down and she walked off toward Highway 90, glassy-eyed, without ever saying a word.

Taylor began to worry that looters might be after his *own* house, so he walked the block and a half home. That's when he found four young men in his yard, picking up his silverware, his prized sailboat-racing trophies, and whatever else they could find. He marched into his house and rooted around in a closet until he found a shotgun and a handful of duck shells. He wasn't even sure the old gun worked, but all he needed was for the looters to think it did. He walked back into the yard and confronted them.

"You put everything down right where you found it! I don't want to shoot anybody, but I will if I have to. Y'all need to just leave. Now!"

Three of the young men dropped what they were carrying and slunk away. But the other kid just stood there, glaring at him. Taylor threw a shell into the chamber and lifted the gun.

"I'll be back!" the looter shouted, threw down the piece of silver in his hand, and took off at a dead run.

Taylor sat down outside his wrecked house in the newly dangerous world, with the shotgun across his knees and a handful of shells in his pocket. One by one, neighbors began emerging from the wreckage of their houses, many in such shock that they hardly seemed to know where they were. One told Taylor that his parents were alive, and out hunting around the neighborhood for him. Taylor got up and walked back down the street to his mother's house. He found her there, hands on hips, standing out in front of her flooded, mud-ravaged home.

Then she turned to him. She did not throw her arms around him, overjoyed to see her only son alive after the great storm. Instead, she just clucked disgustedly.

"Isn't this a mess?" she asked.

"Mama, it's good to see you too!" Taylor laughed, and he just kept on laughing—a big, rollicking tempest of laughter, filled with affection and relief.

2 *P.M. Monday, August 18*

Throughout the morning, Camille trundled north at about 18 miles an hour, raining like fury, ripping down trees and smashing glass in almost every business in downtown Hattiesburg. By the time she hit Jackson, about 150 miles north of the Coast, she seemed to be running out of steam. Wind speed and barometric pressure are a hurricane's vital signs, and her wind speeds were dropping while her pressure was rising, rapidly returning to a state of atmospheric calm. The patient wasn't dead, but she was failing.

The New Orleans office of the National Weather Service signed off on the story of the storm, issuing its last advisory at 11 o'clock Monday. The Kansas City office picked up the story as Camille headed north, issuing the next bulletin that afternoon. It was brief and relatively bland:

KANSAS CITY
BULLETIN 2PM CDT MONDAY AUGUST 18, 1969

REMNANTS OF HURRICANE CAMILLE RAPIDLY WEAKENING . . . HEAVY RAINS AND FLASH FLOODING POSE THREAT TO NORTHERN MISSISSIPPI, WESTERN TENNESSEE, SOUTHEAST MISSOURI, WESTERN KENTUCKY AND SOUTHERN ILLINOIS . . . MANY OF THESE AREAS HAD EXTENSIVE RAINS OVER THE WEEKEND SO THAT ALL FUTURE RAIN WILL RUN OFF QUICKLY . . .

HIGHEST WINDS ARE ESTIMATED 45 MPH NEAR THE CENTER WITH A FEW SQUALLS SURROUNDING THE DYING STORM . . . WINDS AND TIDES WILL CONTINUE TO DIMINISH ALONG THE GULF COAST TODAY AND TONIGHT . . .

NO FURTHER BULLETINS ON CAMILLE ARE PLANNED BY THE KANSAS CITY WEATHER BUREAU

It was almost as though, metaphorically speaking, the weather service were tucking the whole South into bed.

Meanwhile, the nation's attention shifted to the devastation and the rising death toll along the Mississippi Gulf Coast, as the true extent of Camille's destruction emerged from the rubble. At the same time, other distractions, and other stories, began to seize people's attention. In Edgartown, Massachusetts, lawyers said they would open an inquest into the suspicious death of Mary Jo Kopechne, a twenty-eight-year-old secretary who had been riding in a car driven by Senator Edward Kennedy when the car ran off a bridge into a pond on Chappaquiddick Island. The drowning had gone unreported for nine hours, and Kennedy's once-gilded political future was now in shambles. It was reported that the week's death toll in Vietnam had been 244 soldiers killed, 144 missing. The rocks that astronauts Armstrong and Aldrin brought back from the moon turned out to be billions of years old, a real thrill. And outside of White Lake, New York, another afternoon thundershower hastened the end of the mad party at Woodstock. "The great rock festival ended today in the same spirit of peace and sharing that enabled four hundred thousand young people to gather for three days of music and marijuana without a major incident," the Associated Press reported.

Hurricane Camille seemed to slip off the radar screen of public consciousness at the same time she slipped off the radar screens of the National Weather Service. Nothing suited her better. She was a creature of the night, thriving in the darkness, and in the complacency of her victims, and her M.O. was to strike suddenly and ruthlessly. When she had roared ashore on the Mississippi Gulf Coast not long before midnight, nobody could really *see* the damage she was doing; they could only hear the wind and the screaming. Now she drifted northward, slipping out of sight like a lion vanishing into tall savanna grass.

To say that Hurricane Camille had now been reduced to "remnants" was to dramatically underestimate her potential. She was still a massive, unstable system with a circulating eye visible on radar. She was still carrying a cargo of hundreds of millions of tons of water vaccuumed out of the atmosphere and held perilously aloft. Her capacity for killing was still almost boundless, especially if her victims were caught unaware.

The next Weather Service bulletin on Camille was not issued until 6:00 A.M., Thursday, August 21, 1969.

By then it was too late.

PART TWO

~~~

THE EDGE
OF DARK

"They sicken at the calm, who know the storm."
—Old proverb

CHAPTER EIGHT

8:00 A.M., Tuesday, August 19
Massies Mill, Nelson County, Virginia

WARREN RAINES and his big brother, Carl Junior, were so inseparable that summer of 1969 that they'd figured out a way to ride a bicycle as if they were one person. The bike was a cool little low-slung Sting-Ray, a kind of kid-powered hot rod, with swooping handlebars and a long, low banana seat. Carl, who was sixteen, would straddle the forward end of the seat, grabbing the handlebars and steering, but pumping just one of the pedals, with his right foot. Warren, a skinny fourteen-year-old, would mount the banana seat behind him, pumping the other pedal with his left foot. Then they'd take off around the little village of Massies Mill, like some strange two-headed, four-legged boy, peeling down the back roads and driveways with amazing speed and dexterity, at half the effort.

It seemed hard to believe, but in only a week the endless summer would be over, and they'd both be going off to Nelson County High School. Warren, who barely weighed a hundred pounds dripping wet and had permanently tousled summer-blond hair, would be an incoming freshman. Carl, who stood almost a head taller and had darker hair, would be a junior—an upperclassman, an ally against the sharks and bullies who awaited Warren in the scary, unfamiliar ocean of high school.

But a week was an eternity, and now all Warren and Carl cared about was sucking every morsel of pleasure out of what remained of the long, lazy summer. They got up early, gobbled a little cereal at the kitchen counter, and went outside to take a long, lingering look at The Car. It was prominently parked in the side yard beside their small white house, so as to be casually visible from Route 56, the main drag that ran through Massies Mill. Almost all of the hundred or so people in the village lived beside the river, which ran alongside the road, which meant that The Car was permanently on public display.

The Car was a 1954 Ford station wagon that the brothers had been painstakingly restoring all summer. They'd spray-painted the entire thing a fantastically cool new color that Camaro had come out with last year, a neon-bright car-candy color called "Hugger Orange." Then they'd laid a racing stripe down one side, slick as the dickens, and installed a lift kit to jack up the rear end. Okay, so it only had a six-cylinder engine, with three on the column, not much more muscle than an old family station wagon. Still, The Car looked so cool that their friends would come over just to stand there in the driveway and stare at it, as Warren and Carl were doing now. It looked like something you'd see at the racetrack. If you saw The Car on the street, you wouldn't want to challenge it. No way. It seemed to be breaking the speed limit, just standing still. Of course, neither of the boys could even drive it yet (not legally, anyway). Carl had only gotten his learner's permit in May, and wouldn't have his license for a few more months. When that day came, the two of them would go cruising all over Nelson County, and off to school, in their jacked-up, Hugger-Orange, Chevy-eating station wagon. They were counting the days.

This particular golden August morning, they jumped on the Sting-Ray and took a ride down to the river, not much of a ride at all because the river lay not much more than a hundred yards from the house. The summer had been very rainy—it had even rained some overnight—and the Tye River looked a little higher and a little muddier than usual. The boys were accustomed to the river's rhythms, watching it fatten up and rise in the spring or after a rain, and grow slack and shallow in the heat of summer. They'd watched it climb its banks, as it was doing this morning, but because the banks were at least five feet high in most places, they'd never seen it overflow.

In the summertime, the Tye was perhaps thirty feet across and two or three feet deep, with some wonderful deep holes where the river took a turn or hydraulics had dug out deep cool spots where the fish lay in wait, fat and wily. When the water was high, some of the holes were eight or ten feet deep, and the boys could sometimes catch bass or chub, trout or sun perch in the shadowy depths. In the sparkling shallows rustling with horsetails and water hyacinths, they could find crawdads under the rocks, or red-backed salamanders or dragonfly nymphs, hideous to behold. Or, from the gray ledges that overhung the fishing holes in places, they could launch out into thin air, and for one fleeting mortal moment be completely free of earth. Then they'd flop into the freezing depths with a slap, thus ruining all hope of catching a big fish, at least for that day. Even so, flopping in the river was the happiest way to cool off on a muggy day like this one, since the only place in town that had air conditioning was Bowling's Store, which had a little sign on the door with a picture of a penguin holding a cigarette pack: "Come on in, it's Kool inside!"

The Tye River meandered through the Raines brothers' lives, like a long, lazy braid that gave meaning and pleasure to everything, and tied everything together. To the boys, the river was an endless adventure. In the summertime, it was their life. It was so central to their daily routine that they didn't even dream about growing up to become Mickey Mantle or Warren Spahn, like other kids did; they just played a little sandlot baseball, cut a few lawns for two or three dollars a pop, and went back to messing around down by the river. If they weren't swimming in it, they were fishing in it or throwing stones into it or floating things on top of it or just listening to it chuckling and mumuring out the back door. You could actually see it from Warren's bedroom window, down across the back yard and what they called the "back road," that ran between their house and the river itself. In fact, there probably wasn't a single house in Massies Mill that was more than a couple of hundred yards from the river. (In these parts, river is pronounced "riv-uh," in a soft melodious drawl, as if the hard consonants had been softened by the water itself into smooth, sun-warmed curves.)

Nelson County, Virginia, was a bucolic place that morning. The Vietnam War, student demonstrations and the war against the war, hippies, Yippies, drugs, "free love," and all the rest of it seemed a world away. Down at the Kroger in Lovingston, you could buy a can of Campbell's tomato soup for eleven cents, a dozen eggs for forty-seven cents, or a box of Kellogg's Cornflakes for twenty cents. The Volkswagen Beetle, invented by Hitler but adopted by a generation of American college kids, could be had for all of $1,799. The gasoline to run it was 35 cents a gallon. Color television had just appeared, but the color was so bad lots of folks thought it would turn out to be a fad.

Nelson County was a place sheltered from the world and blessed by God. It was traversed along its northwest boundary by the hazy ramparts of the Blue Ridge Mountains, and on its southwest edge by the broad, slow-moving James River, making its way down to the Chesapeake Bay and thence to the sea, about 150 miles to the southeast at Norfolk and Hampton Roads, Virginia. The Tye was one of three stony, smallish rivers—the others being the Rockfish and the Piney—that drained off the ridgetops of the Blue Ridge down into the James. The Tye tumbled down out of the George Washington National Forest, off of Main Top, Three Ridges, and The Priest—at an elevation of over four thousand feet—one of the highest peaks in these parts. It chuckled over the gray boulders of Crabtree Falls, above the little river town of Tyro, then to Massies Mill in the broad floodplain below. Feeding into the Tye, the Rockfish and the Piney were a web of smaller drainages like Davis Creek and Ruckers Run, Cedar Branch and Possum Trot. In among the pitched mountainsides drained by these rivers and streams were sleepy hollows where people grew corn and soybeans, operated small peach or apple orchards, or ran a few milk cows or sheep or horses. Of the twelve thousand souls who lived in Nelson, most were farmers, or depended in some way on the county's agricultural base. Compared to Albemarle County to the north, home of the white-columned University of Virginia and Thomas Jefferson's famous home at Monticello, Nelson was poorer, more rural, more out-of-the-way, more ordinary. It was a lovely, left-behind kind of place, a county you fly by on the highway without even noticing.

And most folks liked it that way.

Local-boy-made-good Earl Hamner Jr. would later create the television series *The Waltons,* based largely on his boyhood memories of growing up in Nelson County during the Depression. Hamner's own family of eight was the model for the fictional Walton family, which lived on Walton's Mountain and ran a small lumber mill out of the house. Each week the story unfolded through the eyes of the eldest son, John-Boy, who aspired to be a novelist. Through him, viewers watched the saga of the family members as they braved the Depression, survived the War, grew up, got married, began families of their own, and learned life's bittersweet lessons. *The Waltons* seemed to strike a chord with the TV-viewing public, perhaps because the picture it painted—the close-knit family, the small farming community with its joys and rigors—seemed alien to modern American life.

The Waltons was not so very far from real life in Nelson County in the late summer of 1969. That morning of August 19, as the Raines brothers rocked around Massies Mill on their dual-powered Sting-Ray, scenes straight out of the TV series unfolded all over the county. Farmers wandered into Lea Brothers general store, which doubled as a post office and sold everything from seed corn and saddles to salt licks and muskrat traps. In Lovingston, the county seat, idlers began their long, hot day of watching the world pass by from seats on the square across from Loving Brothers drugstore. In Wingina, down on the James, men in a lumberyard began loading logs onto railroad flatcars, to be hauled off to the pulp mill. At the rock quarry in Schuyler, men stoked up the wet saws for the day's cutting. At the American Cyanamid plant down on the Piney River, Junior Thompson joked and razzed his brother Buzz as they unlocked the maintentance shack. American Cyanamid, which mined titanium dioxide for various industrial uses, was the biggest employer in the county and was known simply as "the plant."

It was that moment at the very pinnacle of summer, just before the season tips over into harvesttime and autumn. There was a kind of stillness in the air, as if the whole world held its breath, savoring these days of richness. The melons and the sweet corn and the tomatoes were ripe, and everybody's kitchen had some of them—usually homegrown, but sometimes given by a neighbor—on the kitchen counter.

It was the end of baseball, the beginning of football. Almost imperceptibly, the summer was sliding away. Each day was about one minute shorter than the one before; the sun set at eight o'clock now. At night the air was loud with the sound of cicadas. If you looked, you could see the first hints of fall in the woods. The dogwoods were faintly tinged with red-brown, like dried blood. Here and there, you could glimpse flashes of bright red: sweet gum or Virginia creeper, which tended to go straight to crimson as the nights cooled. The horse chestnuts had started to simply turn brown. The locust trees had begun to loose little flurries of small yellowing leaves in a light wind, like handfuls of tossed coins.

Now the oaks and hickories were raining great harvests of nuts, which clattered on cars and rooftops in a high wind. The squirrels, half mad with the late-summer plenty, dashed crazily about, the road-sides seemed littered with the bodies of those whose madness had overcome their caution. A smokiness was in the air, and a faint sense of melancholy. Somewhere in the heart there was already a grieving for the green. Even though all around the woods and fields and mountains were an almost unbroken sea of green, you could feel it coming: the dark days of winter, the change in the light, the turning of the world.

Apples and peaches were the primary crop of the county, and har-vesttime was in full swing. All over central Virginia, in Nelson and Amherst and Albemarle counties, the peaches were ripe and orchards had put out ads to come pick your own: Georgia Bells, Sun Highs, Hale Havens, Blakes, Albertas, and Redskins. The price was generally around $2.50 a bushel (so long as you brought your own baskets). Most of the clingstones were already gone, but freestones like the yellow-fruited Blakes were ripe and sweet. With a paring knife you could slice open a Blake with no effort at all, and it rolled open like a little sunrise, showing its yellow meat and red, corrugated core where the pit came free.

The early-ripening apples were also almost ready for picking: the Ginger Golds, Galas, and Virginia Golds, followed soon by the Jonagolds, the Jonathans, and the MacIntoshes. Around the mostly white county, nut-brown faces of Mexican migrant workers, come north for the apple harvest, had begun to show up in country stores, cheap restaurants, and gas stations. Others had begun to work the ap-ple harvest, too, but their faces could not be seen at all. They worked up in the mountain hollows in the dark of night, stoking up the stills to make brandy out of fallen apples they'd secretly scavenged off the ground and then pressed into cider. Nelson County was famous for its apple brandy, manufactured in the moonlight by people who did not exist.

After visiting the river, the Raines brothers, pedaling madly in tan-dem, took the back road down to the warehouse where their father worked. Their dad, Carl Raines Sr., managed a small business called Miller Chemical Company, which supplied farmers and orchardists with tools and spraying equipment. The business was housed in a huge musty-smelling warehouse not fifty feet from the river, filled with agricultural supplies and tools, apple ladders and baling twine. Carl Senior enjoyed having the boys around so he could keep an eye on them while he worked. The warehouse was magical for kids, filled with places to climb and hide, and sometimes their dad would even let them drive their go-kart around the place, squealing around corners and sometimes popping open a fertilizer bag.

Carl Senior was a gentle, tolerant man who always seemed to have the time to help the boys fix a flat tire or patch a broken bike. He was slow to anger, or to raise a hand for a spanking—it was usually their mother who was the enforcer when the brothers got out of line. Things had to get pretty bad before their father stepped in. In fact, far from disapproving of the boys' high spirits and shenanigans, he had actually helped them build a second, even faster, go-kart from scratch—a machine so high powered that every now and then the brothers would sneak it out on the highway and rev that rascal up to forty-five or fifty miles an hour. Needless to say, they never happened to mention these escapades to their dad, who might have been forced to raise his spanking hand and put a stop to it all.

Carl Junior and Warren had four siblings and their father seemed equally slow tempered with them all. Their nine-year-old brother Sandy loved to watch the TV show *Combat,* and he and a friend next door, Mike Wood, spent a lot of time wearing plastic helmets to fight Nazis down by the river. Little Ginger, who was seven, spent most of her time playing with dolls. Their teenaged sister Johanna, known as Jo, was more-or-less unofficially engaged to her boyfriend, Linwood Holton, and seemed to spend the better part of her life talking to him on the phone. Their oldest sister, Ava, had recently turned nineteen and moved out of the house, to Lynchburg.

This particular morning, the boys got all the way to the warehouse before they realized what should have been obvious from the start: Their dad wasn't even at work today. Some kind of a fancy election was going on, and since Carl Senior was an election official in the Massies Mill precinct, he'd taken the day off to tend to the responsibilities of politics. Whatever that was.

For Warren and Carl Junior, the only responsibility that day was to find some summer fun, so they turned the bike around, headed down to the river, and got back to work.

NELSON COUNTY SHERIFF William Whitehead had already been up for hours, showered and dressed in his crisp service uniform with his .357 Magnum holstered at his side. On his way downstairs from the bedroom, he'd paused to straighten his gun and badge in a hall mirror. At 6'5½" and 270 pounds, Bill Whitehead cut an imposing figure, especially when armed. He was 44 years old, broad in the shoulder and broad in the beam, with graying hair cut in a severe, no-nonsense military style. His handshake was like a vice grip; his gray eyes were direct and unflinching. But that wasn't all you could see in those eyes: There was also fierce intelligence, a wily humor, and a big bear-hug of friendliness.

He strode downstairs into the new part of the house, the part he and Catherine had renovated before they started having babies almost two decades earlier. Catherine was standing in the kitchen, flopping eggs and bacon into the pan, so he gave her a playful peck on the cheek and grabbed a cup of coffee.

The sheriff noticed that she'd thrown in a few extra eggs for the teenage boys, Dick and John, and for nineteen-year-old Nancy, who was home from college. Their capacity for eating was astounding. Also, their capacity for sleeping: They'd all be stumbling downstairs any minute, but only because he'd rapped on their bedroom doors. The sheriff slipped into his favorite easy chair by the window and glanced out, down across the yard to Hat Creek and the tumble of mountains beyond—Brents Gap, Cat Mountain, Mars Knob—lit by amber morning light.

Sitting at the kitchen table that morning, Bill Whitehead looked like the perfect physical embodiment of someone who might be elected sheriff. But for a lawman in a rural southern county, his progressive style had raised a few eyebrows, and a few hackles, over the years. He'd hired a black woman as a deputy—something of a radical act in that particular time and place. And he'd once implemented a controversial plan to employ and pay prisoners at the county jail, something that state inspectors had shut down as soon as they found out about it—then, later, adopted with great fanfare in the press. "I didn't see anything wrong with letting a man earn a few dollars while he was serving his time," the sheriff explained at the time. "It helped bolster his self-respect, and that's the one thing men in jail need most."

That was Bill Whitehead's style: tough but reasonable, firm but humane.

The firm side of his nature was augmented by the .357 Magnum at his side. It was a fairly serious weapon, but "there's no sense carrying a weapon if you're not serious," as he liked to say. He was serious about his job, but he was also proud of the fact that in his nine years as sheriff he had never once fired that gun. That meant that most of the time, he was able to handle anything that came up—domestic squabbles, treed cats, and all manner of disputes from the sorry-ass to the comic—with plain force of character.

Of course, quite often his intimidating physical presence was enough to stop people in their tracks. It wasn't just the gun and the badge. At a distance of a hundred paces, you could tell that Sheriff Whitehead wasn't someone to be trifled with.

He'd grown up on this farm, in the house known as "Willow Brook," as had five generations of Whiteheads before him. The older part of the house, built in 1807, was one of the stateliest dwellings in the county, with high ceilings, grand windows, and no plumbing. It was built at a time when the western boundary of Nelson County extended all the way to the distant, undiscovered sea and local people were still trading with the Indians. To Bill Whitehead, Willow Brook was the center of the universe, and he had no real desire to live anywhere else.

Things were different back when he was seventeen, of course: The Second World War was engulfing Europe, and he and all his friends were itching to get into the fight. He was young, strong, and restless—"full of piss and vinegar," as he says. That's why he left the farm to join the service, serving in the Infantry and the Army Air Corps in North Africa. But though he'd risen to the rank of staff sergeant, he was discharged in 1945 as a private first class, maybe because he'd decked an officer who was giving him grief in a radio mechanics class. Whitehead knew he'd done wrong, and got transferred to another unit after that fight. Still, there was a certain enduring pleasure in knocking the bastard on his ass.

When he came back to the farm after the war, Whitehead spent two years at Lynchburg College, but nothing much came of it. "I was too lazy to do the work," he says simply. Sitting still and reading books in a college classroom just didn't suit him. The best part of college was that he met and married Catherine, in 1948, and they moved back to Willow Brook. For a while, they lived with his parents. Bill Whitehead worked as a roughneck on structural steel jobs around the area. He built the steel framework for a couple of notable buildings in Lynchburg, and the work suited him just fine. He liked clambering over the high, dangerous girders, bolting steel plates with hot rivets. He liked coming home hot and tired, with the feel of a real day's work in his hands and back and legs.

After that, Whitehead tried selling John Deere tractors and other farm machinery for a while, but he lacked the killer instinct to close the deal. He thought just demonstrating the superiority of a disc plough or a combine would be enough to make the sale. But it wasn't, and he hated to push people into things. He preferred to let them make up their own minds.

Whitehead and Catherine renovated the farmhouse, adding a kitchen, a family room, and another bedroom, and then they started having babies. First came Nancy, then Dick and John. Bill began working with his daddy and brother-in-law in the family's extensive apple orchards, which employed several tenant farmers and extended all the way west to Massies Mill. His daddy let him farm part of the property, but it wasn't enough land to make a living, so he bought himself a tractor and a baler and began hiring himself out to bale hay for other farmers "on shares."

"In those days," Bill Whitehead recalls, "very few people had tractors, and everybody wanted to get out of stacking hay." But he liked the sweaty physical challenge of baling out in the hot sun, and he made good money at it, too. He charged twenty cents to cut, rake, and bale a bundle of hay, and he performed this service all across the county from late August through late October. By the end of the season, he'd have several rented barns stacked to the rafters with hay, which he'd sell off gradually over the course of the winter. It was a half-decent way to make a living; he enjoyed the work and was able to support a young family that way.

But when the chance to run for county sheriff came up in November 1959, Whitehead gave it a try. He was well known and liked across the county, and his family had been farmers, teachers, superintendents, and state senators in the area for generations. He won the election, and since that day everybody seemed to know him simply as "Sheriff." Maybe that's why people felt free to call him any hour of the day or night—more than once, he'd been up all night, answering calls around the county. Last night was lucky; there hadn't been a single call, and he'd slept straight through. He felt rested and ready for whatever this day might hand him.

Yep, he thought, gazing out the kitchen window that morning: It was going to be a good day.

1:00 P.M.

The first thing Bill Whitehead did after he left the house that morning was go down to the courthouse in Lovingston to vote. The big political news in Virginia that August day was the bitterly contested runoff election in the Democratic primary for governor. Two men were fighting to become the Democratic standard-bearer in the November general election against Republican Linwood Holton. One was Henry Howell, a fire-breathing Norfolk liberal; the other, a Charlottesville lawyer named William Battle, son of a previous governor and a friend of John F. Kennedy. Howell and Battle, wives in tow, had been crisscrossing the state for days. Yesterday's paper carried a picture of Howell and his wife, Betty, with supporters holding up a cardboard sign: "The Woman Behind the Man: Betty!"

After he cast his vote, Sheriff Whitehead began making his rounds of the county in the patrol car, a beast of a Plymouth with a 440 engine that could outrun all but the most reckless speeders. He stopped for lunch and got a chance to glance at the afternoon papers while wolfing down a sandwich and coffee. The *Charlottesville Daily Progress* reported that two companies of American infantrymen had been badly battered by a North Vietnamese force seven times their size in the foothills south of Da Nang. The 196th Light Infantry Bridgade had suffered about 40 percent casualties, with 15 killed and 50 wounded. The war had turned into a bloody, brutal slog, with every day bringing news like this. Another, more whimsical story reported on the aftermath of an enormous rock festival called

Woodstock that got completely out of hand when four hundred thousand kids showed up at an alfalfa field in upstate New York. It was, the sheriff thought, a damn logistical nightmare: The local authorities had had to fly in food and medical supplies by helicopter after the whole place was declared a disaster area. "There has been no violence whatsoever, which is remarkable for a crowd of this size," the festival's chief medical officer told the papers. "These people are really beautiful."

Whitehead didn't know what to make of any of it—he was just glad he wasn't in charge up there.

The other big news in the paper that day was about a ferocious hurricane called Camille, which had come ashore near Bay Saint Louis, Mississippi, around midnight on Sunday, a day and a half earlier. The paper reported that rescue workers in the coastal town of Pass Christian had pulled twenty-three bodies from the wreckage of a luxury apartment building called the Richelieu, which had been completely obliterated by the storm. The storm's death toll now stood at 128, but a state senator who was coordinating the civil defense efforts said it was sure to go much higher. "We know there are more bodies," he observed. Military helicopters were being used to fly in massive amounts of food and water to the survivors. But the devastation was so extreme it was difficult to comprehend: Some small coastal communities had simply disappeared. Nothing was left but their names. "There are no homes there," one local parish commissioner told the Associated Press. "There are no grocery stores. Nothing, period."

Of course, the Mississippi Gulf Coast was nine hundred miles away from Nelson County. That was almost as far away as Vietnam, as far away as Woodstock. There were violent summer storms in these parts, sure, and high water too, but hurricanes never came this far inland. In most parts of the county, there weren't even any rivers to speak of, just little chuckling farm-ditch creeks, so even serious inland flooding was unlikely. Besides, the weather forecast was right there in the Charlottesville paper, bland and benign as a blue summer day: "Rain is likely tonight, ending tomorrow. The low tonight will be about 70, the high tomorrow in the 80s. Thursday will be fair and cooler."

Even so, Sheriff Whitehead checked the U.S. Weather Bureau forecast when he stopped by the office later in the afternoon. The storm had been downgraded to a tropical depression as it headed north across Tennessee, Kentucky, and West Virginia. It had dumped a couple of inches but this had been a god-awful dry summer down there in the Deep South and they were probably grateful for the rain.

6:00 P.M.

It did rain that day of August 19,—off and on, all day, in big, thudding spatters. Then the sky would clear and the stuffy midsummer heat would settle down again, like a wet sheet.

IVANHOE STEVENS put in a good day's work that day at the Central Virginia Electric Cooperative, providing power to all the people in the county who lived in rural areas (which was almost everybody). Then he went home to work in his garden by the creek in Stevens Cove. His garden was a blessed spot, a place he liked to come to rest his soul at the end of the day. From there beside the creek, he had a serene vista of the Blue Ridge Mountains to the west, including the towering cone of The Priest. The fat pods of his okra were beginning to swell, so Ivanhoe spent some time that evening spraying them to keep the worms out. Then he pulled a few weeds and just lingered in the garden, resting his bones and looking around. A light spattering of rain came over the Blue Ridge, so he stopped his work and gazed up over the mountain, with starbursts of rain spattering in his face.

It was then that he noticed the clouds. They were coming in over the Blue Ridge from the west in one angry, roiling mass, piling higher and higher in the sky, impossibly high, like an illustration in a fanciful children's book. He'd never seen anything like it. He later described them as looking like "a hornet's nest." The clouds were so curious that he walked into the house and asked his wife to step out to take a look. Then they both stood outside the back door awhile, staring up into the sky as the great cloud masses came swarming over the mountain. Ivanhoe Stevens watched them until the sky darkened into twilight and then he went back indoors.

NOT FAR across the county, down at the old Lovingston Elementary School baseball field, Bobby Ray Floyd and the Nelson County All-Stars were having a good night. The All-Stars, the local slow-pitch 16-inch softball team, were just absolutely tearing it up this year. They'd just won the regional tournament down in Lynchburg, beating out teams from Amherst, Roseland, Shipman, Piney River, Arrington—all over the place. Now they were getting pumped and ready for the national tournament, in Waukegan, Illinois, against fifteen of the best slow-pitch softball teams in the country.

Ever since he was a little kid, all Floyd really wanted to do was play ball—to be like the players in the Big Show, like Hank Aaron, or Joe DiMaggio. Winning that tournament and heading to the nationals was like a little bit of heaven. What made it all the sweeter was that he'd been playing with these boys on the All-Stars team for years. They were his best friends, and in some cases his relatives. Making it to the tournament would be something they all shared, and the possibility of winning it was the one thing in his mind that warm August twilight, as the sun sank down behind Bald Knob and the whole ragged skyline of the Blue Ridge to the west.

Floyd was twenty-eight and married, with two children. Like most of the other folks in the county, he'd been born here, and, like many others, he'd never really felt like leaving. He was content to stay home, manage the family business, a little appliance store on Front Street in Lovingston, and after work and on weekends, try to get famous as the world's greatest slow-pitch shortstop. It was the top of the ninth inning when the sky began to darken ominously over the ballfield, and Floyd remembered that the papers said a storm was supposed to be blowing in tonight.

The sky continued to darken, and weird, leaden cloud-masses started moving over the mountain. Then it began to thunder. When a few lightning bolts cracked open the sky, Bobby Ray, Roger Ashley, Berks Fortune, Billy Hill, Buren Drumheller, and the rest of the All-Stars decided to bag the practice and drive on over to the Village Inn, in Lovingston, for something cold to drink. Big drops of rain began thudding on the windowpanes while they knocked back a few cold ones in the restaurant. Then thunder and lightning started clattering down the sky. The All-Stars decided to call it a night, postponing practice until Wednesday. As they left the Village Inn, somebody called out, "Well, boys, see you tomorrow night—God willin' and the creek don't rise!"

It was just an old Southernism, something people said without thinking much about what it actually meant.

OVER AT Nelson County High School, Vernon Lewis heard from the football coach about the strange clouds. Lewis was the director of the high school band, in addition to his regular duties as pastor of the Woodland Baptist Church. He was a slender, forty-three-year-old man who looked every bit the Baptist preacher, with his thinning hair, old-fashioned glasses, and conservative, fuddy-duddy suits. In preparation for the opening of school and the upcoming season, the football team was out on the practice field running drills. The band was playing Sousa marches in the band room when the football coach stepped in the door.

"There's a big storm coming over the mountain—it looks pretty bad," the coach told Lewis. "Think I'll cut practice short. Why don't you come outside and have a look."

Lewis stepped outdoors and looked up over the mountain to the west. The coach was right: The sky looked fierce and ominous, with immense, dark clouds stacking up into the upper atmosphere. You could already see flashes of lighing igniting the firmament and hear the distant rumble of thunder. Lewis decided to finish up the practice and send the kids home early.

As the youngsters filed out of the band room, an especially pretty seventeen-year-old girl named Audrey Zirkle came up to him. The year before, she had been chosen Miss Nelson Teen, the county's junior beauty queen. She was a radiant, outgoing girl. Everybody liked her.

"Well, I'll see you sometime tomorrow!" Audrey sang out.

Vernon Lewis would remember that comment for the rest of his life.

8:30 P.M.

After supper that night, Warren Raines flopped down in front of the TV and flipped idly through the channels. On the news, there was something about this big hurricane way down in Mississippi, wherever that was, and how this one man's refrigerator had been found blocks away from his house. Warren didn't listen for very long before switching to something of more interest: *Gunsmoke*, with James Arness as the slow-talking sheriff who was always right. Finally he turned off the television and wandered out onto the front porch to join his father.

Warren's brother Carl Junior, had gone off to a 4-H meeting and wouldn't be back until ten o'clock or so. Sandy and Ginger were already asleep. His mom was in the kitchen. His older sister Jo was probably off somewhere talking to her boyfriend on the telephone. So it was just Warren and his father there together on the porch. A summer thundershower had begun, and they sat chatting about mundane things—school, the apple harvest, The Car, what an election was. Eventually they stopped talking and just sat there on the porch of the little white house in Massies Mill, listening to the sound of drowsy summer rain drumming on the roof.

CHAPTER NINE

8 P.M., Tuesday, August 19
Lovingston, Virginia

AT THE SAME MOMENT that Warren and his dad sat listening to the rain in Massies Mill, Colleen Thompson was helping her three children get ready for bed in a travel trailer parked outside her mother-in-law's house, which sat on a hill beside the highway just north of Lovingston. The kids—Bonnie, Dale, and little Eddie, who was blind—always thought it was great fun to sleep in the travel trailer when they came to visit Gramma Lena. Their dad, Jake, parked the trailer in such a way that its windows lined up with those of the house, so the kids could talk to people inside Lena's little two-bedroom home through the windows. Eddie and Dale were ten, and Bonnie, the oldest, was three weeks shy of her twelfth birthday, so they were still young enough to revel in the novelty of this setup. In fact, there was something about this arrangement that seemed kind of crazy and cozy and exciting—almost like one of those children's television shows, where dolls and puppets pop their heads out of windows and say goofy things. The kids got so revved up, chattering to Lena or her daughter Grace through the window, pretending they were on TV or living in a doll's house, that it was all Colleen could do to get them settled down enough to get into bed.

Colleen, Jake, and the three youngsters had driven over to Lovingston, the Nelson county seat, a few days earlier to visit Lena, Jake's mother. The Thompsons came visiting quite frequently, making the four-hour drive from their home in Hampton, Virginia, at the mouth of the Chesapeake Bay. They came with the travel trailer hitched behind the car, because that was the only way Jake and Colleen's family of five could fit into Lena's little home. At the foot of the hill perhaps five hundred feet from her house, was a little stream called Muddy Creek. In the summertime, it wasn't much more than ankle-deep. Still, the kids loved to get down there and dam it up or make little boats out of sticks, or just splash around in the summer heat. Occasionally, after a sudden thundershower, Muddy Creek would swell up and spill over the highway. The hill down to the creek was so steep that when Jake parked the travel trailer in the driveway, he had to jack up the rear end and chock it with cinder blocks to bring it level with the windows in the house, just as the kids liked it.

When the Thompson family came to stay, the little house was stuffed to the rafters. Lena lived there with her divorced daughter, Grace, and her two teen-aged boys. Grace's boyfriend, Buzz Thompson (who shared a last name but was not related), also stopped by fairly often, sometimes staying overnight, sleeping in a lounge chair. (When everybody was there, that made ten people in all.)

Crowded as the house was, everybody seemed to get along famously. Lena enjoyed seeing her granddchildren, who warmed her heart and made her laugh. She was not much of a "go-er," she was just an old gramma who stayed home and liked to cook what the kids liked to eat. The three children seemed to enjoy their grandmother's company just as much as she enjoyed theirs.

The only odd thing that had happened on this trip was Lena's dream. She'd had it the night before, and all that August day she couldn't stop talking about it.

"I saw Colleen in a lake of water with nothing but her head sticking out!"

Lena kept repeating this story, pronouncing Colleen's name as if it were spelled "Coal-leen," in a broad, gentle drawl. And then she'd laugh and laugh.

"I saw Coal-leen in a lake of water with nothing but her head sticking out!"

It wasn't like Lena to say things like this, though. She wasn't one for having crazy dreams, or making things up, or calling attention to herself for no particular reason.

In response, Colleen couldn't think of anything to do but laugh dismissively.

"Aw, now, Lena, don't you be saying that! That's just a crazy old dream."

But Eddie, Dale, and Bonnie picked up on Lena's fanciful mood. They began gleefully elaborating on her preposterous yarn. It had been an unusually wet summer, and they'd had rain off and on all that August day, including one hard, sudden downpour in the late morning. Even so, the whole idea of Colleen's head bobbing around in a biblical flood was so outlandish it kept everybody in stitches all day.

"It's gonna flood, Mama! We're gonna have us a flood!"

Then they, too, would laugh and laugh.

JAKE AND COLLEEN had been married in 1949, twenty years earlier, and they had adopted all three of the children. Eddie was the first one—two months old at the time, and blind. When he was three, they requested another child. They wanted a little girl, but when the adoption agency told them it had a brother and sister whom it did not want to separate, Jake and Colleen decided to take them both. That's how Dale and Bonnie had become part of their family.

It was a small, close, old-fashioned family, bound by ties not of blood but of love, affection, and faith. The cornerstone of their lives was their faith in God; and Jake and Colleen had tried to bring up the children in "the nurture and admonition of the Lord," as the Bible instructed.

Eddie was the first of the children to accept the Lord. He made an altar call at a church that didn't even have altar calls. The Thompson family was attending a Presbyterian church at the time, and one morning Eddie just got up, dragged his mother out of her pew, and walked to the front of the church.

"I want to accept the Lord," he told the preacher. And he did, right there. Later that day, Colleen heard the two boys talking at home.

"What will happen if I die before I accept the Lord?" Dale asked in a small, fearful voice.

"You'll go straight to Hell," Eddie told him.

Dale accepted the Lord right soon after that.

It was the Reverend Jerry Falwell, pastor of the Thomas Road Baptist Church in Lynchburg and famed televangelist, who was instrumental in bringing Bonnie to the Lord. He was preaching a revival at Smith Memorial Baptist Church, near Williamsburg, just before the Easter Sunday that Bonnie was baptised. When the family went to visit Gramma Lena in Nelson County that August, Bonnie told her father,

"I want to go to Lynchburg to hear Jerry Falwell preach. I want to hear him." So Jake took Bonnie to Lynchburg, a half hour down the road, to hear Falwell preach on Sunday morning.

Two days later, on the morning of Tuesday, August 19, Jake drove down to Lynchburg General Hospital to get the news about his dad. His father, Hampton, was in the hospital for an operation to remove a cancerous tumor from his lung. The whole reason for Jake and Colleen's trip to Lovingston was that, while Hampton was hospitalized, Jake needed to help Lena run his parents' little store: H & H Grocery, on Route 151 down in Piney River. Jake had taken time off from his job as a civilian aircraft maintenance worker at Fort Eustis, the big Army base, to drive his family over to Lovingston. When he got to the hospital, he found that the doctors had not been able to remove all the cancer.

"Do you think it's all right to tell my mother what his condition is?" Jake Thompson asked one doctor. "She's got a heart condition, and I don't want to upset her."

"It's best just to tell her what you know," the doctor said. "She'll worry if she knows, and if she doesn't."

So Thompson had driven back up to Lovingston and told his mother the news. She seemed to take it with faith and fortitude—maybe because the prognosis was not entirely unexpected, since her husband had ignored doctors' warnings for years. After he broke the news to Lena, Thompson headed down to Piney River to help out at the store.

Grace's boyfriend Buzz got off his shift at the American Cyanamid plant down in Piney River at four o'clock that day. He, his brother Junior, and their father were on a maintenance crew at the sprawling plant. Junior worked late that afternoon, helping to replace a piece of overhead pipeline that slurried titanium dioxide ore into the plant. He was working outdoors, looking up, so he watched as the late-afternoon sky grew ominously grayish-green. He could see massive storm-clouds roiling up from two directions, and when they converged, the sky grew darker than he'd ever seen it. Then it began to rain, hard and furious, so hard it hurt your face when it hit. There was something strange about those clouds, and stranger about the rain: It was the coldest rain Junior Thompson ever remembered in the middle of August. It was so cold his teeth started chattering. The rain commenced to fall so hard the men on the rigger crew dashed into the maintenance shack to get out of the wet. Then they decided to call it quits for the day.

After his shift was over, Buzz Thompson drove down to Lynchburg with $600 cash in his pocket, because he was trying to buy a new front end for a vehicle he was working on, and he'd heard from a friend that one was for sale down there. As it turned out, the front end didn't fit, so he drove back up to Lovingston to Grace's house to visit and maybe have a bite to eat. By the time he got there, around eight o'clock, it was raining.

Buzz decided not to take a chance driving back down to Piney River, a distance of perhaps twenty miles. He figured he'd just sleep over in the lounge chair, as usual. Since Jake was off tending the store in Piney River, fate chose that moment to put seven people in Lena's house and the travel trailer parked beside it.

That's when it began to rain in earnest.

8:30 P.M., Roseland, Virginia

Sheriff Bill Whitehead didn't get home until around 8:30 P.M. After the polls closed at seven, he'd waited around for an hour or so until the local vote was counted. It looked like Bill Battle was solidly in the lead against Henry Howell, the senator from Norfolk, to become the Democratic nominee for governor. Virginians had been putting Democrats in the governor's mansion for a century, but this time the Republicans had an impressive candidate in Linwood Holton. If Battle wound up winning the nomination, he'd have one hell of a fight on his hands, the sheriff thought.

He sat down at the kitchen table for a quiet supper with Catherine, who'd worked that day as a guidance counselor at Nelson County High School. As they ate, he could hear the rain picking up, a steady, accelerating drumbeat on the low tin roof overhead. They had just finished eating when the phone rang. It was one of his deputies, Ron Wood, calling from down in Piney River.

"Sheriff, just thought you should know that we've got kind of a situation developing down here," Wood said. "Some folks called the fire department to come pump out their basements—one guy's basement just collapsed—but the creeks are coming up so fast the firemen can't even get to the firehouse."

"You suppose I should come down there? These people need my help?"

"I'm not sure there's much you can do, Sheriff. I'll just try to keep in touch with these folks and let you know how it comes out. There may be nothing to do except wait for the water to go down."

"Well, then, we'll just wait her out," the sheriff told Wood. "But you call me if it starts to get out of hand down there, Ron."

Just then an enormous thunderclap shook the house, and White-head glanced out the window. A lightning flash lit up the yard with its surreal glare, then another. Catherine was deathly afraid of electrical storms, and he wondered if she'd be able to sleep at all tonight, if this kept up.

The storm continued to worsen as the couple got ready for bed. The rain on the tin roof steadily escalated into a deafening clatter. He couldn't remember it ever raining so hard. The phone rang again. It was Ron Wood:

"My uncle called me from his house in Lowesville, over there on the James, said he was surrounded by water and he wanted me to come rescue him. He was afraid he couldn't get out. So I took my truck down there, but I couldn't even get to the house. I've never seen the river this high, Sheriff. And it looks to me like it's still rising."

"Do you want me to come down there?" Whitehead asked again.

"Sheriff, I don't think you can go anywhere. The roads are all blocked. No sense in your trying to come out at all."

Bill climbed into bed with Catherine, but by now the whole house seemed to be shaking in the storm. The rain and thunder were relentless. Every time there was a thunderclap, he felt his wife jump. Then, during a slight lull, he thought he heard a new sound: an eerie, steady roaring, like a freight train passing overhead, or the sound of jet engines revving at top speed.

"I thought you said there weren't supposed to be any high winds out there tonight," Catherine grumbled.

"Well, that's what the weather service said."

"But, *Lord,* listen to that wind blow!"

9:00 P.M., Davis Creek, Virginia

Outside his small house next to Davis Creek, a couple of miles north of Lovingston, Tommy Huffman and his brother Russell worked until dark on an old dump truck the two of them owned and rented out on the side. They could use the extra money: Russell made a meager salary at the stone quarry down in Piney River, mining road stone; Tommy worked up at the University of Virginia in Charlottesville, on the heating and air-conditioning systems. Tommy was a gaunt, rangy man who liked to joke that he was so skinny because he was born in the Depression. The joke wasn't far from the truth: He'd always "made do" with whatever came along, working as a carpenter or a railroadman, doing some farming or construction jobs.

The dump truck was parked beside the little brick house Tommy Huffman had built himself on weekends and vacation days over a period of four years—so many Saturdays that he and his wife, Adelaide, came to call it their "Saturday house." Russell lived down the hill closer to the creek, with his wife and eight children. Tommy and Russell had grown up on Davis Creek, and their mother was still across the creek on the old homestead with another brother, Jesse, who had married and had seven children but had never left home. Another brother, Houston, also lived in the hollow with his family. In fact, so many Huffmans lived along Davis Creek that for as long as anybody could remember it had been known as "Huffman's Hollow."

Bending over the engine compartment of the truck that night, in the glare of a shop light suspended from the open hood, Tommy and his brother were so intent on their work that they barely noticed the rain starting. It was gentle and cool—cold, even—and on this warm evening actually rather pleasant, so they just kept on working until dark. Then Russell went home and Tommy came indoors for supper. It was, he remembered later, "just at the edge of dark."

Afterwards, Tommy flopped down on the couch to watch a little television. A black man with strange hair, called Jimi Hendrix, was on *The Dick Cavett Show* that night. So was the "psychedelic" band Jefferson Airplane, with their black-haired vixen of a lead singer, Grace Slick. On *The Tonight Show,* Johnny Carson offered a more staid lineup: Dean Martin, Raquel Welch, Joe DiMaggio and comic

Shecky Greene. It was shortly before ten when Tommy heard a ruckus at the back door. It was Bunny, the white Persian cat, mewling and scratching like the dickens out there. It was odd, he thought, because Bunny was strictly a country cat, and was never let indoors. When you grew up on a farm, the whole idea of letting animals into the house seemed strange. But the cat wouldn't quit.

"Daddy, can't we let Bunny inside tonight?" his eighteen-year-old daughter, Ann, implored. "It's really starting to rain out there!"

"Well, just this once," Tommy told her. "Mind you don't let her up on the bed, though."

Ann opened the door and the cat, soaking wet, bolted indoors.

"Look, Daddy, she's got a kitten in her mouth!"

And so she did. Ann made her a little nest in a closet, and after tucking away the tiny kitten, the cat returned to the door and begged to be let back outside. She was gone twenty minutes, and then back at the door, scratching and mewing—with a second kitten in her mouth.

Tommy Huffman stared at the cat. Something about this behavior gave him the faintest inkling of a disturbance in the proper order of things.

"You know," he remarked to Adelaide, "something ain't right. That cat *never* wants to come inside. What's goin' on out there?"

EDDIE, DALE, AND BONNIE THOMPSON went to sleep out in the travel trailer that Tuesday night, despite what soon became a thunderous clamour of rain flailing on the metal roof. Colleen, Lena, and Grace sat up late, just talking about everyday things. Gradually the rain grew so loud they could barely hear each other speak. You had to holler if you wanted to talk. Colleen finally went off to the trailer with the kids, since she would never have dreamed of leaving them out there by themselves. But she felt uneasy. The ferocity of the rain, the *violence* of it, stirred some deep maternal anxiety. As she was getting ready for bed, she decided to leave her bra on underneath her nightdress. She wasn't exactly sure why. Then she climbed into bed.

But Colleen slept fitfully. Great claps of thunder shook the trailer. The rain on the roof was unlike anything she'd ever heard. She was amazed that the children seemed to be sleeping right through it. Outside, through the little windows of the trailer, she could see flashes of the most peculiar kind of lightning—it was bluish, almost like electrical sparks.

Finally, unable to sleep at all, she sat up in the bed and swung her feet onto the floor. *Wow.* That was a surprise. Her feet splashed into a small lake of water, ankle-deep.

The hot-water heater must have broken—that's the only way there'd be this much water, she thought. A moment later, she withdrew that thought. There was no way that much water could come out of a little hot water heater in a trailer.

Then she felt something more ominous: The trailer itself seemed to shudder ever so slightly, as if it were beginning to move. Had the trailer begun to float? It seemed impossible. Muddy Creek, all of six inches deep, was way down below the house, perhaps five hundred feet away. The house sat far up on the hill above the highway; if water was moving the trailer, then the highway would be deep underwater. She knew that, in a hard rain, the creek sometimes formed a small lake down there, especially since the highway department had put under the road a culvert that quickly filled up with debris, forming more of a dam than a drain. But in order for the trailer to be floating, the water would have to be twenty-five or thirty feet deep. She opened the door and looked outside.

In the weird, bluish glare of the lightning, which seemed to be flashing along level with the ground, she could see that the trailer was indeed afloat. All she could see in every direction, was a lake, or a river, of fast-moving water, filled with drifting debris.

"Eddie, get up! Dale! Bonnie! It's a flood!"

Colleen grabbed blind Eddie, instinctively reaching for the one who always seemed most helpless, and threw him over her shoulder. She charged out through the torrent, fighting her way to the porch of Lena's little house. It was perhaps forty feet from the trailer to the front door of the house, but she managed to get Eddie through the door and inside. Then she waded back out to the trailer. To her amazement, Bonnie was still in the bed.

"My Lord is with me and I'm going to sleep," Bonnie murmured.

"Bonnie, get up! The trailer is going to wash away!"

ABOUT THE SAME MOMENT, Ann Huffman woke her mother, Adelaide, in their little house on Davis Creek.

"There's a leak in my bedroom ceiling," Ann told her. "Water's coming down all over the floor."

"Tommy, did you hear that?" Adelaide whispered, shaking her husband awake. "The roof is leaking in Ann's room."

Tommy had worked carefully, over many weekends, to build their "Saturday house," and he knew he'd buttoned that roof up tight—two courses of tarpaper beneath each course of shingles.

"If that roof's leaking, something ain't right," he mumbled, though he did not get up.

Adelaide climbed out of bed and followed Ann into her bedroom, where water was pouring through the ceiling into the center of the floor. She fetched a kettle out of the kitchen and put it under the leak. In the dim glow of a nightlight she noticed Bunny nestled in Anne's closet with a swarm of kittens around her.

She climbed back into bed with Tommy, who hadn't gotten up. But she could not sleep. The rain on the low tin roof sounded like someone was whopping it with a flail—a hard, metallic pounding. Then, over the roar of the rain, she heard a muffled sound.

"Adabah!"

Then she heard it again, more clearly.

"Adelaide!"

"Tommy," she whispered. "*Tommy!* Someone's outside hollering my name!"

Tommy staggered out of bed as Adelaide hurried to the back door. When she opened it, a parade of sopping, bedraggled bodies poured in the door. It was Russell, Tommy's brother, with his wife, Maude, and eight of his nine kids. The kids looked scared, their hair plastered flat by the rain, noses and mouths tucked into their clothes so they could breathe. As they burst into the house she could see that three or four of the kids were badly winded, desperately gasping for breath, almost as if they'd just been pulled out of a swimming pool on the brink of drowning.

"The creek come up so fast, by the time I got these young'uns in the car it was too deep to drive," Russell said. "We got out of the car and the damn thing just floated away, headlights still on. Half-sunk in the water, just floated away! We come scramblin' up the hill, but I think the house is gone now, too!"

Maude looked stricken in the glare of the overhead kitchen light.

"Where's Mitchell?" she murmured. "Where's my boy? He went up to the Shifletts to spend the night about seven, and now I don't know where he is . . ."

Her eyes were blank, unseeing. Eight of her children were safe, but the ninth was all she could think about. Just then Tommy stumbled into the kitchen, pulling his nightshirt around him. Adelaide was still having difficulty taking it all in—the near-drowning children, the floating car, the pounding on the roof, the fear and confusion, Maude's missing son. Suddenly a low rumble ran through the house, end to end, like a seismic shudder.

"What you doing with the furnace on, this time of year?" Russell asked.

"I ain't got no furnace on," she said. The rumble seemed to grow and multiply, until it had become a great roaring like the sound of a squadron of fighter jets bearing down on the house. The floor and windows rattled. The children, still gasping and coughing, stopped to stare around in terror. Adelaide ran to the back door and pushed it open.

"Oh, *lands,* Tommy, come here!" she cried. "What's that noise? And—*pee-ew!* What's that horrible smell?"

Tommy stepped out the back door, ducking his head into the rain. He'd farmed these Nelson County mountains his whole life. He recognized the smell immediately—the smell of disturbed mountain earth. It was rich, and unpleasant, like ripe manure, the smell of deep mountain soil that's lain undisturbed for centuries. Something was happening out there that was turning the world upside down; the earth itself had been opened to the core.

The earth itself was screaming.

COLLEEN THOMPSON grabbed Bonnie and Dale out of the bed and the three of them fought their way out of the floating trailer, which had now drifted around to the side of the house. They got inside the house and pushed the back door shut. For a moment, the living room was safe and dry, except for the water they'd sloshed into it. But within moments, water began seeping under the door and up through the floor.

Colleen, the kids, Grace, Lena, and Buzz stood watching as water rushed into the room. Colleen glanced at Buzz, whom she knew was terrified of water. Once, when he had visited them on the Chesapeake Bay, her husband had taken Buzz fishing. But even in two or three feet of water, he got scared and seasick. Now water was rising up around Buzz's knees, but if he was frightened he did not show it. In fact, Colleen recalled later, it was surprising how calm everyone was. Nobody seemed to panic—though there was every good reason to.

"I'm going to help Grace and Lena up to Meyers's house!" Buzz announced. "They'll be safer up on higher ground!" Meyers Thompson, Jake's uncle, had a house several hundred yards up the hill.

Buzz grabbed Grace, threw open the screen door at the back of the house, and charged up the hill in the raging darkness. He returned about ten minutes later, with his hair streaming down his face in the rain, breathing heavily. By now the water had gotten so high that the refrigerator capsized and began floating through the room, like a porcelain coffin. Bonnie climbed up on top of it, strangely calm, floating as if on a life raft. Colleen lifted Dale up into a window well, to get him up out of the rising water. Then the lights went out. Colleen knew where Dale was, but she couldn't see Bonnie or Eddie.

"Bonnie, where are you?" she yelled.

"Mama, I'm all right," she heard Bonnie say, serenely.

"*Help me get Lena out!*" Buzz shouted. Colleen pushed mightily against the back door to help Buzz get Jake's mother out of the house to safety. But the force of the incoming water was so powerful, it trapped her between the door and the wall. Then the whole house shuddered. It groaned and began to move. Like many old houses in Nelson County, Lena's was simply set down on a block foundation, rather than being actually attached to it. Now the rising water had lifted it off the blocks and it was floating away, down the hill towards the highway.

In the dark, they heard the windows begin to explode, either because the house was rocking and shifting in the flood or because the inrushing water had trapped air in the room and the air pressure was blowing them out like overfilled tires. Buzz returned a second time, forcing his way into the room through chest-deep water, breathing heavily from the effort. He was a big man, in his mid-thirties, but the strain of dragging two people uphill through a raging torrent was taking its toll. This time, he took blind Eddie out of the house, half-dragging, half-carrying him up the hill, and set him under a tree. The rain was coming down so hard it was almost impossible to breathe. The torrent and thunder were deafening.

"Eddie, you set right here! Don't you move! You stay there until I come back for you!"

"Okay, Buzz," Eddie said meekly. "I'll stay here until you get back."

Then Buzz Thompson, so terrified of water that standing in two feet of it made him seasick, charged back into the storm towards the house. He made it to the front porch, where he leaned up against one of the uprights. Colleen could hear him gasping for breath in the dark.

"I can't do any more," Buzz gasped. *"My strength is all gone!"*

By now, at least, the house seemed to have stopped moving. It had apparently lurched and floated down the hill to the edge of the highway, two or three hundred feet away from its original location. It appeared to have snagged against the crown of the highway. The water indoors was almost up to Colleen's throat now.

"Maybe we'll still be all right in here, if the house has stopped," she heard Buzz say. Of course, where else were they supposed to go? Outside the house, right smack into the flood and the darkness? By now, it was too late to do anything except keep your head above water and pray.

That's when the house exploded. There was a terrific noise, the sound of a series of debris-dams up the mountainside collapsing under the weight of thousands of tons of water—earth, boulders, trees, and water exploding down the mountainside and ramming into the side of the house like a tsunami. One minute Buzz stood, exhausted, leaning against an upright on the porch; Bonnie floated on the capsized refrigerator; Dale was in the window well; and Colleen was pinned behind the door. The next moment, everything was gone—the entire recognizable world had detonated violently. There was only darkness, and water, and the sound of kitchen cabinets, rafters, joists, walls being ground into splinters.

Colleen went under the water.

"Lord, if I must die, let it be fast," she thought. Then her whole body went limp. As she was rolled over and over, colliding with logs

and splinters and debris, she simply surrendered to her gentle faith
that He would protect her. And she began reciting the Twenty-third
Psalm:

> *Yea, though I walk through the valley*
> *Of the shadow of death,*
> *I will fear no evil, for Thou art with me . . .*

At his house in Roseland, Sheriff Bill Whitehead got up out of bed
and went to the window. Outside, the world appeared to be eerily
bright, but there was so much water pouring down the storm window
he could barely see anything. The interior window was already open,
so he reached down and opened the storm window to get a better
look at what was going on.

It was then that he beheld a scene so unlike anything he'd witnessed that it simply did not register.

There were continuous flashes of lightning—not bolts of lightning
coming down out of the sky, but lightning flashing *sideways.* These
surreal, ground-hugging flashes were exploding so continuously that
the world seemed as bright as day, each flash hanging in the air for
ten, fifteen seconds, suffusing the air close to the ground with an unearthly glow.

But what made his eyes nearly pop out of his head was Hat Creek,
which was normally a foot or so deep, meandering along a hundred
yards or so below the house. He'd jumped across it as a boy. Hat
Creek was now a quarter mile or more wide, a raging, muddy torrent
that completely covered the yard and everything in sight. It looked
more like the ocean or the Chesapeake Bay, with huge, white-capped
waves six or eight feet high. And the water was moving at an astounding speed. He could see enormous trees racing by, wrenched out of
the ground by their roots, and bits of houses and barns, and what
looked like a terrified cow. He simply could not believe what he was
seeing: barns and livestock flying by. Huge white-capped waves—on
Hat Creek.

Struggling to take in the scene, he now realized that instead of the
screeching hurricane wind he'd expected to find outside, there was
barely a breath of wind at all. The limbs of an immense old sycamore
tree were hanging absolutely still, except for the lowest branch, which

was now bobbing furiously in the torrent. Days later he would measure the distance between that limb and the dry ground. It measured twenty-five feet.

What he had thought was the roaring of the wind was in fact the roaring of the water. Then came another surprise: Of all the great trees that had stood around the old house, only the sycamore was now standing. The rest had been ripped out of the ground by the flood.

"My God!" he gasped to Catherine. "Every tree has washed away! There's not but one tree left!"

The severity of this storm was beyond anything he had ever seen, beyond his comprehension. It was beyond anything he had ever heard his mother or daddy talk about, and they'd lived around here all their lives. Increasingly alarmed, he and Catherine woke the children. Dick and Nancy got up willingly, but John just grumbled and tried to go back to sleep. By then, the power and the phone had gone out. Stumbling around the house, they realized that water was now cascading in through the storm windows, overflowing the windowsills and spilling onto the floor. By the light of candles and flashlights, they all started mopping the floors, but the water just kept pouring in.

The fact that his home was beginning to fill up with water made Whitehead wonder about his seventy-eight-year-old mother, who lived alone in a white frame farmhouse on the property, up at the top of the hill beside the road. His father had built the house in 1911, and Bob had grown up there. He had not worried about her until now, because her home was on higher ground, perhaps as much as a quarter mile uphill from the old family farmhouse where he lived with Catherine and the boys. But this flood was unlike anything he had ever seen. If the raging torrent started taking down the hillside, his mother's house would eventually come down with it.

"Dick," he shouted to his oldest son, "come on with me, let's go up and check on your grandmother."

They ran outside into the storm. The rain was so heavy it was barely even riven into individual drops; it was just one solid body of water dropping out of the sky. So much water was in the air the sheriff had to cover his mouth so he could even breathe. He and Dick climbed into his police cruiser, the old Plymouth 440, and went sliding and clattering up the road to his mother's house. He got out beside the building and with the cruiser's headlights on, tried to open the back door. But it was locked. In the pouring rain he started banging on the side of the house with a pocketknife. Finally, his mother came downstairs to the door and let him inside.

"Mama, you've got to get up and get dressed—the creek is flooding something awful!" he told her once he'd stumbled inside.

"Aw, now, you just calm down," his mother said, unperturbed. "I've seen it rain days and days, and the water only got up so high. I remember when I was teaching school back in the twenties, when I was boarding over to Miz Gant's, I saw pig pens floating down Hat Creek with the pigs still in 'em!"

"Mother," the sheriff insisted, "you've never seen anything like this! *This is something you just can't imagine!*"

CHAPTER TEN

2 A.M., Wednesday, August 20
Massies Mill, Virginia

WARREN RAINES woke up when he heard the telephone ringing. It was scary to hear the phone ring in the middle of the night, especially on such a night as this, when it sounded like the house was a foundering ship, plunging through a storm at sea. Outside, rain clamored against the roof. He heard his father, down the hall, in his parents' room, talking to someone on the phone.

As he groggily came awake, Warren remembered sitting on the front porch of his family house in Massies Mill earlier in the evening, listening to the rain and talking with his dad. Drowsing and talking as the summer thundershower had pattered through the leaves outside, neither one of them could possibly have known what was occurring in the lightning-riven darkness high above the house. There had been no warning whatsoever—no sign, no clue, that anything was amiss in the world. The only signs they saw or heard or felt were those that reinforced their belief in a benign and comforting universe: the sound and smell of summer rain through the screens; the stirring of wind in the trees; the distant bark of a dog; the low murmur of their own voices; and a feeling of sweet sleepiness beginning to steal over their bodies. There was no way they could have known that dark armies were massing ten miles above their heads. Or that, in the face of such primeval power, a man and a boy sitting on a porch were as inconsequential as dust.

Warren enjoyed his dad's company, so he lingered out there a long while before wandering off to bed around eleven o'clock. He'd gone upstairs to the bedroom he shared with his brother Carl Junior, kicked off his sneakers, flopped down onto his bed fully dressed, and promptly fallen asleep.

Now wide-awake and scared, Warren crept down the hall to the door of his parents' bedroom, where a light was on and he could see his dad sitting on the edge of the bed, talking on the phone. All the other kids had been awakened too, so Warren stood in the hall beside Carl Junior, Sandy, Ginger, and Jo. They didn't know if they were supposed to be alarmed or not, so they just stood there in the hall in their bare feet, glancing at each other and waiting for a cue from their father.

"Don't worry about it, kids—go on back to bed," Raines told them. "Must be a prank call. Some lady says Massies Mill is flooding and her car has floated away."

The kids, trying to read their father's mood, found his tone calm and even slightly amused. A prank call. Warren remembered having made a couple of those himself.

Even so, they could all hear the rain pounding on the shingle roof. None of them had ever heard rain come down on the roof like that. And when it thundered, the sound was so violent it rattled the windows.

"Why don't we take a look outside, Carl, just see what's happening out there?" Warren's mother, Shirley, suggested. The little family trooped over to one of the two windows in the bedroom, the one from which they could see down to the main road, Route 56. It was two o'clock in the morning in a tiny rural town, but while they stood there they noticed two or three cars come past. That was odd. Where was everybody going in the middle of the night? Odder still was that there was so much lightning outside—the flashes were almost continuous—that the yard was lit by an eerie electric-blue light, almost as if the end of the world had come and a great blue-white light was spilling down from the gates of heaven. The yard, meanwhile, had turned into a small lake. It did not appear to be terribly deep, but that meant either that it was raining like the dickens, or the Tye River had flooded its banks. Nobody had ever seen that happen before. Warren looked out the other bedroom window, which faced the backyard and the rest of the neighborhood. From here, he could see that the neighbors' houses were islands, completely ringed by rising floodwater.

"Kids, you'd best get dressed," Raines said, his tone still calm, but grave. The children obeyed without further word. Warren went to his bedroom and pulled on a pair of rubber boots, olive drab and midcalf-high, and headed downstairs. He didn't bother to put on any socks, because he figured he'd be back in just a little while. From the landing, he could see water seeping underneath the front door, spreading across the oak floor.

The phone rang again. Warren heard his dad talk briefly, then turn to his wife with the receiver held against his chest.

"It's Page Wood, across the street. He wants to send the four kids over. He feels like he's got to stay there with Francis. He wants to know, if we decide to leave, would we take their kids along?"

Frances, Mr. Wood's wife, was wheelchair-bound and unable to leave the house.

"Why of *course*, Carl," Shirley said. "You know that."

"No problem, Page," Raines said into the phone. "Send 'em on over."

Even with water spreading across the living room floor and that eerie electric-blue light flashing through the windows, the mood in the house was relatively calm. Warren and Carl Junior thought it was kind of a lark, something new and exciting, like a fire drill at school. The littler kids, Sandy and Ginger, picked up on their older brothers' mood and trooped along behind them, calm and obedient, helping to pick things up off the floor and make preparations for the flood.

Moments later, the back door burst open and the Wood children came into the house, soaked and scared. Eighteen-year-old Donna Fay carried Gary, who was four, with Teresa and Mike, holding hands, behind her. Mike was six or seven years old, a friend of Warren's little brother, Sandy.

"Go start the car and pull it around front," Raines said to Carl Jr., who went outside to start the family's '68 Ford station wagon, while Warren helped his mother move a prized wingback chair up onto the landing. She'd just bought that chair and she hated that its feet had already gotten wet.

"Okay, everybody, let's go get in the car and head for higher ground," Raines told his wife and the children, who with the addition of the Wood kids now numbered eleven people. "We can drive up Pharsalia Road and just stay up there until the water goes down."

The turnoff for Pharsalia Road, leading to higher ground, was perhaps two or three hundred yards up Route 56 from the Raines's house. Once they got in the car, escape would be easy. But when Warren tried to push open the porch door, he discovered that the water, now knee-deep, was moving so swiftly he had to lean all his weight into the door just to force it open. The house was perhaps three feet below Route 56, and water seemed to be pouring down off the road into the front yard. The house was now standing in the middle of a swiftly moving river.

The rain was coming down so hard it was not like rain at all, but more like a solid slab of water falling down out of the sky. Warren had to cup his hand over his nose just to breathe. It was as if he were literally underwater, as if it might be possible to drown standing up. He waded out to the idling station wagon and clambered over the backseat into the car's cargo compartment, Carl Junior and their little brother, Sandy, crowding into the space beside him. The Wood children and Johanna Raines took the backseat. The adult Raineses got into the front seat, with little Ginger between them.

Although Carl Junior had left the car idling, when Raines eased it into gear, even before he pushed the accelerator, the old Ford's engine died. Raines slipped the car back into park, turned the key. The engine ground but wouldn't catch. Tried it again. Nothing. Maybe water had gotten into the distributor cap, Warren thought, or the spark plugs got soaked. Outside the back window, he could see that the water on the road looked deeper than it had just moments before when they climbed into the car.

"Okay, kids, we'll just have to walk," Warren's father said firmly. He was still calm, but there seemed to be an edge in his voice.

They climbed back out of the station wagon into the hammering rain. Warren's rubber boots instantly filled up.

"We'll just walk up to higher ground," Raines told the children, his voice rising to a shout to be heard above the roar of the rain. "Let's just stay on the road and walk up to the center of town, then we'll turn by Lea Brothers' store and go up the hill. Worst that could happen, we'll just spend the night on somebody's porch. Okay, everybody stick together. Let's go!"

They started walking up 56 toward Pharsalia Road. Lightning flashed continually around them. The thunder was deafening. Raines was holding little Sandy's hand; his wife was carrying Ginger in her arms. Donna Fay Wood was carrying her little brother Gary. The medium-sized kids—Warren, Carl, their sister Johanna, and Teresa and Mike Wood—sloshed along on their own, trying to be grownup and brave. But Warren was scared, terrified actually, and his water-filled boots seemed to weigh a ton. For the first minute or two the water was only calf-deep, but then it climbed to Warren's knees and a minute later to his thighs.

The kids yelled back and forth over the din of the storm, just making contact with one another, making sure everybody was all right.

"You okay, Carl? Comin' along there, Michael? Okay, let's keep moving!"

They came past their neighbor Buen Wood's house, and even over the roar of the rain, Warren could hear Buen yelling at his wife. He was always yelling at his wife.

"Turn the damn lights back on, will ya? I can't see!"

A second later his wife, Lola, was hollering at Warren's family from the front porch.

"Ya'll come on, come on in here with us!"

They'd walked perhaps thirty yards down the road when suddenly, as if from nowhere, a surge of water rose to Warren's chest. The current was coming up behind them, streaming diagonally across the road, back towards the riverbed, pushing them forward and towards the road's left shoulder. Suddenly Warren was in chest-deep water, and then his feet left the ground and he was clawing at the dark torrent, half-running, half-swimming, trying to grab on to something to keep from being swept away. He grabbed and clawed at the low brush and briars along the roadside. He managed to latch on to something, maybe a honeysuckle bush or a little paradise tree, but against the ferocious onrush of the water it was like grabbing a twig in a hurricane. He glanced downstream and in the weird, heavenly glare of the lightning, he could see his mother standing there with little Ginger in her arms, his sister Jo and Donna Wood beside her. They were an eerie tableau, completely surrounded by rushing water, glistening in the lightning light.

"I can't hold on!" Warren screamed. *"It's giving way!"*

"Go ahead and let go," his mother yelled back. "We'll catch you!"

Warren hesitated a moment, afraid to hold on, afraid to let go. Then he obeyed his mother and released his grip. A second later, when the current had swept him to the place where his mother had been standing, she was gone.

IN THE DARKNESS miles above the storm-lashed figures in the flood, something utterly extraordinary was occurring. A great multitude of meteorological complexities had fallen into place at the same time, like the tumblers in a complex lock. And when they all lined up at once, the resulting cataclysm was so extreme, and so improbable, that a report from the U.S. Department of the Interior would later call it "one of the all-time meterological anomalies in the United States." A report from the Hydrology Office of the U.S. Weather Bureau would later note that such a thing would probably not recur for "well in excess of a thousand years."

Warren Raines and his family could be forgiven for failing to understand the peril they were in, because even the United States Weather Bureau did not fully understand what was unfolding in the tumultuous atmosphere above Nelson County, Virginia, that night. After Kansas City's weather bureau signed off on the storm with a nonchalant bulletin the day before, Camille seemed to have vanished from the face of the earth. She did not literally vanish, of course; and the weather service did not completely ignore what was occurring as she down-shifted into the predictable stages of decay, dissolution, and death. But because it was assumed that Camille posed no further imminent danger, nobody was paying sufficient attention to realize that the tragedy that had unfolded on the Gulf Coast of Mississippi was about to have a second act.

The United States Weather Bureau, in fact, had two radar stations tracking Camille's progress as she moved up across western Tennessee, made an abrupt arc to the east, and began barreling across Kentucky and West Virginia, aimed directly toward the mountains and foothills of bucolic central Virginia. But Nelson County, content with its remoteness from city life, was also far from the atmospheric surveillance provided by Weather Bureau radar. The nearest radar stations were located near Washington, D.C., about 150 miles to the northeast of Nelson County; and Pittsburgh, more than 200 miles almost due north. These automated weather radars sent a beam through the atmosphere in great sweeping revolutions, like the searchlights at a county fair, taking pictures as they went. Because the radar stations were so far away, however, Nelson County was hidden behind the curvature of the earth, and the circling beams only skimmed the very tops of the great rain clouds massing over the county.

"Not much of the storm's intensity or movement could be accurately gauged below the sweep of the beam, but the fact that persistent cloud tops were even detected at those great distances suggests that the thunderclouds must have been towering giants," NASA meteorologist Dr. Jeffrey B. Halverson wrote in a paper about the storm. In retrospect, Halverson adds, when you go back and study the radar images that were recorded the night of the storm, something else raises a warning flag. The cloud-top images record great ragged masses of intense storm activity, which were not unexpected. But in images taken two hours, four hours, and six hours later, the areas of most intense activity have hardly moved or changed at all. They were stuck in the sky, unleashing their fury on the same small target for hours on end. Within the zone of stasis, the towering tops of individual thunderstorm clouds (three to five miles in diameter) could be seen periodically rising up and dissipating. It was as if the very pistons of the rain machine could be seen surging up and down, detectable even at these great ranges.

At the time, though, no one in the Weather Bureau radar stations in Washington or Pittsburgh seemed to sense the danger, or to understand the horror, of what was going on beneath those ominously motionless thunderclouds. No flash flood warnings—or warnings of any kind—were ever issued. And there's no evidence that anybody in the Weather Bureau was seriously worried about what was happening.

Yet a near-world-record rain, a catastrophe of unprecedented proportions, was now occurring in Nelson County. Why? A whole array of elements conspired to cause the great rains there, Dr. Halverson later concluded, after analyzing surface and upper atmospheric weather charts, and satellite and weather radar data collected that terrible night.

One of the primary elements—the "powder keg" that fueled the explosion—was an immense mass of extraordinarily humid air coming up from the Gulf and even as far south as the intertropical convergence zone, near the equator, and the rain forests of South America—two enormous moisture sources only rarely drawn upon by hurricanes this far north. The air and ground in central Virginia were also extremely wet because the summer of 1969 had been a very soggy one, with abundant rains falling from a succession of much-weaker storms over the previous days and weeks. The soil in Nelson County was nearly saturated. Moisture evaporating from fields and forests baking in the hot sun added further to the air's humidity. All of this taken together gave rise to an opaque, hazy air mass in which afternoon and evening dewpoint temperatures soared to an astounding 75 to 78 degrees Fahrenheit. ("Dewpoint" is the temperature at which the water in the atmosphere will condense as drops on a surface.) Any summertime dewpoint in excess of 65° Fahrenheit registers as uncomfortable. Low 70s become oppressive, and mid- to upper 70s are rarely ever observed. In fact, the moisture content of the air was approaching the theoretical maximum for the afternoon's air temperature. In essence, this was hurricane fuel, of the highest octane possible.

At the same time, a weak frontal boundary (a contrast between cool and warm air masses) lay across the state from west to east, like a cliff face of denser air. As more wet, humid air was drawn up against the cliff face by inflowing winds, it was trapped there and began to accumulate.

Now, stealing in across the Blue Ridge Mountains from the west were the so-called "remnants" of the great storm once called Camille, the immense counter-clockwise spiral that was drawing much of this humid air into the region. Though decaying, Camille was still one of the greatest storms on record, still malignant, still furiously rotating and laden with hundreds of millions of tons of water. Her disintegrating vortex drew hot, wet air into the low-pressure center from all directions and began spinning it up into the upper troposphere. The massing of such extreme humidity so close to a tropical vortex was akin to throwing a spark on a keg of black powder. As Camille's remnants crossed the Blue Ridge and began to draw in this super-high-octane fuel, the explosion was not far behind.

Added to this volatile mixture of rocket fuel and rotating energy was the jet stream, a high-altitude river of air coursing along from southwest to northeast at an altitude of thirty-five thousand feet. As it happened, for a few chance hours the ever-changing jet stream began spreading apart like an oriental fan, creating a void in its center. And due to the physics of the atmosphere, air is automatically drawn upwards into a void—so this new configuration of currents created yet another force drawing wet air aloft.

Then there was the landscape itself. The lovely steep ridges and narrow valleys of Nelson County created an "orographic" effect, mechanically lifting these wet air masses as they collided with the mountainsides.

A basic tenet of meteorology is that rain develops when moist air is forced to rise. As the air's moisture content increases, or the air is forced to ascend more vigorously, the rains will become heavier. Warm air with a very high humidity will essentially rise on its own, because of its own buoyancy and a property of the summertime atmosphere called thermal instability. All of these elements were now at work, along with those previously mentioned—so that a whole array of different forces was now lifting the entire complex of moisture-laden weather systems aloft.

A number of meteorological paradoxes was associated with Camille's passage through Nelson County. The first relates to her intensity. Moving across Tennessee, Kentucky, and West Virginia, Camille had been losing power and coming unraveled so rapidly she had almost lost the attention of the U.S. Weather Service. Two days after making landfall in Mississippi, her rainfall had dwindled to a few inches: her once-terrifying winds had gentled to occasional thirty-five-mile-an-hour gusts. Her lowest central pressure, 1,007 millibars, would barely have raised a forecaster's eyebrow. As she banked eastward toward Virginia and the Atlantic, there was no reason for forecasters to expect any further worries from what now seemed like a tamed monster.

But in the years since Camille—at least partly *because* of Camille—meteorologists have learned that a hurricane's capacity for releasing phenomenal amounts of rain is only loosely related to its intensity. The current U.S. rainfall record for a twenty-four-hour period is 42 inches, which fell over Texas from a weak tropical system named Claudette in 1979. This rain did not fall out of the screaming fury of a Category Five, but from a garden-variety atmospheric disturbance. Camille, too, appeared to be weak and depleted—but she was only coiling for the strike.

Meteorologists now surmise that something more menacing was also going on deep inside Camille's core, where it completely escaped the notice of weather forecasters. While Camille's lower altitudes were rapidly calming and slowing due to the effects of friction and thermodynamic cooling and drying, in the higher altitudes, the eyewall was still whirling furiously. Even two days after making landfall, the inertia in the rotating winds of a Category Five hurricane is extreme. But this furiously churning core would have been difficult to detect, given the technology of the time: Weather balloons were routinely launched only twice a day from stations spaced hundreds of miles apart, so the raging upper-altitude core probably slipped relatively undetected through the network as it hooked eastward across central Virginia. And the distant radar scans were only clipping the very tops of the cloud towers, leaving Camille's secrets unrevealed. As a result, as was her way, she deceived; she beguiled; she misled. She was not what she appeared to be.

The second paradox was one of direction. The tropical remnants of Camille arrived from due *west*. Experience has long taught forecasters to monitor the Atlantic side of the eastern United States for tropical troubles. This is the usual direction from which gales blow unabated off smooth water, the direction from which towering storm surges sweep onshore, the direction facing towards Africa—where the worst tropical tempests are born. And typically, these tempests arc into the Eastern Seaboard as part of a broad, clockwise gyre of steering air currents that span the western Atlantic. At the westernmost point of this great arc, hurricanes brush the United States coast, or spin northward up the Piedmont, or are steered northward along the spine of the Appalachians. The tropical threat almost always approaches from the east or south.

But shortly after midnight on August 19, the terrible rains arrived in central Virginia by way of the Ohio Valley. This is in the manner of a great stealth attack, a great crashing of atmospheric elements against the back door. The giant arc that wheeled Camille around the Atlantic had shifted more deeply inland than usual, then hooked sharply into the Virginias. Even though it would seem reasonable that by the time she reached the Blue Ridge her great thunderheads would be mostly emptied of rain—she'd been "raining out" for two days over land, and also moving steadily farther away from her moisture source in the humid Gulf—such was not the case at all.

She deceived; she beguiled; she misled.

Camille's final paradox was her speed. Because of the phenomenal rainfall that occurred in one small quadrant of one small county, it was often later assumed that Camille must have stalled or remained nearly stationary over this one godforsaken spot. What happened in Nelson County came to be referred to as flooding caused by a "parked cloud." But this is not entirely correct. Later analysis of surface pressure patterns proves that Camille was indeed on the move as she crossed the Blue Ridge. She was moving because her circulation was caught up in the west-to-east flow of the jet stream, which was dragging her eastward over the mountains. The critical problem—the thing that was to prove fatal to so many—was that for a brief period of time, the terrain and all these atmospheric elements conspired to create a near-perfect, utterly inhumane and utterly implacable "rain-making machine."

It was this additional, final process that was needed to wring an astounding 31 inches of water—more than *two feet*—out of the atmosphere in six to eight hours. (By some anecdotal accounts, the rainfall may have been even heavier.)

As the parent vortex of Camille approached the Blue Ridge in the early evening, there was a point at which low-level winds out of the southeast began to pick up, drawing fantastic amounts of low-level moisture from the atmospheric power keg south of Charlottesville. By midnight, as these great wet air masses were drawn into the larger storm system, they intercepted the abutments of the Blue Ridge head-on. Weather charts show that they were drawn into the storm at the absolute, optimum angle—ninety degrees—that will sustain maximum uplift of air. And the exact point of intersection between these inflowing, moisture-laden southeasterly winds and the mountains lay precisely over Nelson County.

As moist and unstable air was shoved vigorously upward, thunderstorm cells began to blossom over the tallest mountain peaks. As storm cells erupted deep into the troposphere, the tallest clouds bloomed all the way up into the jet stream, which was crossing the sky from west to east about seven miles above the earth. These thunderclouds were swept toward the east, carried along in the swift current. While moving east, a torrential cargo of rainfall developed inside the core of each cell. Normally, in a maturing thunderstorm cell, it takes fifteen to twenty minutes for heavy rains to condense and fall to the surface of the earth. If the cells were moving to the east at a good clip—say, 35 or 40 miles an hour—then the time required for each storm cell to manufacture its load of rain explains why the heaviest accumulations fell not directly over the Blue Ridge, but over the lesser mountains eight to ten miles *east.*

So for several ghastly hours, this process of birth, maturation, and death of ferocious thunderstorm cells was repeated over and over again, within a zone measuring roughly twenty-five miles north-south by seventy-five miles east-west and centered squarely over the little town of Massies Mill. It was not so much a "parked cloud" as a whole series of rain-laden clouds being created one after another, each of them violently rising, bubbling upward, dumping its cargo of rain, then making way for the next cloud to rise and dump its load. The machine was continuously fed by the swirling mass of humid air churning into the parent tropical vortex. For a brief window of time and for one unlucky corner of the Blue Ridge, nature had conjured the perfect, self-reinforcing rain-making machine. Camille's vast, sprawling energy had become focused down to a virtual pinpoint: a handful of humble river towns in one southern county.

And God have mercy on anyone who found himself there that night.

CHAPTER ELEVEN

3 A.M., Wednesday, August 20
Massies Mill, Virginia

WARREN RAINES was flailing in the torrent, gasping and choking, trying to grab something to stop himself from being engulfed completely. He'd swept past the point where his mother and sisters were standing when his mom told him to let go. Now they had vanished and the dark current had him, churning him helplessly down into the river channel. Suddenly he grabbed on to a tree trunk. He clung to it desperately, holding on for all he was worth. He could tell that the trunk was about five feet around, and that it was vibrating feverishly against the force of the deluge. He wrapped his arms around the tree and hugged it while the dark current sought to pry him free and carry him away.

He hung on to the trunk in that fashion for twenty, perhaps thirty minutes, trying to gather his thoughts and think what to do, trying to imagine what might have happened to the others. They must be safe, simply because he could not imagine anything else. They had made it to dry ground or they were clinging to a tree like he was. But what on earth was happening? It was only minutes ago that he was safe at home in his dry, cozy bed. Now he was desperately grasping a tree in the middle of a world he could not imagine, where everything safe and familiar—even his own mother—had been swept away. Around him, the near-continuous lightning flashes illuminated onrushing water coming at him at astounding speed, bearing with it huge, looming objects—uprooted trees, cars, even entire houses. There was no time to be frightened. He clung to the tree, fiercely concentrating on the parade of objects that was being swept toward him, trying to avoid being crushed like a bug. It was like playing defense in football. A house came past, not ten feet away. If the house collided with his tree, he would be slammed underwater and drowned. Where would he go, if a house came straight at him? What could he grab on to that would offer any safety at all?

Suddenly he felt the tree shudder, and then slowly it begin to yaw all the way over until its crown had pitched into the water. Apparently the current had toppled the tree, but its roots—at least for now—had held. The tree, a weeping willow, had long, drifting, whiplike branches and he grabbed on to these, scrabbling for a hold. He found himself standing on the now-horizontal trunk, waist-deep in water. He pulled himself forward on the loose branches until he was able to grab on to a limb while the upended tree seesawed madly in the current.

He glanced down at his wristwatch, one of his most prized possessions, which had a face that glowed in the dark. It was 2:15 in the morning. The face of the watch, and the time, were the only things he knew for certain. He had no idea where he was. He had no idea what had happened to his mother or Ginger or Johanna, or his dad or his brother Carl, Jr. or his little brother Sandy, or the Woods children. He was a skinny, fourteen-year-old boy clinging to a tree in a flood, and for all he knew the world had ended, like in the Bible. He thought that maybe this was the end of time, that Massies Mill and Charlottesville and Richmond and the whole United States were gone. Maybe the angel Gabriel would blow his trumpet and then Jesus would come down out of the sky. Maybe this really and truly was the end of the world, like he remembered from Sunday School.

Then he'd think: No, couldn't be—this whole thing will rain itself out in a little while and the sun will come up and everything will be all right and I'll have a whopping good story to tell.

For now, though, he was in the middle of a raging flood and in the weird bluish lightning light he could see all kinds of stuff flying at him from every direction, another house, tipped over on its side like a listing boat, rushing by in the stream; a whole tree, yanked up by its roots. Here came a car, or a telephone pole, or a terrified cow thrashing madly to keep its head out of the water, eyes white with fear.

Not too far off from where he was clinging to the branch, he noticed the warm glow of electric lights from a soda-pop machine on the front porch of a still-standing grocery store. He knew the store, of course—it was Bowling's store, where he and Carl went every day in the summer to buy a cold drink or balloons to attach to his bicycle spokes.

Suddenly he thought: *If that drink machine goes in the water I'm going to get electrocuted.*

There was a house right next to the store and from where Warren was, he could see somebody leaning out of a lighted upstairs window, apparently measuring the water depth with something that looked like a curtain rod. It was Johnny Bowling, whose parents owned the store. They were off in Virginia Beach, and Johnny and his sister were home alone. Warren was not more than 150 feet away from him, but it might as well have been a hundred miles. There was no way to reach him at all. The sound of the water was so loud there was no way he could even shout at the boy in the window.

Just then all the electric lights went out, and the boy in the window disappeared. Warren looked down at his watch: It was 2:30 A.M. At the same moment, an electric kitchen wall clock in his family's house stopped. Warren Raines would later find the clock and store it in his attic, frozen at 2:30. To this day he has never plugged it back in.

Off and on, over the roar of the deluge, Warren kept thinking he heard somebody shouting. Sounded like somebody high up above him, maybe somebody in a tree. He couldn't quite make out what the person was shouting. All he knew was that he was freezing to death, and that the relentless rain did not show any sign of slowing. He had to cup his hand over his mouth just to breathe. Maybe he'd drown without even falling into the water. Maybe this really was the end of the world.

Just then, he made out the voice, shouting down from a tree, fifty or sixty feet away.

"Warren! Hey you, Warren!"

"Yeah! Who's that?"

"Don't you know who I am?"

"No, not really!"

"It's me, Carl Junior—your own *brother,* you dope!"

Now, in the strobe-like lightning flashes, Warren could just barely make out a small figure perched up in a rooted paradise tree.

"Jeez, Carl—gosh, am I glad to see you!"

"You okay down there?"

"Well, I'm freezing to death."

"What are we gonna do?"

"I don't know—just hang on, I guess!"

"Where's everybody else? Where's Mom and Dad?"

"I don't know."

They shouted back and forth for a while, but they could not reach or even see each other very well. There was nothing to do but hang on, try not to freeze to death, and wait for dawn.

3 A.M., Wednesday, August 20
Roseland, Virginia

The Nelson County Water and Sewer Authority had two hourly stream-recording gauges in operation in the wee hours of August 20, 1969: one on the Tye River and one on the Rockfish, two of the primary waterways in the county. (A third, on the Piney River, had been removed for bridge construction.) The U.S. Geological Survey also operated two crest-stage gauges on Cove Creek, a smaller drainage. As the water rose that night, the gauges on the Tye and the Rockfish faithfully recorded the magnitude of the rising flood; then, sometime after midnight, both ripped free of their moorings and washed away. (They were later recovered miles downstream.) Only the crest gauges on Cove Creek survived the night intact.

As a consequence, scientists investigating the aftermath of the storm had only incomplete data with which to reconstruct both the rising and falling waters during those chaotic hours when the roof of the world seemed to have collapsed. Still, using the Nelson County gauge data, and discharge estimates from eighteen other gauging stations in the region, they were able to construct a remarkable flood hydrograph of that night.

The chart for August 19 shows a nearly level line between noon and about 6:00 P.M., indicating a small but steady drumbeat of rain, resulting in slightly elevated stream levels. After 6:00 P.M., the line gradually tilts upward until around midnight, indicating gradually rising water levels. Then, shortly after midnight, the line suddenly bolts straight skyward, at a nearly vertical pitch, reaching an astounding, brief peak about three o'clock in the morning of August 20. For only a matter of minutes, the very air had turned to water. Millions of tons of water descended from the black ramparts of the sky in a solid slab, falling into rivers, streams, and drainages, raking open the earth and drowning everything in its path.

It must have been near that astounding 3:00 A.M. peak when Sheriff Whitehead's elderly mother finally agreed to get dressed and get in the car, so the sheriff could take her down to the main farmhouse where she might be safer. She wasn't happy about it, though.

"*Pshaw*, boy, there've been rains like this before!" she insisted, despite all evidence to the contrary.

The matriarch finally got dressed and came back. The sheriff trundled her to the car. Then he and his son Dick drove down to the main house through what appeared to be a solid wall of rain, shot through with horizontal lightning.

"I'm going to drive out to the highway and see if I can get a better sense of the situation," the sheriff told the boy.

"Can I come?" Dick asked eagerly.

"Okay," his dad said. "I might need you, because there's no telling what we might find."

He liked the boy's company. Dick was a big, rawboned kid, a wrestler on the high school team who was fond of physical challenge and a bit too ready to take a dare. He reminded the sheriff of himself at that age. Still, he didn't share with the boy the anxieties that were gnawing at him now. This thing that was happening—at some point it had become obvious that it was more than just a bad storm. It was as if the foundations of the mountains were being shaken. Suddenly he was in a world where lightning flashed sideways and every solid object seemed in danger of washing away.

Truth be told, he was as surprised and frightened by what was happening as anybody—but he was the sheriff, a man of action, father figure to a whole county. People depended on him. His job was to *do something*. When Ron Wood, his deputy, had called from down on the Piney River earlier in the evening, should he have been quicker to react? If a guy's basement had collapsed and the water was so high they couldn't get the fire truck through, shouldn't he have known events were quickly getting out of control? How bad *was* it out there? Were there people stranded, or even drowning, at this moment? Had he been decisive enough, brave enough, sure enough? Was he already too late to help?

In the battering rain, Bill Whitehead steered the old Plymouth 440 back up the long driveway, past his mother's house on the hill, and out onto Virginia Route 151, the main road that ran past the family homestead of Willow Brook. He turned left and eased the car down the hill towards the bridge over the Tye River. The sound on the roof of the Plymouth was like a tinny kind of thunder; he could barely see the road in the rain. The bridge, fashioned of concrete and structural steel, normally stood thirty-five or forty feet above high water. Abutting the road on both ends of the bridge were concrete sidewalls four or five feet tall. As he eased down the hill towards the crossing, his high beams threw a bright trail right across the chasm where the bridge normally stood. But there was no bridge, and no concrete sidewalls. All he could see were veils of rain descending into his high beams, and what looked like an ocean of water, with whitecaps cresting higher than the waves in Hat Creek. Not only was the bridge gone, he noticed now, but the deluge was grinding away at the concrete abutment and the road itself.

As Whitehead watched the rushing torrent in his headlights, he saw a telephone pole come flying downstream with such speed and force that it struck the submerged concrete side railing of the bridge, was hoisted clean up into the air, jackknifed, and came down with a splash into the water on the lower side of the bridge. Then it simply disappeared in a flash, swept away. The sheer brevity of this event was an astounding sight, one he had trouble comprehending. That pole must have been twenty-five or thirty feet long and weighed three hundred pounds or more. But the water was moving so fast it flipped the pole into the air like a matchstick and then swept it away.

"Lord," he murmured to Dick. "There are people in trouble tonight."

That was all he could think of to say. What he could *do,* he was not yet sure. He turned the car around and headed back up 151 towards home, and as he passed his own driveway he noticed headlights. At first he thought it might be Catherine, coming out to look for him and Dick for some reason. But as he got closer, he could see that it was Wilson White's pickup truck. The sheriff pulled in beside the truck, stopped, jumped out, and leaned in the window. Sitting in the backseat, his face pale and frozen, was his old friend and neighbor Tinker Bryant.

"Tinker's house has washed away, and his whole family with it!" Wilson shouted over the roar of the rain.

Tinker leaned up close, so that the sheriff could see the utter shock in his face.

"I can't find my wife! I can't find the three girls!" he shouted. *"My house is gone—it's completely washed away! Bill, please! Get some help and come see if we can find my family!"*

The sheriff pulled out the hand mike on his police radio.

"This is Bill Whitehead on Route 151 in Roseland. Jimmy! Bobby! Can you hear me?"

But there was pandemonium on the line. Every small community in the county was being flooded, and everybody was on the emergency radio channels. You could barely understand a word.

"Jimmy Godsey, Bobby Napier, come in, please! We got a rescue situation up here in Roseland. Tinker Bryant's house washed away and his wife and girls are gone. If you can hear me, get down here quick as you can."

Normally, the sheriff oversaw a staff of three regular deputies, a radio dispatching station, and the county jail. Two deputies, Jimmy and Bobby, would be on duty tonight, but over the hysteria and static on the emergency frequencies, he wasn't sure he was getting through to them. Finally Jimmy Godsey's voice came through, weak and distant.

"Message received, Sheriff," he said. "We're on our way, but the roads are flooding something awful down here. I'm not sure we can make it over!"

Tinker and Wilson went on ahead in the truck while the sheriff raced back to the house to enlist the help of Catherine and John, his other boy, and then drove back up to the little village of Bryant, near Tinker's house. As they neared Bryant they came upon a great heap of debris scattered across the highway. He stopped the car, leaving it running with the headlights on. Muddy water was pouring over the highway, which was blocked by trees and debris. He and Dick got out in the pelting rain to pull the rubbish out of the road—pieces of beds, sopping mattresses, pillows, a sad little pink child-sized suitcase, fragments of a roof and a wall. Standing there in the surreal glare of the headlights, in the pounding rain, the sheriff suddenly realized it was the remains of Tinker Bryant's house.

Tinker's wife and daughters were nowhere to be seen.

3 A.M., Wednesday, August 20
Muddy Creek, Virginia

Colleen Thompson did not know how to swim. She disliked water almost as much as Grace's boyfriend Buzz did; she didn't even like getting water on her head in the shower. But now she rolled, over and over, limp and helpless, in the torrent.

She'd go under and then come back up again, gasping for breath. She'd see flashes of lightning on a lake of water, choking with floating logs and houses and debris. The water was so thick with debris she barely had to swim. She kept pushing away trees that rolled up against her, rasping and ripping at her skin. Coming out of the water at one point, she saw some shadowy silhouettes and heard people shouting. She couldn't make out what they were saying. (Much later, she figured out who at least one of the people was: local-boy-made-good Jimmy Fortune, who would later play with the big-time country-western band The Statler Brothers.)

Then Colleen went under again. Twice, she heard a terrible crashing sound, like the roar of jet engines. Vast mudslides were pouring down the mountainside into the river that was sweeping her away. The first time, she didn't know what the sound was, until the mudslides swept her under, tumbling and smashing against trees and boulders, and then released her. The second time she heard that sound, she was prepared, and moments later was swept under the water in a roar of cascading rocks and rubble. Somehow, some way, she was released from the mudslide a second time, and swept on down the river like a fleck of flotsam. She came through a third, smaller mudslide, and washed out of that one too, the Lord only knows how.

What had once been Muddy Creek was now a ferociously raging river, an avalanche of water. It swept Colleen Thompson miles downstream. Suddenly, it seemed to veer sharply to the right. Somehow, she caught sight of a small tree on the riverbank, grabbed hold, and pulled herself out. She lay there shivering in the dark. She was wearing nothing but her bra and her wristwatch. Her nightdress had been sucked off her body, leaving only the piping around her neck. She stood up and tried to walk a bit, but her knees were weak as a baby's. She'd lost her glasses, but it hardly mattered because it was too dark to see anything anyway. She had no idea where she was.

3 A.M., Wednesday, August 20
Lovingston, Virginia

Bobby Ray Floyd awakened when his wife, Margaret, reached over in the bed and gave him a shake.

"Can you hear that?" she asked. "I think we've got water coming in the basement."

Floyd sat up in bed. Though the bedroom was up on the second floor, and though they'd never had a drop of water in the basement in the nine years they'd lived in the house, he could hear the water now. It sounded like *lots* of water. He grabbed a flashlight and went down to check. He peered down the stairwell into the dark cavern of the basement. *Damn.* It was knee-deep. Water seemed to have poured down into a window well, popped open a basement window, and now the place was rapidly flooding. Outside the house, the yard was filled with water; it was also seeping under the back door and pouring down the stairwell into the basement.

Floyd threw on a rain slicker and charged outside, looking for help. It was a surreal scene, so much bluish-white lightning he didn't need a flashlight to see at all. "It was just dancing all the time," he recalled later. There was no wind at all; just rain, unlike any he'd ever seen in his life, like a lake was simply dropping down out of the sky in one solid mass.

Down the street, he saw some of his pals from the Lovingston Volunteer Fire Department using a portable pump on the firetruck to try to pump out a neighbor's basement. He knew all these guys because he served with them on the volunteer fire squad—Billy Hill, one of the All-Stars; Billy's cousin Johnny Ponton; Johnny's brother Al, and their father, Herman Ponton. Floyd ran down there in the rain. He could quickly see that the basement pumping operation wasn't working. The gas-powered pump drew up around 250 gallons a minute, but the water was rising so fast it overwhelmed the pump's ability to keep up.

"My basement's flooding, too!" Floyd called out to them over the roar of the rain. "Why don't y'all come try to pump me out!"

The men drove the fire truck up to Floyd's house, hauled out the pump, snaked the big suction hose down the basement stairwell, and cranked the thing up. It was no use. A river was running right through his house. It appeared to be clear water; no mud or rocks or rubble. Where was it coming from? The water in the basement was now so deep the freezer had begun to float, along with chairs and buckets, his National Guard fatigues, and his prized, newly reconditioned pool table. Floyd looked frantically at the open basement window, but water was pouring in so fast it would have taken five or six men to force the window closed—and the glass would have broken out anyway.

"I've got some plywood out back—let's try to built some kind of barrier to block the water from coming down the hill!" Floyd shouted to the others.

Floyd, Johnny Ponton, and Billy Hill tried to brace two sheets of plywood upright, forming a kind of crude prow that would slice through the water like a ship's bow and keep it from flooding into the basement window well. It was hopeless. The water knocked the whole thing down, like a house of cards. Now mud and rocks and rubble seemed to be coming downstream, too.

Floyd suddenly got the idea of driving down to the store to get some nails to pound the plywood sheets together, so he jumped in the car and headed downhill in the roaring rain. He could barely see to drive, and the water in the road was so deep he was afraid he'd stall out. He jerked the car around and was driving back up the hill when suddenly an enormous wall of water, rocks, mud, broken trees, and jackknifing cars came avalanching down. He yanked the car frantically out of the way of the mudslide, stopped in his driveway, and ran back into the house.

Inside, it was pandemonium. The elecricity was out, and in the glancing lights of flashlights and candles, Billy Hill and Johnny Ponton came charging up out of the basement, soaking wet, gasping for breath. Floyd couldn't help but notice that they'd tracked mud all across his brand-new carpet.

"We barely got outta there," Hill gasped. "Mudslide busted through the window and knocked us clear across the room."

Later, when they measured it, they realized that the mud and rubble that smashed through the basement window had knocked the two men thirty-two feet across the floor. Then the room flooded all the way up to the ceiling, and the only way they escaped alive was to feel their way out by holding onto the floor joists above their heads.

Margaret Floyd was standing in the hall, holding little Chris in her arms. Beside her stood three-year-old Susan, eyes wide, wearing nothing but a summer nightgown. Around them stood the hulking, sopping men, covered with mud. Then Floyd heard something rumbling outside the house, a great roaring that shook the floor. It sounded like a freight train approaching.

"Get out of there!" Floyd heard his uncle Herman shouting. "There's another one coming!"

Johnny Ponton grabbed Chris from Margaret, Floyd grabbed little Susan, whom he liked to call Suebell, and they all ran out of the house and started running across the street, heading blindly towards a two-story building that seemed to hold the prospect of safety. It was then that a second, much bigger avalanche of water, mud, cars, and debris swept Floyd off his feet and he found himself flung down the mountain, struggling to grab something, struggling to keep Susan alive.

"Suebell, you hold on to Daddy real tight! Don't you let go for anything!" he shouted.

Susan was clutching him for dear life as he flung outward, trying to grab on to something. He kept slipping underwater; he'd roll under and then come back up, choking. His elbows, hands, and shins kept smashing into debris, but the water kept rolling him down the mountain. Finally, suddenly, his feet landed flat on a bank and the force of the water jerked him straight upright. He managed to keep his balance against the raging torrent, wading out of it until he could grab on to something that was solid. Susan was soaking wet but she was alive. He dragged himself up the street to a house—its front porch was very nearly underwater—and banged on the door. He knew who lived there: Mildred and Lucy Whitehead, a pair of unmarried sisters.

"Please, open the door!" he shouted. "It's Bobby Floyd. Please let me in. I got my little Suebell here and we need some help."

He beat on the door and kept yelling for a long time before the sisters, frightened, let him in. They were cowering inside by candlelight. They took Susan out of his arms. The little girl was strangely serene; her near-death experience didn't seem to bother her a bit. (To this day, Susan remembers the old women who cleaned her up with cold water that night.)

Floyd borrowed a flashlight and waded back up the hill towards his house. It was still raining something awful, but the mudslide seemed to have stopped; nothing much was moving except the water.

Floyd found his wife and baby Chris in the home of the high school principal, Mr. Colley, along with Colley's wife, Billy Hill, and a few others. Together, they spent the rest of the night in that house. Billy Hill helped Floyd clean up his wounds. The skin was torn off his fingertips, his elbows, shins, and feet were shredded. Floyd was so torn up from his tumble down the mountain that he would be unable to walk for thirty days afterwards. For now, though, there was nothing to do but cower inside the house and hope it, too, did not get washed down the mountain by whatever was happening out there.

3 A.M., Wednesday, August 20
Tyro, Virginia

A few miles upriver from Massies Mill, in the little town of Tyro, John Henry Fitzgerald stirred in bed. When his hand flopped off the edge of the bed and landed in water—*cold* water—he sat bolt upright in alarm.

"*Frances!*" he hissed at his wife, who was sleeping beside him. "Get up!"

John Henry and Frances Fitzgerald lived in a little three-room cinderblock house with an attic, about a hundred yards from the Tye River. Next door was a small rental house and a little store, called the Mountain View Tearoom, which despite its fancy name was just a modest country store that sold mostly canned goods and staples. John Henry was a big bear of a man over six feet tall, but when he jumped out of the bed into the water it was almost waist-deep, nearly level with the bed. Now truly frightened, he waded into the front room, where they'd left the two-month-old baby, John Henry Junior, whom they called "J.H.," sleeping in a bassinet. He switched on the light and beheld a surreal sight: The sofa, chairs, and all the other furniture were gently bobbing in a lake of water in the living room, like sailboats at anchor. And in the midst of all this lay J.H., sound asleep, basking in his floating bassinet like Jesus in the bullrushes.

When Frances came sloshing into the room her heart seemed to stop. The world outside was moving in slow motion. She could see the bassinet floating in the room, but she could not see whether her baby was dead or alive. She saw her husband reach down and pick up the baby and hand him to her. When she touched her child, she could feel that he was completely dry and sound asleep, as if nothing had happened at all. She nearly collapsed in relief. She realized at that moment that, had there not been a plastic liner in the bassinet that kept it afloat like a buoy, the baby would have drowned. She'd used that bassinet for both of her little girls, but she'd never gotten around to installing the plastic liner in all those years. It had only been since J.H. was born that her husband's sister had taken the trouble to add the plastic that saved her baby's life.

Moments later, the electricity went out. The flooded room was plunged into darkness. The electric clocks stopped. It was 2:20 A.M. Through the windows, Frances could see the spooky lightning flashes, arcing low across the ground. She peered outside into a world now become completely unknown to her. The Mountain View Tearoom, named by her mother in a moment of gaiety many years before, the little rental house next-door, occupied by Calvin Allen and his family, the children's beloved tire swing, hanging from an oak tree outside the back door—all the familiar signposts of her world now seemed as surreal as a dream. Oddly, she could see a light on the front porch of the store, still shining through the storm.

"I want to go out there," she said to John Henry. "I want to go over to the store and see what's going on."

"You can't go out that door!" he snapped back, snatching her by the arm.

Out there, the world was as hostile a place as the moons of Jupiter. The sky, the earth, the river—they had all been raked open and churned into a deadly, fast-moving river of water, mud, rocks, trees, houses, debris, and bodies both human and animal. Cowering inside the flooded house, with her baby in her arms, there was no way Frances Fitzgerald could quite grasp that if she ventured outside, she would surely be killed. She might be swept away and buried, and her body never found. Her husband, who was only twenty-seven and who had never experienced a flood in his life, remained determined to prevent her from leaving. Going outside the house meant death. That much he knew for certain, and he stuck to it, firmly and without panic.

Suddenly, standing there in the darkness waist-deep in water, Frances remembered a strange scene from earlier in the evening. Her two little girls, Angie and Anita, had run out of the house and over to the store when they saw their grandmother pull up in her car. It was perhaps eight o'clock at night and just beginning to rain—a soft, pattering summer thundershower. But the girls, four and seven, had become terrified of the rain. They dragged their grandmother back to Frances's house and insisted that they be allowed to spend the night with her. It was odd, because the girls never did this. Their grandmother loved them, but she was old and Frances knew well enough how exhausting two small children can be. Occasionally she'd allow one or the other of the girls to stay overnight with their grandmother, but never both of them at once. This time, though, the girls were absolutely insistent.

Finally even Grandmother joined in. "Frances," she said firmly. "I'm taking these children with me tonight." Then she took them and left.

Now, standing in the darkness in the rising floodwater of the living room, to Frances Fitzgerald the whole incident seemed eerily prophetic. If they'd stayed here, the children might already be dead. John Henry opened the refrigerator door as it lay floating on its side, extracted some milk for the baby and handed it to his wife. Then he sloshed his way into the bedroom, fished a pocketknife out of a pair of pants hanging on the bedpost, clambered up onto the top of a wardrobe in the corner, and began cutting a hole in the sheetrock ceiling. Frances stood holding J.H. in one hand and a flashlight in the other, as the water steadily rose around her. When her husband had cut a big enough hole in the ceiling, he helped her and the baby climb up onto the rafters in the attic. Then he followed her up, pausing a moment to grab her mother's Bible off the bedside table. John Henry had never been a churchgoer, but this was a night when the Good Book might come in handy.

The Fitzgeralds spent the night on the attic rafters with that Bible, a flashlight, and the baby, cradled in a pillow. The rafters were terribly uncomfortable to sit on, and they kept shifting their weight, in the process inadvertently knocking pieces of sheetrock out of the ceiling until by morning only two sheets were left intact. Once, while she was holding the baby, Frances shifted her position, suddenly lost her balance and the baby tumbled out of her arms. Her husband grabbed the child just as he was about to fall into the water below.

John Henry kept shining the flashlight into the flooded bedroom beneath them, and they could see clearly that the water was rapidly rising. All the furniture and appliances were floating, along with the baby's bassinet, their bed, the TV, and everything else. If the floodwaters filled the little cinderblock house up to the ceiling, they could easily rip the house off its foundations and wash everyone away. The house would simply collapse.

"Here, hold the flashlight," John Henry told Frances, and she grabbed it along with the baby while her husband squeezed his body down through the rafters and in this awkward position kicked out a window in the bedroom with one foot. That would at least relieve the water's force a little, and maybe save their home. Moments later, the whole attic shuddered when something enormous crashed into the back of the house.

John Henry grabbed the flashlight and shone it into the dark cavern of the attic. They could now see that a huge tree had fallen on top of the roof, taking off the corner of the bedroom and the whole back side of the house. If there was enough structure left to hold the house together, Frances thought, it might actually be a godsend because it would allow the floodwater to rush through the house.

Neither of them talked very much. It was obvious that death was at their door and there was no real need to discuss it. Besides, John Henry was a country man, more at ease behind the controls of a 'dozer or a front-end loader than sharing his fears and feelings with his wife. If he understood better than she did how much danger they were in, he never said a word about it. He wasn't a religious man either, but every once in a while he'd give Frances a little light punch in the shoulder and ask her to pray. She went to church and read the Bible, so he reckoned maybe she had better connections than he did. And pray she did, fervently, silently, all night long.

Frances had no way of knowing how much time had gone by when she noticed a weak and watery dawn beginning to appear through cracks in the roof and walls of the house. John Henry lowered himself down through the rafters, onto the floating stove and then into the water; it was chest-deep. He waded through the flooded house and out into the yard, which was now a muddy lake filled with debris, including all their furniture and beds and the baby's bassinet.

Their beloved little cinderblock house by the river had been smashed open at one end, as if an angry giant had dealt it a blow. The house looked like a small, sad, sinking ship, submerged up to the edge of the roof. A car belonging to their neighbor, Calvin Allen, had floated onto the front porch and was now wedged across the door, apparently having blocked the flow of floodwater and perhaps even saved their lives.

The low bridge across the Tye had been washed out, and on the other side of the river John Henry could see people standing along the bank. They were so far off, and the high water was so noisy, that all he could do to communicate with them was make a sweeping gesture with his arm. Later, he learned that the onlookers interpreted his gesture to mean "they're all dead," so they assumed that Frances and the baby had been swept away. With the whole house almost completely submerged, it seemed to them unlikely that anyone could have survived. This erroneous news quickly spread to John Henry's mother's house, on higher ground up the river, where his two daughters had begged to spend the night. When they heard that their mother and baby brother had been drowned, the girls collapsed in tears with their grandmother.

Though Frances's prayers for her family's safety were answered that night, many others were not so fortunate. For some reason having to do with the way the river eddied around a bend near the Fitzgeralds' house, as the water receded that morning it deposited enormous piles of debris around the yard. And scattered through the spindrift were human bodies, splayed like ragdolls in the postures of death. Two women, naked and hanging off the brush as through crucified, were found along the riverbank. There was a man's body tied up in the fence across the highway from the house. And Audrey Zirkle, the lovely young girl who had spoken to Vernon Lewis at band practice the night before, was found buried a few hundred yards up the riverbed, just her small hand emerging from the sand.

CHAPTER TWELVE

5:00 A.M., Wednesday, August 20
Roseland, Virginia

SLABS OF SILVERY RAIN descended into the glare of the headlights from Sheriff Bill Whitehead's police cruiser, which was now stopped on the flooded highway beside the sad debris of Tinker Bryant's house. With their heads lowered to keep their faces out of the rain the sheriff and his two boys, Dick and John; a state police sergeant; Jimmy Godsey and Bobby Napier, from the rescue squad; Wilson White; and Tinker himself grimly cleared a path through the wreckage. Each was hoping that he would not be the one to find the bodies of Tinker's wife, Grace, or any of his three pretty teenaged girls, Frances, Patricia, or Lou.

Once the road was clear, Godsey and Napier set off on foot, with flashlights, working their way up the swollen stream channel below Tinker's house. Everyone else got back into the police car and Whitehead drove slowly up the road to the spot where Tinker's house had stood, up on higher ground above the creek. It was an astonishing sight. What had once been only a barely noticed country rivulet, not much more than a spring branch, had been so suddenly and vastly magnified by the downpour that it had swept the house away completely, as if it had never been there at all.

Now, with the aid of flashlights, the sheriff's party worked their way down the stream channel, searching and calling as they went. In a short while they met Godsey and Napier. Nobody really had to speak. It was obvious that no one had found the four women. The men stood there in the pounding rain, in the surreal glare of the flashlights, with torrents of muddy water cascading downhill around them.

Bill Whitehead walked up the hill and rapped on the door of a

After Camille, the bridges and highway at Woods Mill, in Nelson County, Virginia, were destroyed by massive erosion and logjams. (Tom Gathright)

On the night of August 19, 1969, a fast moving slurry of water, mud, and debris brought immense boulders down the mountainsides near Davis Creek, ripping open houses and burying many people alive. (Tom Gathright)

Hurricane Camille Memorial Wall outside Episcopal Church of the Redeemer in Biloxi, Mississippi. The memorial bears the names of 172 people killed or missing when Camille devastated the Mississippi Gulf Coast. The list of dead includes three female bodies that were never identified, now known as Faith, Hope, and Charity. The flagpole was bent by 200 mph winds when Camille came ashore. (Stefan Bechtel)

One of the heaviest rainfalls ever recorded—nearly 30 inches in less than eight hours—lifted houses off their foundations and tipped them over in the night. (Tom Gathright)

Davis Creek, usually a tiny stream, became so swollen with rain the night of August 19 that it shredded immense tree trunks. (Gene Ramsey)

Mudslides and erosion were so extreme that people were swept out of their beds in the night. Many bodies were never found. (Gene Ramsey)

Nelson County mountainsides, normally completely forested, were exposed to the bedrock by massive mudslides. (Gene Ramsey)

Warren Raines's family home in Massies Mill, Virginia, was inundated by the flood, and the family attempted to flee—though, in a tragic irony, all would likely have survived if they had simply stayed home. (Gene Ramsey)

Warren Raines *(right)* was fourteen and his brother Carl was sixteen the night Hurricane Camille flooded their family home in the little town of Massies Mill. The boys' parents and three siblings were killed in the flood. "August twentieth is a date that will be branded in our minds until we die," Warren says today. (Gene Ramsey)

The flood lifted this house in Massies Mill off its foundation and dropped it on top of a car. (Gene Ramsey)

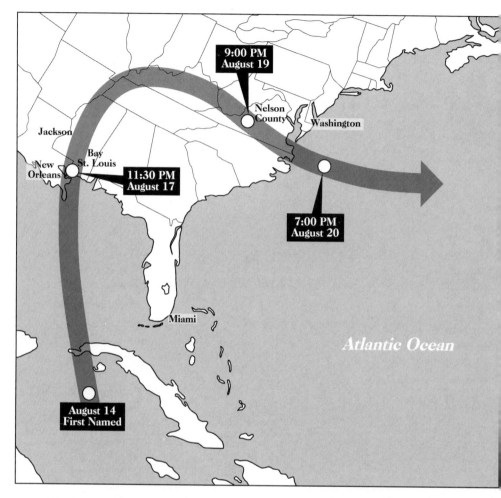

Hurricane Camille's storm track, from her official birth in the Caribbean Sea south of Cuba on August 14, 1969. She made landfall in Mississippi shortly before midnight on August 17, struck Nelson County, Virginia, after dark two days later, and eventually swept out into the North Atlantic, leaving more that 300 people dead or missing in her wake. (Will Cypser)

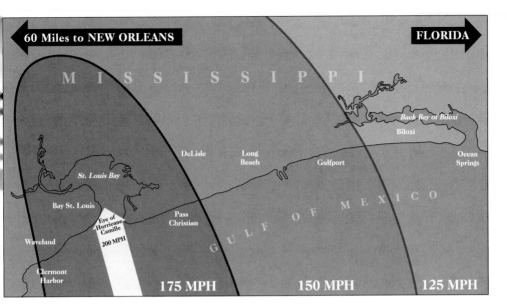

Camille came ashore about 11:30 P.M. on August 17, 1969, near the mouth of Bay St. Louis, Mississippi. She was the only Category Five hurricane to strike the mainland United States in the twentieth century, with winds in excess of 200 mph. (Will Cypser)

Satellite photo of Camille shortly before landfall. (Photo courtesy NOAA)

Boat washed ashore in Biloxi, Mississippi, after Camille struck the coast, killing more than 170. (Photo by Fred Hutchings, The Hurricane Camille Photograph Collection, McClain Library and Archives, University of Southern Mississippi)

A tire swing and a chair are all that remained of this house in Bay St. Louis, near the eye of Camille. (Photo by Fred Hutchings, The Hurricane Camille Photograph Collection, McClain Library and Archives, University of Southern Mississippi)

City hall was one of the few buildings left standing in downtown Pass Christian, Mississippi, the morning after the storm.   (Photo by Fred Hutchings, The Hurricane Camille Photograph Collection, McClain Library and Archives, University of Southern Mississippi)

The Richelieu Apartment complex in Pass Christian was only a few hundred yards from the beach. (Chancey Hinman)

Richelieu Apartments after the eye of Hurricane Camille came ashore almost dead-center on the building, The highest storm surge ever recorded leveled the complex, with only three known survivors. (Chancey Hinman)

Trinity Episcopal Church in Pass Christian, built in 1849, had withstood eighteen hurricanes before Camille. (Chancey Hinman)

What remained of Trinity Church after Hurricane Camille. It was here, in an auditorium attached to the sanctuary, that church caretaker Paul Williams tried to ride out the storm with his family. (Chancey Hinman)

"The eyewall of a hurricane is as different from our normal atmosphere as our atmosphere is from the atmosphere of Jupiter," says Dr. Hugh Willoughby, a senior scientist with the International Hurricane Research Center. (Photo taken from Skylab, courtesy National Climatic Data Center)

house occupied by a neighbor, George Bond, and his son. The Bonds' house sat up on considerably higher ground, and when George and his son came to the door, they were surprised to learn that Tinker's house had washed away. They immediately volunteered to join the search party. At the sheriff's suggestion, the Bonds began searching through the wreckage on the far side of the creek while the sheriff and his party worked their way downstream along the opposite shore. Together, they all worked down the creek to Whitehead's house, and a mile or two further downstream, as a faint dawn brightened over the devastated landscape. Tinker Bryant's family, along with his house and everything in it, seemed to have been swept away.

Sheriff Whitehead returned to his police cruiser and nosed up the highway through thunderous rain. But like everyone else who was out and alive on this horrendous night, he discovered that the roads were blocked by high water and debris in every direction. He could drive a mile or so north up Route 151, towards Bryant, where the road was blocked; then he could turn around and drive back, until the road became unpassable thanks to what normally was a tiny rivulet called Possum Trot, which had now become an angry, muddy torrent. In effect, he was stuck on a two-mile stretch of Route 151, like a rat trapped in a maze. He couldn't get out on any side roads because the creeks had washed them away. "It was impossible to get anywhere," Whitehead recalled later. For a man of action, it was infuriating. There was nothing he could do except drive up and down the road and try, mostly without success, to reach the outside world on the radio.

At one point, the sheriff went down to Mac Giles's store, a bit to the south on 151, and sat in the police car with the headlights on, watching the floodwater eating away at the roadway. The water came pouring over the road, driving immense piles of flotsam and a tangle of downed power lines before it. As it cascaded down over the far side of the highway, the water rapidly eroded the embankment, and as it dug deeper and deeper into the road's foundation, the road itself began to collapse. Bite by bite, like a voracious monster, the flood ate completely through the embankment, then completely through the highway, and then suddenly a great muddy spasm of water exploded through and the now-broken road became a river channel. The sheriff shifted his police cruiser into reverse and backed away, fearing the astounding power of this thing.

Afterwards Whitehead had gone back home to check on his own family. They were safe at Willow Brook, the old homestead beside Hat Creek, though the creek had now transmogrified into water without end. He and his sons had gone down to check on a boy who worked on the farm who lived in a trailer beside the creek. If he was asleep, he definitely needed to be roused. But it turned out there was no way they could reach the trailer—from the place where the police car could go no farther, it was fifty feet across what was now a swift-moving, debris-choked torrent. The sheriff turned on his police siren, laid on the horn, even tried hollering on the bullhorn. But there was no sign of life in the trailer. The boy was either asleep or dead.

In the midst of all this, Whitehead was frantically trying to get through on the police radio, but it was virtually useless with so much pandemonium on the line. He had trouble even getting through to his own deputies. In all the small towns and counties surrounding Nelson—Waynesboro, Staunton, Charlottesville, and Albemarle County; Buckingham and Amherst counties—everybody used the same radio frequency. And now 39.50 megahertz was pure bedlam. "Every sonofabitch and his brother was trying to talk at the same time," the sheriff said later. He kept trying to find out whether his messages had been heard, whether anyone out there understood what was happening in Nelson County, whether any help was on the way. One thing he did begin to realize: It was not just Hat Creek and the Tye River that were overflowing. The whole region seemed to be disappearing underwater. Something truly monumental was happening. And the town was his responsiblity. If things went wrong—and they had—he'd be the one to take the heat.

Finally, Whitehead found a working telephone and called the sheriff's department down in Amherst, a small town in the next county, on the other side of the James River.

"We've got a drastic situation happening up here!" Whitehead shouted over the line. "We need help!"

"Well, yeah, it's been raining quite a bit down here, too," the dispatcher said.

"You don't understand—we've got a major flood here! Whole houses swept away! Most major roads are overflooded. You can't get anywhere! There may be people up here who need to be rescued, but we can't get to them!"

The dispatcher did not seem quite able to believe what the sheriff was telling him.

"Look," Whitehead said finally, "I need you to call Sandy White, at Civil Defense, over in Salem. Get him out of bed. Then I need you to get back in contact with me, to let me know you've gotten in touch. This is an emergency situation. We're going to need a lot of help over here. We're going to need helicopters. Tell Sandy White to start trying to find some. *Do you understand?*"

The Virginia Department of Civil Defense, envisioned primarily as a vehicle for responding to nuclear war, had divided the state into five regions. Sandy White was the regional coordinator of emergency response in the areas that included the city of Lynchburg, and Amherst and Nelson Counties, all the way down toward Danville, on the North Carolina state line. The sheriff had worked with White the year before, in 1968, during a staged trial run of the civil defense response to a nuclear disaster. White might be able to mobilize the sort of resources the sheriff was thinking might be needed—not only helicopters, but heavy equipment, earth-moving machinery, and medical help. If the flood had simply washed Tinker Bryant's house off the face of the earth and his whole family with it, the devastation across the rest of the county was going to be catastrophic.

Sandy White, it turned out, was not in bed when the Amherst County Sheriff's Department dispatcher got him on the telephone. He was in his office. White told the dispatcher to relay this message to the sheriff over in Lovingston: "Don't worry, the floodwaters are all up at Covington and Clifton Forge, and it will be two or three days before they get all the way down to Nelson County."

Covington and Clifton Forge, about sixty miles to the west of Lovingston, were two towns that sat in steep mountain valleys along the Jackson River, one of the headwaters of the James, which meandered through mountain passes on its lazy way into the southern reaches of Nelson County. If what White said was true, it probably *would* take a couple of days for all that floodwater to make its way to Nelson. But what White did not understand was that the floodwater was already *in* Nelson, pouring down out of the sky in what would later prove to be a near-world-record eight-hour rainfall. The apocalypse was not on its way. It had already arrived.

It was almost comical. Here was the regional coordinator of civil defense, telling the sheriff that what was happening was not happening. No one the sheriff talked to that night could quite understand what was going on in Nelson County.

And who could blame them? Even the *sheriff* couldn't believe it.

*6:00 A.M., **Wednesday, August 20***
Massies Mill, Virginia

Clinging to the toppled weeping willow tree where he'd spent the night chest-deep in water, Warren Raines was so cold he began to wonder if it was possible to shiver to death. He was wearing only a T-shirt, shorts, and the ill-fitting rubber boots he'd slipped on when his father told the family to flee the house in the middle of the night. He hadn't even put on any socks, because he figured he'd be back in the house, and back in his own bed, before you knew it. It would be like a fire drill at school. But it hadn't worked out that way at all; something truly awful had happened and now he was deathly cold and alone and on the verge of slipping into shock.

Around him, a ragged dawn began to rise over Nelson County and a world transformed. As the light came up, Warren could see that something almost beyond comprehension had happened in Massies Mill. His old familar world—Bowling's Store and the back road, The Car and the river, his family home and all sense of comfort and safety he had in this world—had turned into nothing but muddy, onrushing water; massive mounds of debris ten or fifteen feet high; wrecked, knocked-over houses; dead cows; and a few dazed-looking people wandering around on the shore. And there was the strangest smell in the air, the smell of dank, muddy earth and pulverized tree bark, and of things that had lain underground for ages, now ripped open and laid bare. It had been raining relentlessly all night, and it was still raining.

"Warren! Hey, Warren! You still alive down there?"

It was Carl Junior, calling down from his perch in the paradise tree.

"I'm about froze to death! Can't stop sh-sh-sh-shivering!"

"No kidding, man! I'm freezing up here too!"

"When's it ever gonna stop raining?"

"I dunno. Just hang in there and somebody will rescue us soon!"

But it was an hour or more before a couple of men from town with a johnboat and ropes spotted the boys clinging to their trees in the river and came out to get them. Just before the boat got to the tree where he'd spent the night, Warren glanced back up to the north and spotted an immense black cloud massing over the mountain. It looked like death.

"It's coming back again!" he shouted, his whole body convulsing in fear.

But for some reason the cloud steadily lightened and dissipated, and the rain began tapering off as the men loaded the boys into the boat and transported them to shore. When the brothers climbed out of the boat, they were dumbfounded at what they saw. Massies Mill was a scene of total devastation. There were wrecked houses sitting in the middle of the road, houses sitting on top of cars, houses smashed into other houses, and upended cars and uprooted trees everywhere. As the floodwater began receding back into the river channel, fish flopped in the middle of the muddy road. The whole world was upended.

"Why don't you boys go inside my house and get yourselves cleaned up and get you some rest?" one of the men asked kindly. They knew the man, of course—everybody knew everybody in Massies Mill. Warren and Carl Junior, too cold and dazed to disobey, went into his house, cleaned up a little, and lay down on a bed. But they were up again in a couple of minutes.

"We're not going to stay here," the boys told their host. "We've got to go find our family."

They walked down the road to the Miller Chemical Company warehouse, where their father worked, Warren plodding along in the ill-fitting rubber boots that had now begun to raise blisters on his heels. Carl had gotten into some glass somehow and his feet were lacerated, so he was limping too. The boys went to the warehouse out of some vaguely misplaced homing instinct—it was a "home away from home," where they'd always felt safe and close to their father. But as a practical matter, it had a big upstairs storage attic where the family might have gone to escape the flood. Their dad always carried his keys with him and would have been able to open the building. Besides, it wasn't too far away from the place where Warren had last seen his mother and sisters.

But when the boys got there, they discovered to their amazement that the entire massive building, big as a barn, had been lifted up by the flood, moved 150 feet, and deposited in the middle of the Route 56 highway bridge into Massies Mill. The road into town was now completely blocked, with the cavernous building, tilted at a crazy angle, sprawled across the bridge. They crept into the warehouse, now eerily dark. Everything inside was strewn about and half buried in several feet of mud. It smelled like fish.

"Mama! Daddy! Y'all here?" they shouted into the dimness.

No answer.

"Anybody here?"

Silence.

6:00 A.M., Wednesday, August 20
Muddy Creek, Virginia

Colleen Thompson was completely naked except for her bra and her wristwatch, and covered with mud and bruises from head to toe. She'd lost her glasses. She was freezing. And she had no idea where she was (though it would later turn out that the flood had carried her four miles downstream from where she'd been washed out of Lena's house). Trying to keep herself warm, and feeling vaguely immodest even in the dark, she stuck sticks and branches into her bra to form a crude kind of dress. Then she knelt down under a tree and waited.

As a weak dawn light came up, she could see that she was surrounded by woods, and that what had once been Muddy Creek was now a swift-running, silted-over floodplain that had ripped open the earth overnight, littered with boulders and trees and chunks of broken houses.

She stayed under that tree, half naked, and bleeding and covered with mud, but apparently not in shock, until about four o'clock in the afternoon. That's when she heard voices, shouting, from somewhere nearby.

"I'm over here!" she shouted back. "Down here, in the river!"

A young man appeared up the hill. It was the son of Preacher Dean, pastor of Ridgecrest Baptist Church. Despite her primitive dress, Colleen felt ashamed when the young man made his way across a log to fetch her on the far side of the river. Noticing her modesty, he laughed.

"Oh, *forget it!*" he snorted. "Let's just get you out of here!"

He helped Colleen up the hill into the rectory of the church. She was a pitiable sight. The preacher's wife handed her a housecoat to cover herself with, and then tried to clean the awful gashes on Colleen's arms and thighs and feet, where she had been ripped and pummeled by logs. (The bra had shielded her from at least some of the bruising.) But the wounds were too fresh and painful to be touched, so the preacher's wife quit trying to be helpful.

Moments later, they heard the driving *thok-thok-thok* of an approaching helicopter, and the preacher's wife rushed out into the churchyard and waved. A big tandem-rotor Marine chopper descended onto the yard, its prop-wash flattening the grass. The preacher's wife helped Colleen into the big bay doors of the helicopter and then she was whisked up into the sky and down to Lynchburg General Hospital, twenty miles to the south.

When she was wheeled into the hospital emergency room, one of the first people Colleen saw, sitting up on a gurney, was her ten-year-old son, Dale. He had bandages on his chest, and he looked wan and pale, but he was overjoyed to see her.

"Mama, where have you been?" he cried.

"Dale, you don't want to know!" Colleen told him.

"Where is Gramma? Where is Grace? Where's Eddie?"

"I know Buzz got Lena out, he got Grace out, and he got Eddie out," Colleen told him. "But if they got to safety, I don't know. I don't know what happened to Buzz. And I don't know what happened to Bonnie."

Dale had an amazing story of his own to tell. He'd been found not far down Route 29 in an enormous pile of debris that had been swept downstream by the torrent. He'd been trapped inside a corner of the roof, pinned inside this V-shaped remnant by a nail stuck into his chest just above the heart. He'd been found at ground level, but high water marks on the trees around him showed that the water around him had been twenty feet high. In effect, this fragment of the roof had created a small air pocket in which he crouched while the river raged around and over him. Had he been able to break free of the spike in his chest (which left a scar that is still visible to this day) he probably would have been killed. As it was, he'd broken one leg just above the knee. The leg, badly set in the hospital, would later have to be rebroken and reset, and Dale would spend months in a full-body cast.

Colleen found out the next day that Eddie had survived, crouched under the tree where Buzz had left him. In the wee hours of that terrible night, just before dawn, Lena said she heard somebody calling. She thought it might be Eddie. As she had the day before, when she had related her prophetic dream, she just kept persisting.

"I hear somebody calling out there!" she'd told the others.

Huddled in the darkness of Jake's uncle's house at the top of the hill, the rest of them thought Lena was distraught. They thought she just wanted somebody to be alive.

"Now Lena, you know you can't hear Eddie calling, with all that noise out there."

None of them could hear anything except the roar of the mudslides and the storm. Finally, though, when no one else seemed prepared to go back outside, Lena insisted, "Well, if you won't go, I'm going out there! I'm going to go look for Eddie."

Jake's Uncle Meyers got a flashlight and walked down the ravaged streambed a quarter mile or so, and there he found Eddie huddled under a tree, just where Buzz had left him. The blind boy was soaking wet, and crying.

"Where's Buzz?" he asked. "How come Buzz didn't come back and get me?"

Enormous trees had washed up all around the boy, some of them splintered like matchsticks from the force of the flood. But Eddie didn't have a scratch on him. It was a kind of miracle, because if he had moved, he would have been killed. Something else was strange about the place Eddie was found: It was much too far away from the house for Lena to have heard him calling.

Even more amazing, was two days later, while Colleen was still in her hospital bed. She wasn't sleeping at all because she was in such terrible pain—her entire body was battered and bruised, one foot had been severely lacerated, she had a terrible kidney infection, and her sinuses had been so packed full of dirty mud and gravel that the doc-

tors had to go in through her nose to wash out the sinus cavity. As
she lay in bed, unable to sleep, Bonnie appeared to her, just as plain
as day. Colleen Thompson knew very well what a dream was, and this
wasn't a dream. It was her daughter Bonnie, standing there in front of
her. Bonnie was radiant, full of joy.

"Mama, I just had to come back and see you one more time,"
Bonnie said, her little upturned face aglow. "Now I've got to go back."
Then she seemed to rise up toward the ceiling, luminous and calm,
and disappeared.

Though searchers scoured the Nelson County riverbeds for weeks
afterwards, and three times authorities called the Thompsons with
news that they had found her, to this day Bonnie's body has never
been found.

MRS. SADIE THACKER BOWLING, 83, lived in a trailer beside Bowling's
Store in Massies Mill with her retarded son, Duval, whom she affectionately called "Mutt." The two of them had had a terrifying night—
in fact it was only by God's grace, she believed, that she'd lived to see
the dawn at all.

Mrs. Bowling had been awakened in the night by the storm, and
when she reached out of bed to turn on the light, her hand splashed
in water. She saw her two white shoes go floating by. She turned the
light on; but it almost instantly went out again. She got out of the bed
and waded through waist-deep water into Mutt's room to awaken
him. Mutt, who was sixty-one but had the intelligence of a small child,
had always been terrified of storms. He was dazed and frightened, sitting up in bed as the floodwater rose around him.

"Oh, Mumsy, what's going on?" he asked her, as the trailer rocked
back and forth in the flood and rain thundered on the tin roof.

"Who takes care of you?" she asked him.

"God takes care of me," he said.

"God will take care of us. Don't be afraid. Now come on with me
to my room and we'll sit there together."

The old woman helped Mutt wade into her room. At one point,
she stumbled and fell in the water, felt it up around her throat. *I'm
drowning,* she thought. But she dragged herself up again, and she
heard Mutt singing a hymn: "God will take care of me . . . !"

The two spent the night clutching each other, as the flood ripped off the door of the trailer, then the plate glass window. Then the whole side came off and Sadie Bowling felt the trailer being swept downriver, bouncing and banging against things. She later said it felt as if the trailer "was being ground up in a machine."

Eventually, as the water receded, she sat down on a chair in the kitchen. Mutt laid his head in her lap, and she patted him gently. He complained that he was cold, and she tried to warm and comfort him. As the daylight came up, the trailer gradually stopped rocking. The water drained out of the room. When she finally had the nerve to stand up and peer outside, Mrs. Sadie Thacker Bowling realized that the trailer was now about 150 feet downriver from where it had been the night before. It was lodged up in a tree outside Lea Brothers general store.

The only thing that was missing was her pocketbook, which contained $300—all the money she had in this world.

But she and Mutt, though cold, wet, and frightened, were alive.

EDNA CAMPBELL and her eighteen-year-old daughter, Iris, were alone in their house in Lowesville, near the James River, that night. Even though it was raining hard, Edna's husband, Ward, had left the house shortly before eleven o'clock, going off to his regular shift at the American Cyanamid Plant in Piney River. The two women went to bed shortly after Ward left the house, but they had trouble sleeping because of the thunderous storm outside, and the day-bright lightning flashes. It was 1:30 in the morning when Edna went downstairs to check on things and found water pouring in under the door and even through the windows. She called Ward at work to ask him to come home, but he reported that the roads were already closed by high water and there was no way to reach them.

"You and Iris go on upstairs and just stay there," Ward told them. "You'll be safe."

Still frightened and unsure of what to do, Edna called her brother Gordon, who lived nearby. He suggested they go over to the Piney River Baptist Church, which was only a few hundred yards from the house. But when Edna peered out the window, she could see in the electric glare of continuous lightning flashes that attempting to cross even that short distance would almost certainly be fatal: A raging river separated her front door from the sanctuary of the church. Shortly afterwards, around two in the morning, the electricity went out. Edna grabbed a flashlight and with her daughter dashed upstairs.

But the storm was unrelenting. Although theirs was a seven-room frame house on a solid foundation, now it began to shudder in the onslaught of the flood. The water seemed to follow them upstairs: In the flashlight beam, Edna could see it mounting the steps. She and Iris climbed into bed and hugged each other, hoping and praying that they would be saved.

That's when the whole house exploded. With a crack, the roof collapsed on top of them, pinning them to the bed, and mother and daughter found themselves being swept down the river in a tangle of broken rafters and debris. It all happened too fast to even know what was happening; all they knew was that, eventually, the remnants of the bed upon which they were riding seemed to lodge in a tree. They were still pinned beneath what remained of the roof, but Edna, holding the flashlight, managed to work herself free, climbing out into the branches of the tree. Then she labored mightily to free her daughter from the wreckage. Edna was a small woman and her daughter was portly, so this task, in the hammering rain in the middle of the river, both of them freezing cold and bruised over every bit of their bodies, was one of those heroic deeds of which humans are capable, perhaps once in a lifetime, in the direst of circumstances. Once Edna had wrenched Iris free, the two of them clung to the debris pile, counting on Edna's wristwatch the hours until dawn.

"We were surrounded by a great roaring," Edna said later. Around them, immense piles of detritus—uprooted trees, ruined houses and barns—built up into a kind of dam, at least partly deflecting the force of the flood. As a faint dawn began rising in the sky, they could see that the beaver-dam of wreckage and the broken roof they were clinging to seemed to be braced by two small trees, and that if either one of them gave way, they'd be swept down the river and probably drowned. There was nothing to do but hold on for all they were worth and hope the twin trees would hold.

They held.

By seven in the morning, it was daylight and the two women could see people on the riverbank trying to figure out a way to rescue them. It took hours to get a boat across to their perilous perch in the tree—a spot that later turned out to be a mile downstream from where their house had once stood. The house itself and everything inside it had utterly vanished. The only thing left was a cement front porch, tilted over and washed into the yard. All that remained of the Campbells's possessions, acquired over a lifetime, were the flashlight Edna had in her hand, a Bible, and a cedar chest with one wobbly leg. All the rest of it, Ward said later, was "washed away clean."

CHAPTER THIRTEEN

Morning, Wednesday, August 20

THAT WEDNESDAY MORNING, a painter in Charlottesville got up early and went outside to feed her cat. Overnight there'd been violent thunderstorms and torrential rain, and she'd seen a good deal of lightning in the sky in the direction of Lovingston, which was down across the county line to the south. She noticed a few branches down in her yard, and mud puddles where the ground was low. It seemed to have been a fierce but unremarkable summer shower; now the sky was clearing, and patches of blue were appearing overhead.

But there was something else in the air which she sensed immediately—an eerie silence, as if the world had been entirely stripped of sound. It took her a moment before she realized what it was: There were no birds in the trees, on the ground or anywhere else. They were gone. At this point, she later recalled, she'd heard nothing on the radio or television about what had happened down in Nelson County. But she couldn't shake the feeling—like a ghostly finger grazing the back of her neck—that somehow, somewhere, something had gone wrong in the world.

A mere twenty miles to the south, people were waking up to a world that had gone so badly wrong that even thirty years later, many would still choose not to speak of it. Over in Tyro, the man known to everybody as "Captain Billy" Massie had had his lawn mowed by a teenager the night before. He'd stood out there in the early evening, admiring the new-mown grass, thinking how pretty it looked in the golden light. He went to bed at his usual hour but was wakened in the night by the storm, walked downstairs and stood at the head of the basement stairs, dumbfounded, as his entire basement filled with water in five minutes. A calm and unexcitable man, he'd rolled up the rugs in the living room, dragged them up onto the stairs, and gone back to bed.

But now, when he walked outside his house in the morning light, he was surrounded by a completely disorienting sight. His new-mown lawn was buried under two feet of mud. The Tye River, which normally flowed past his house on the opposite side of the road, was now *behind* his house. The road itself seemed to have disappeared. Sprawled in the front yard was the dead body of a man. And further away, where the road used to be, were the bodies of two women, their ears, noses, and mouths filled with muddy gravel.

Grisly scenes like this were repeated all across the county. At first nobody grasped the magnitude of what had happened.

Sheriff Whitehead, who had been up all night leading a so-far-unsuccessful search for Tinker Bryant's wife and three daughters, had also been frantically trying to reach the outside world by radio. For the most part, he'd met with pandemonium or disbelief; even when he got through to the proper authorities, he could not seem to quite communicate the disaster in his county.

What neither Bill Whitehead nor anyone else understood at that moment was that the greatest devastation was restricted to a relatively compact area, roughly a hundred miles long and twenty-five miles wide. Outside of this area, such as in Charlottesville to the north or Amherst to the south, there'd been heavy rain and lightning overnight, but nothing approaching the catastrophe that was unfolding in Nelson County. And no place in Nelson County, it seemed, had been more badly hammered than the little towns of Massies Mill and Tyro, on the Tye River, at the foot of the four-thousand-foot crests of the Blue Ridge. The unimaginable amounts of water that had fallen overnight had been focused and concentrated by the great drainage basins of the mountains, dumped into the branching arterial network of creeks and rivulets that fed into the Tye, and then hurtled downstream, and down the mountain into the sleeping hamlets below. The hydraulic force of this blow had nearly wiped Massies Mill off the map.

Devastated roads and bridges had trapped Sheriff Whitehead in a small quadrant in the western part of the county near his home in Roseland all night, but by eight in the morning, as the water receded, he was able to nose his Plymouth 440 police cruiser down a debris-strewn road to the edge of Massies Mill. He'd begun to get scattered reports on the radio that there were people clinging to trees and houses in the river, and he was heading down there to help. It turned out that a small party of local men—Walter Scott Evans, Bill Flippin, Garland Wright, and Walter Hoffman—had already rescued people who had been stranded on the roof of flooded homes, or were clinging to bits of wreckage from ruined houses or trailers. This small party had also managed to rescue Carl Raines's two boys out of the trees where they'd spent the night. Warren and Carl Junior were freezing and frightened, but otherwise seemed to be unhurt. So far, the men told Whitehead, they had found no trace of the boys' father, his wife, or his three other children. Two of the Wood children had been found: little Mike, clinging to a roof, and his fifteen-year-old sister, Theresa, who'd been washed half a mile downstream but was saved when her arm got caught in the fork of a tree. Theresa told her rescuers that when she was being swept downriver she felt sure she was going to drown; then when her arm got caught she felt sure it was going to be ripped completely off, the floodwater was so strong.

It was not clear that the rest who had fled the Raines house that night had been so lucky.

The Miller Chemical Company warehouse, where Carl Senior worked, had been transported by the flood into the middle of the Route 56 bridge and now sat there, dank, desolate, and badly listing to one side. The sheriff and a group of other local men walked into the dark building. Warren and Carl Junior Raines came up to them.

"Have you seen anything of our mother and daddy?" they asked. "Have you seen our sisters? Have you seen our little brother, Sandy?"

"I never felt as miserable in all of my life as then, being able to tell them absolutely nothing, whether they were dead or alive," Whitehead said later.

By this time, the sheriff was besieged by calls for help from all sides, whether by wan and terrified people who came up to him in the street or by reports he was getting over the radio. All around him were scenes of almost incomprehensible devastation, and cries for help—many of which he could barely hear, because the roar of the receding water seemed to drown out all other sound. The water, which had risen to perhaps twenty feet above normal at the height of the flood, had already receded to six or seven feet above normal. The air was filled not only with sound but also with the smell so many people remembered later: that rank, rich, slightly unpleasant smell of freshly turned, deep earth and pulverized bark and trees. It was a smell that told the sheriff one thing: There were massive landslides on the mountain, which meant there was death and misery on a scale he had never encountered in his life, even in war.

All that night and morning Whitehead had been on the radio, begging for helicopters from anybody who would listen, because it was now clear that people were going to be stranded by destroyed roads and bridges all across the county. One of his cries had been heard in adjoining Augusta County by the sheriff there, John Kent. Kent comandeered a helicopter, surveyed the damage in his own county, evacuated a few people, and then sent the chopper over to Nelson, where'd he'd learned from monitoring radio reports that things were very, very bad. The chopper came flying up the Tye River over Massies Mill, where Whitehead spotted it and signaled the pilot to land. When the chopper put down in a field, Whitehead climbed aboard and they took off over the devastated county, the Nelson County sheriff still on the radio responding to a cacophony of cries for help and reports of people stranded, injured, dead, or missing.

What unfolded below Whitehead now almost surpassed belief. He knew this county as well as anyone, had lived here all his life, but there were places that were so transfigured by the floods and mudslides that they were unrecognizable. All across the green, undulating mountainsides, in the folds between the ridges, you could see places that looked like naked wounds, where the red Virginia clay was ripped open like raw muscle, with the white bone of bedrock showing through—wounds that would still be clearly visible thirty years later. A U.S. Department of the Interior study would later determine that the entire area between the Tye and Rockfish Rivers, about sixty-five square miles, was "completely devastated by debris flows and floods." Debris flows are a kind of landslide or earth-lava made up of a mixture of water-saturated rock detritus, rubble, and soil with a consistency similar to wet cement, which move rapidly downslope under the influence of gravity. Because they are so high in density and travel so rapidly, they are capable of moving immense boulders, houses, or anything else in their path. Almost every major drainage channel down the mountainsides had turned into a debris flow chute. From the air, thousands of "failure sites" could be seen, where the mountainsides had collapsed and their cargo of soil, boulders, trees, and rubble had thundered down into the valley below.

Everywhere Sheriff Whitehead looked, he could see flooded or destroyed roads and bridges, which meant it would be impossible to reach many parts of his county except by air. But as the chopper turned north of Lovingston and passed over Davis Creek, the sheriff grew silent. Davis Creek, like little Hat Creek that ran behind his house, was normally so tiny and so shallow a tall man could step over it without breaking stride. But Davis Creek had turned into a vast, flotsam-choked gorge, a raw, red canyon, stacked full of mud and boulders, half-buried houses and cars, and enormous downed trees as big around at the base as truck tires. Most of the debris flows seemed to have traveled relatively short distances, but in Davis Creek (and also the Freshwater Cove area), debris flows had left rubble-strewn devastation stretching downslope more than two miles.

The outflow from this cataclysm had swept down across U.S. Route 29, the main road out of town to the north, and simply swept huge sections of it away. It was a newly improved divided-lane highway that had just been completed in May—and big chunks of it were simply gone, or in the process of collapsing into the scoured-out riverbed below.

There was no telling how much human misery lay down below.

The pilot and the state trooper who were onboard the helicopter told Whitehead that earlier, they'd spotted a group of people on a riverbank, put the chopper down nearby, and found the people frantically trying to dig out a man who had been buried in mud and debris up to his neck. He was still alive but his wife, buried in the mud nearby with a jagged board rammed into her back, had already died. The rescuers were desperate for equipment—a power saw, gasoline, shovels, mattocks, anything to free the man's body from the suffocating grip of the mud and debris. Whitehead directed the pilot to land near Lovingston, where he borrowed tools and equipment from somebody from the Central Virginia Electric Cooperative. Then the chopper headed back towards where the man was buried, in the Davis Creek area. The pilot dropped the chopper onto the gravel of the riverbed and Whitehead jumped out with an armload of tools. But the weary rescuers, their faces streaked with mud, just looked at him blankly. The man, whose name turned out to be Robert Martin, had just died.

It was too late.

WHEN CLIFF WOOD got up at daybreak that morning, around 6:00 A.M., he looked out at his 120 acres of corn disappearing under water and thought, We're ruined. Wood was a rangy local diary farmer and vice chairman of the Nelson County Board of Supervisors—an important position in a rural area—who lived in a comfortable brick house on the bluffs overlooking the James River, on the southern edge of Nelson County. The house sat high enough on the bluffs to be spared from the flooding, but down below, on the James River floodplain where he grew corn to be used for silage for his Holsteins, his whole crop was going under. Floods were not unusual down there—it was a floodplain, after all—but never in his life had he seen anything like this. He had never seen it flood to this level, this quickly; the entire valley below was under water. Normally after a big rain, it took a day or two for high water to wind its way down the big river through Lynchburg, but that wasn't the case this morning: high water had already arrived, and it was rapidly getting higher.

Luckily, Wood's wife, Louise (whom he affectionately called "Ease"), was at home and safe; so were his teenage daughters, Jane and Ellen. Even his house was safe. But his corn crop would be flattened by the flood and completely ruined.

"I was very fortunate—my corn was underwater, but my family was all right," he recalled later. "That makes this easier to talk about—plenty of people in this county don't want to talk about it at all."

The James River is a great, slow-moving waterway that drains ten thousand square miles, wending its way lazily and circuitously across the state, moving eastward, gathering volume from innumerable smaller drainages until it dumps its cargo into the Chesapeake Bay at Hampton Roads. It is one of the great watercourses of the East, which in colonial times served as a primitive interstate highway, plied by watermen in long, narrow boats called "bateux," which carried goods to market.

The Wood family farm sat on the bank of the James where two of the main rivers that drained Nelson County—the Tye and the Rockfish—fed into the big river. Wood had seen high water often

enough to know that you could tell which of the two rivers was flooding worse simply by observing the color of the floodwater. The
Rockfish River, which emptied into the James at Howardsville upstream of Wood's house, drained the forest soils of the mountainous
regions, so the floodwater tended to be a kind of grayish-tan. The
Tye, which emptied into the James at Norwood about three miles
downstream of his house, drained lower-elevation parts of the county
that were predominantly reddish Piedmont soils, and this floodwater
was red as rust. There must be horrendous flooding on the upper
reaches of the Tye, back up at the foot of the mountains around
Massies Mill, he thought.

(Wood later spoke to his uncle, who lived on a bluff overlooking
the James several miles upstream of Norwood. He said so much reddish floodwater, choked with logs and debris, poured down the Tye
that morning that the James came to a standstill and then actually began *backing up,* pushing the water at least three miles upstream.
Eventually this reversed flow began to slow; then it came to a standstill; then the James resumed its stately flow to the east. The amount
of hydraulic force it would have required to make the mighty James
River flow backwards staggers the imagination. But it's not impossible. In that particular place the gradient of the river is nearly level for
several miles, and at midsummer the amount of water in the river
would be relatively low. But the primary driver of this extraordinary
event would be the amount of water flowing down the Tye, calculated
by one expert observer at one hundred *million* gallons. Cliff Wood,
who was only forty-two in 1969, had never seen anything like this
flood in his lifetime—but his uncle was eighty and he'd never seen
anything like it, either.)

Wood got in his truck and drove down towards Howardsville, a
small town not far from his house. Howardsville was completely underwater. All the buildings on the south side of the river were gone,
including some that had been there two hundred years: the post office,
stores, the sawmill, all gone. The train station was gone, and the railroad bridge that crossed the Rockfish River from Nelson County over
to the neighboring county of Buckingham had collapsed into the river.
"The river was raging," he remembers, "and there were logs leaping
into the air as they came into contact with the fallen bridges, leaping
into the air like salmon." Oddly enough, the road to Howardsville was

clear, and the sky above was clear and blue as heaven. People had driven their cars down from Shipman and other places and stood on the bluffs overlooking the town, marveling at the flood like water tourists. As they watched, the river kept rising, and it would continue to rise until it crested around 2:00 P.M. the following day, as Camille's spent cargo of rain made its way down through Lynchburg and the mountain counties to the west, like a pig passing through a python.

Wood commandeered a johnboat and, with several others, rescued an old lady named Mrs. Belcher, who'd survived by climbing through the attic and up onto the roof. She told Wood that she had some relations who lived down on the Gulf Coast of Mississippi and had been relieved to find out they were safe.

"I never expected to be the one washed out of my house!" she told him.

The phones were down, so the only way Wood could gather information was to drive around the county (as far as he could get on the flooded roads) and talk to people. So he did. Since he was a civic official, this was a semi-official information-gathering trip. And gradually, as he drove around the county and talked to people, Wood began putting together a fragmentary story of what had happened. At first, it had seemed like just another flood—a mighty big flood, the biggest in his lifetime, but just another flood nonetheless. But gradually a darker picture began to emerge. People told him there was bad flooding in the Beech Grove area, and at Reids Gap, and Tyro and Davis Creek. The Green Acres neighborhood had been flooded and Bobby Ray Floyd and his family had nearly drowned. Tom Burnley and his whole family had washed away at Norwood. Mr. and Mrs. Wooten had washed away. Most of Massies Mill had washed away. Down in the river town of Wingina, on the James, Wood ran into Walter Tucker from the Rural Electric Co-op. Tucker told him that even Lovingston had flooded. Lovingston! It was a town on high ground miles north of the James, with only a stream that dried up in hot weather. How could *Lovingston* flood? But when Wood drove over there, he discovered it was true. The IGA supermarket was destroyed. Whole mountainsides above the town had collapsed, with landslides cascading into the streets. Something truly unbelievable had happened.

"It looked like there had been a war, and we lost," Wood said.

In fact, the analogy was apt. Wood had been on active duty in the miltary for three years, during the latter days of World War II and then later as a reservist in Korea. He had seen what war looks like. He'd been stationed around Manila, in the Philippines, where war had raged for years and where the Japanese occupiers had brutalized the local population. There was "a lot of destruction, a lot of misery." Later, in Korea, he'd worked in Seoul at a time when as many as a million refugees had come streaming down from the north because the North Koreans and the Chinese had ravaged the countryside, taking everything, destroying rice paddies, civilians be damned. There was hunger and privation and destruction on a massive scale. He remembered thinking then, as a young serviceman overseas, how hard it was to imagine what it would be like if something like this happened in his home community back in Nelson County.

Well, now it had happened. And it looked a lot like war. Around him was destruction on a huge scale, with ruined roads and bridges and buildings. There were an unknown number of victims, killed or badly injured, and others—women, children, old people—stranded out in the hollows in need of help. There would be problems providing clean drinking water and food and medical supplies. There would be problems with disease and perhaps vermin, in the festering summer sun. The rescue operation would have to be massive. And the task of rebuilding—well, at this point, it was too daunting even to think about.

"The disaster itself, the flooding, was over in eight hours. But the rescue and recovery was just beginning. It was a sad place to start," Wood said later. "One of the unique things about Camille was that the rain started after dark and ended before daylight—it all happened in darkness and the people who died, died in total innocence. That was the thing that really got you."

WHAT HAD OCCURRED overnight would later go on record as the worst natural disaster in the history of the Commonwealth of Virginia. And so many innocents died in it at least partly because the whole thing was so improbable. Among the many peculiar aspects of the storm, one of the oddest was that all this hurricane-induced rainfall had occurred so far inland. In a scientific paper about the floods, U.S. Weather Bureau hydrologist Francis K. Schwarz later pointed out that the most intense rainfall from hurricanes that blow in off the Gulf of Mexico almost always occurs within a hundred miles of the coast. But Camille dumped her deadly cargo in central Virginia, *eight hundred miles* inland. Schwartz looked at all previous hurricane and tropical storm tracks on record, to see if any of them had regained tropical storm intensity after such a long overland trajectory, but "no case as remarkable as that of Camille could be found."

Down on the Gulf Coast, the heaviest rainfall associated with Camille was 9.4 inches, measured at Picayune, Mississippi. By the time she was 150 miles inland, her rains had rapidly diminished to little more than 3 inches. In western Tennessee and Kentucky, the heaviest reported rains were between 2 and 3 inches—all gratefully received, after a persistent drought. It was only after Camille's revolving low-pressure center crossed the Blue Ridge into Virginia and collided with the various weather systems lying in wait there that the great deluge commenced.

How much rain actually fell? Soon after the storm, the U.S. Weather Bureau sent a survey team into the devastated region to collect "unofficial" rain measurements. That is, rain caught in small plastic commerical rain gauges, empty trash cans, fuel barrels, and so on. Four of these receptacles contained more than 20 inches of water and one, found near Massies Mill, contained 27 inches. There were other, anecdotal reports not collected by this team that suggested even higher rainfall amounts. A local farmer named John McCarthy who had an empty 55-gallon barrel on his pickup truck before the storm found it was almost full of water, 31 inches deep, after the storm— and his truck was not even in the center of the storm. The Weather Bureau team heard about one report of 31 inches in five hours, measured at the junction of the Tye and Piney rivers (not too far from Massies Mill). If verified, this would have amounted to a new world record—but the survey team could not confirm this measurement because neither the person who made the observation nor the container that was used could be identified. "However," they concluded, "a reliable measurement of 23 inches was obtained for the same general vicinity, indicating that the rainfall was extreme, and that 31 inches may have fallen." A report from the U.S. Department of the Interior adds that "many of the total rainfall determinations are minimums . . .

The buckets, milk pails and other open containers used to measure the rainfall overflowed and the total rainfall is not known."

The official, confirmed rainfall record for the Camille storm, according to the Virginia State Climatology Office, is 27.35 inches in about nine hours. But even if it "only" rained 27 inches, consider this: The average monthly rainfall in the state is between 3 and 4 inches per month, meaning that nine *months* of rain fell between dusk and dawn on a single night. There is good reason to believe the rain was actually heavier than that—perhaps *much* heavier. It is indeed possible that a world-record rainfall fell that night in Nelson County, although the precise truth will never be known.

But it was not the rain that was the deadliest element of the storm. It was the debris flows triggered by the rains. Towering above the peaceful fields and orchards of Nelson County were the steep slopes and narrow hollows of the Blue Ridge. The torrential rains made weapons of the landscape, turning the bucolic mountains into massive missile-launchers aimed directly at everything and everyone that lay below.

Most of the landslides and debris flows were later found to have occurred on mountainsides underlain by rocks known to geologists as the Lovingston Formation, composed of granitic gneisses and other rocks dating back about a billion years. Lying atop this slick, shallow bedrock was a thin mantle of rich mountain soil and saprolite (sometimes called "rotten granite" because it easily crumbles), which had built up since the last Ice Age ten thousand years ago. The interface or "cleavage surface" between the mantle of topsoil and the underlying granitic bedrock was fairly thin and fairly weak, according to geologist Thomas Gathright, of the Virginia Division of Mines, who extensively studied and photographed the geological aftermath of the storm. This was a critical weakness, but something that would normally go entirely unnoticed, like the weak link in a chain. It was only after the whole system came under severe stress—stress unlikely to have occurred in these mountains for at least the previous thousand years—that massive, catastrophic collapse took place.

The "set-up" for the catastrophe had actually been occurring for months previous to Camille's arrival. The summer of 1969 had been very wet, and this thin mantle of rock and soil had become almost completely saturated with rainwater. (There had, in fact, been a heavy rain the morning before the storm.) The overburden of soil was now wet and viscous as pudding. At the same time it lay steeply tilted on the mountainsides, like an immense wedding cake on a perilously tilted table. When the great rains of that August night occurred, the soil on the mountainsides reached a "tipping point." The mantle shook loose, and a kind of high-density, fast-moving slurry of dirt, boulders, and trees began cascading down the slope, peeling away everything in its path. Gathright says that geologists have never conclusively established whether the landslides began at the top of the mountain ridges and then cascaded downward; or whether raging creeks and rivers dug out the foot of the slopes, thus undermining the slope's foundation and triggering a collapse that traveled upwards. It all occurred in deep darkness, in the middle of the night, and nobody saw it happen—so many critical details will forever remain unknown.

But a hint of what was happening up in the dark mountains on that terrible night was glimpsed by a state trooper whose patrol car was stopped on U.S. Route 29 near the mouth of Davis Creek. In the pounding rain, he could see that floodwater was pouring across the Interstate at such velocity it was tearing away at the highway itself. Then, suddenly, with a roar, an immense logjam of trees, boulders, and soil avalanched across the road, pushed by a wall of water. The pile of debris, high as a house, completely blocked the road, but the force of the water was so powerful it was actually moving the mountain of rubble. For a short period of time, only water came down the mountain. Then, with a roar, another logjam catapulted across the road.

What clearly was happening, Gathright says, is that as the great mass of soil, rocks, and trees cascaded down the mountain and into steep-sided hollows, debris logjams or dams built up, which immediately backed up tons of water. Once the pressure built up to bursting, the debris-dams violently disintegrated, sending walls of rubble-filled water down the mountain. There was, in effect, a series of massive detonations or explosions followed by thunderous avalanches, which caused the earth-shaking roar people heard down below, as well as the strange, pungent smell of deeply turned earth, as two-hundred-year-old trees were pulverized like pencils, and boxcar-sized boulders that had lain in place for thousands of years came loose and were

THE EDGE OF DARK   205

swept by rivers of fast-moving mud into the valley below. For those caught in the middle of this great grinding geological process, there must have been a brief window of terror that came before death.

The astounding force and violence of this geological event helped geologists rethink their whole idea about the nature of geological evolution over great spans of time. Prior to the time of Camille, it was generally thought that geological landforms are shaped primarily by incremental processes like wind, water, and erosion operating over millions of years. But many geologists now believe that sudden, catastrophic events like floods, earthquakes, and volcanoes are actually the primary forces that shape the earth, Gathright says. One geological study later concluded that about two thousand years of erosion had occurred in that single night in Nelson County. And almost forty years later, mountainsides scoured clean and reshaped by that cataclysmic event are still clearly visible.

It may be that our world has been formed more by drama than by tedium, and what happened that frightful night is more the norm than an anomaly. And that, however infrequent and unlikely, such an event is guaranteed to happen again.

RIGHT NOW Cliff Wood had a pressing practical problem that is commonplace in war: How do you communicate? How do you talk to anybody, get help, get organized, or even figure out the extent of the damage, without the ability to communicate?

"The amazing thing was that we were just cut off from the world," remembers Phil Payne, who was a Nelson County teenager at the time. "There were no cell phones. Some of the local phones were down, and there was no long-distance service. A couple of people had short-wave radios, but that was about it. We had reverted to a pre-technological era. I mean, the sheriff from Augusta County flew over in a helicopter and saw our devastation and reported it, because we couldn't. Because we couldn't communicate, or get above it like that, it wasn't until late the afternoon of that first day that we really started to grasp what had happened."

Wood comandeered a Jeep from the county and he and Bob Goad, the commonwealth's attorney, tried driving up U.S. Route 29 to see how far south they could go, to try to get a better sense of the extent of the damage. A few miles up the road, at Freshwater Cove

Creek, the road was completely washed out and there was a half-buried car down in the creekbed. A man standing by the road said somebody had drowned in the car. Wood and Goad turned around and drove north, up past Lovingston, where a house sat forlornly on the median strip and people were already out trying to clear the road with a motley assortment of tractors and bulldozers and farm equipment. At Woods Mill, the highway was washed out and blocked by massive mounds of debris, some of them twenty feet high or more. Crowds of dazed-looking people stood beside the highway. Nobody seemed to know what was going on. When Wood and Goad got to the place where Davis Creek crossed the highway, the road was blocked by an immense logjam of downed trees. Wood got out of the car and spoke to a man, who was crying, and who told him that things were just awful up in Davis Creek.

Wood was getting back into the Jeep when an immense, important-looking man approached him and Goad.

"Jim Tribble," he said. "I'm from the state office of civil defense."

Tribble, who weighed in at 240 pounds and stood over six feet tall, had flown in on a helicopter. He had an air of authority about him, and he was in a hurry. He'd served in the Marine Corps in the South Pacific and in China and he had an abrupt, miltary bearing. He was looking for whoever was in charge.

"Who are you?" he asked Wood.

"I'm Cliff Wood, vice chair of the county board of supervisors."

"Are there any other supervisors around?"

"No, nobody else can *get* here."

"Well, would you say this is a disaster?"

"Yes, it sure is! Right now my guess is we need food for four thousand people, a third of the population of this county. Is that a disaster, or not?"

It was not a trick question, or an idle one. Tribble had been sent to Nelson County by the state's civil defense office to get an official declaration from some local authority, to set the wheels of government in motion. It was akin to the president officially declaring a "disaster area," which sets in motion the release of federal money. Tribble would relay Wood's comments to his boss, Minor Hawley, director of civil defense in Richmond.

Help, it seemed, was on the way.

"LET'S GO BACK HOME and see if everybody's there," Carl Junior Raines suggested to his little brother Warren, after they talked to the sheriff at the warehouse where their father worked. "We can get us some dry clothes, too."

So the boys walked back down the road towards home. People were wandering around the streets of Massies Mill, some of them clearly in shock, hardly seeming to see anything. By now it was nine o'clock in the morning, the faint dawn had turned into a brilliant blue summer day, and the floodwater was rapidly receding back into the river. In fact, it was amazing how quickly the water retreated, leaving what looked like a debris-strewn muddy riverbottom where their pretty little town had once stood. By nine-thirty in the morning, all the swift water was back within the banks of the Tye.

When they got close to their home, the boys could see that it was at least still standing, though the downstairs windows were all broken out and it was standing in a lake of muddy water. The big house next door, had come off its foundations and wedged into some trees in front of their house, apparently blocking some of the river's flow into their own home. The home of Mr. Wood, their neighbor who had chosen to ride it out, had been moved fifty feet but was still standing. Another house had been dropped down on top of a cow, which was now grotesquely squashed. And the station wagon that the Raines family had tried to use to make their escape, was also crushed beneath a house, sticking out from under the foundations like the end of a hot dog protruding from the bun.

Carl Junior and Warren crept through the front door of their family home. Something horrible had entered the house while they were gone, leaving a dank fishy smell in the air and knee-deep mud in the front room. Their mother's precious wingback chair, which Warren had helped her lift onto the landing to keep dry and safe, was lying on its side in the middle of the room, half-buried in muck.

"Daddy? Mama?" they shouted. "Jo? Ginger?"

Silence.

The brothers made their way into the kitchen, the soul of the house, where their mother and Jo used to love to talk while they cooked. A high-water mark, etched in muck, stood halfway up the wall at about the five-foot level. The mark neatly transected a handwoven potholder hanging on the wall, sad and alone. The kitchen, so recently submerged, smelled foul.

Just then, they heard a thumping noise upstairs, where the bedrooms were. They charged up the stairs and found the family dog, Bo, a sweet-tempered black Lab, sprawled on their little brother, Sandy's bed. Bo was glad to see them, as always. He thumped his tail like mad and lathered up their faces with his tongue. He was normally an outdoor dog, but somehow he'd gotten inside and found his way to the only place in the house that had been spared by the flood. In fact, glancing around, Warren and Carl Junior could see that the upstairs bedrooms were completely untouched. Sandy's plastic helmet and plastic guns, Ginger's baby dolls, Warren's hotrod posters and stamp collection and unmade bed—they were all there in casual disarray as though nothing had happened at all. It was only when you looked out the window that you realized the world would never be the same. Warren did not quite let himself think the thought, but it hung there in the air anyway: If they'd just stayed home, everything might have been all right.

The boys changed into some dry clothes and went back downstairs. The house was creepy. As they left quickly by the back door, Warren noticed a ghoulish sight: One of the family housecats had been trapped and drowned behind a screen door.

The boys went back out into the ruined town, wandering among the other zombie-like survivors, looking for their family. They found The Car, or what was left of it, a few hundred yards down the road from their house. Tipped over on its side and completely ruined, it looked like it had been in a trash compactor. Funny, considering all the work they'd poured into that car, but when the boys saw it like that neither of them even seemed to care. They just shrugged and kept walking. All that mattered now was one increasingly frightening question:

Where's the family? Where is everybody?

About a quarter mile down the road from the house, they found their Sting-Ray bicycle, badly bent, emerging out of the mud. They cleaned it off, straightened out the handlebars, climbed aboard in their standard way and started double-pedaling around the village, talking to everybody they saw, trying to get information, trying to find their family. Everybody seemed to feel sorry for the boys, and almost invariably offered some helpful and encouraging news.

"Your family is okay, they came and took them down to Lynchburg General Hospital."

"Everything's fine, they're safe and they're trying to get word back to you boys."

"The state police were here and they took them up to Charlottesville, and they'll be back in the morning."

But Warren had a queasy feeling in the pit of his stomach. He and Carl Junior didn't believe these people. There was no way all this junk could be true. People were trying to be nice, but the truth was that nobody knew where their parents were at all. Something was wrong—really, really wrong.

Where's the family? Where is everybody?

CHAPTER FOURTEEN

Thursday, August 21
Nelson County, Virginia

IF A STORM of Camille's magnitude were to strike central Virginia with such devastating force today, by Thursday afternoon—more than forty hours after the rains began—CNN, Fox News and The Weather Channel would have had reporters on the ground in Nelson County, broadcasting live worldwide. Storm-watchers would be able to download streaming video of survivor interviews off the Internet. And bloggers in cyberspace would be chatting up a storm, posting comments, sharing information, and second-guessing the police and the weather service.

But in 1969, by Thursday afternoon much of the news about what had happened in Nelson County came from regional and national newspapers—and much of it was still fragmentary or erroneous. "As far as can be determined, there are no communications either in or out of the stricken area either by telephone or radio . . . ," the Lynchburg paper reported. The Associated Press said Massies Mill was reachable only on foot, and "those who have walked into the area had not returned by noon today." News outlets had to make do with estimates and second-hand information. The Associated Press reported that by late Wednesday, thirty-eight people were known to have drowned and thirty-two more were missing, but because bodies had been found floating in rivers, inside wrecked buildings, and in cars washed off highways into deeply flooded fields, the numbers were sure to rise. "State police reported that the town of Massies Mill, for all practical purposes, has been completely washed away." Railroad and highway transportation were at a standstill in Nelson and adjoining Amherst counties. Three miles south of Lovingston, a full-sized tractor trailer disappeared under a mountain of mud that cascaded from a cliff onto one lane of U.S. Route 29. In nearby Louisa County, an earthen dam at a large man-made lake gave way and a twenty-foot wall of water drowned an estimated four hundred head of cattle. In the town of Glasgow, about thirty miles southwest of Lovingston on the James River, Fire Chief A.W. Ferguson said, "everything is a disaster, everything. All the businesses on Main Street are wiped out, and three-fourths of the houses are flooded."

The Charlottesville *Daily Progress* reported that local people were recovering from "the worst flood in at least a generation." Virtually every business in Scottsville, on the James, had been destroyed. A curfew was declared in the town to control huge crowds of people who had come to see the damage, including water 20 feet deep downtown. In Richmond, the state capital, the James was enormously elevated by early Thursday, and the Weather Bureau said it would crest at 34 feet—25 feet above flood stage. Thursday afternoon, helicopters were attempting to locate a frame house with an undetermined number of people on top of it, reported floating down the James south of Scottsville.

At the same time, in the face of all this, it was remarkable how quickly the news of the quotidian crept back into the papers. It was as if the sheer magnitude of the catastrophe called forth a longing for the comfortingly trivial, the unimportant, the ordinary. Side by side with news of Camille's devastation, there was news of a tow-headed local boy who'd made it all the way to the national Soap Box Derby Championship in Akron, Ohio. News of church suppers postponed, of people dying and getting engaged, of Johnny Unitas throwing two touchdown passes to carry the Baltimore Colts over the Buffalo Bills. A store offered back-to-school discounts on metal lunch buckets with thermos included, only a dollar, seventy-six.

Meanwhile, the news from the Gulf Coast, while more complete than the news from Virginia, was getting grimmer by the hour. The official death toll now topped 170, but based on the level of destruction, Mississippi Governor John Bell Williams said it might go far higher, perhaps to 500 or even 1,000 deaths. Martial law had been declared on the storm-ravaged coastal strip.

In Gulfport, a Red Cross aerial survey said there was total destruction on the waterfront, with at least two thousand homes completely destroyed and two thousand more with major damage. Three immense tankers had been driven aground in the harbor, and after a cat food factory was ripped open and its contents scattered across the beach, swarms of rats began overrunning the habor area. In Pascagoula, an influx of snakes emerged from the flooded bayous. "We've had to organize to fight them," a state senator said.

The hardest-hit area was the fifty miles of coastline from Waveland, Mississippi, east to Pascagoula, near the Alabama state line. Pass Christian, Bay Saint Louis and, Waveland were "all but destroyed," it was reported.

Ronnie Caire, a newspaper publisher in Pass Christian, said of the town: "It's gone. There's nothing there. It's just gone." He said he had inspected his own home, but, "I just turned away and left it for anyone who wanted it."

Twenty-three bodies had reportedly been pulled from the wreckage of the Richelieu Apartments, a luxury complex on the beach in Pass Christian. The stench of death hung over the Coast and officials, fearing an epidemic, ordered the survivors of Pass Christian evacuated. Military buses and Navy choppers handled the enforced evacuation to nearby Gulfport. Parnell Mckay, head of Civil Defense there, said bodies were being uncovered so fast Wednesday that nobody kept count. The adjoining waterfront communities of Long Beach and Henderson Point were virtually wiped out.

In Plaquemines Parish, Lousiana, where winds hit 200 miles per hour when Camille made landfall, there were early estimates of $50 to $100 million damage, not counting ripped-out levees. From Port Sulphur south along the Mississippi River to Venice, a stretch of thirty miles, every structure received extensive wind and water damage. An estimated five thousand head of cattle were drowned. President Richard Nixon declared parts of Louisiana and Mississippi major disaster areas. Vice president Spiro Agnew, on a helicopter tour of the ravaged coast, announced that the federal government would probably provide more relief than in any previous disaster in history.

Governor Williams said the damage zone had been quarantined to limit the flow of people, especially sightseers, who were turning the area "into a carnival." The state adjutant general, Walter Johnson, reported: "I've got two thousand men under arms, and I've got to bring in another two thousand. Sightseers are jamming in—looking for bodies, I guess." Charged with administering martial law over a six-hundred-square mile area of Mississippi, Johnson vowed to crack down on looters and profiteers. Men were hauling in ice and selling it for a dollar a pound. Striking back, one man opened an artesian well and began giving water away. Others hauled the water a few blocks down the street and began selling it for a dollar a gallon. Johnson said of the profiteers: "They're raising the price of food, especially milk, sometimes by as much as one hundred percent. Under martial law this will not be allowed." Some supermarkets selling bread for fifty cents a loaf would have to go back to last Saturday's prices or be prosecuted, he added.

THAT THURSDAY, Warren and Carl Raines got a ride back to Massies Mill from a friend of their father's named Tom Bruguiere. Bruguiere, who managed Dickie Brothers Orchards, had found the brothers wandering around the sad, flooded wreckage of the town on Wednesday evening and invited them back to his house to spend the night.

"Boys, come on, you're going with me," Bruguiere told them.

"But we've got to find the rest of our family!"

"You can work on that tomorrow. Y'all got to go somewhere tonight—you can't just stay around here."

Tom Bruguiere lived two or three miles out of town, up toward the mountains on higher ground, which had been mostly untouched by the flood. His wife fed the boys supper and fixed them a place to sleep in a guest room. They were so exhausted that slipping in between clean sheets felt heavenly. But "when we laid our heads down on the pillow that night, we knew that was probably it," Warren says today. "If we hadn't found our family by now, we knew the chances of finding them were pretty slim." The brothers did not talk very much, holding the grief of this terrible knowledge inside.

The next morning, Bruguiere took the boys back to Massies Mill to resume their search. But things did not look good. The town was filled with people wandering around dazedly, looking for lost family members. Everything was covered with mud. Everything had been violated. Everything was upside down and smelled bad. Of the forty or so buildings in the village, only two were habitable. Others were completely gone, or scattered about, or rammed into one another, as if a giant, spoiled child had been playing in the mud. A group of men with chainsaws and earth-moving equipment had begun dismantling the Miller Chemical Company warehouse, which was still teetering on the bridge.

The boys were walking down the muddy street when a state trooper pulled up in his patrol car. Trooper Ed Tinsley stepped out. Tinsley, a thirty-two-year-old ex-Marine, had gotten a call from a police dispatcher the morning before, ordering him back to duty in Amherst County.

"What's going on?" Tinsley had asked the dispatcher.

"Once you get down there, I think you'll see," the dispatcher replied.

When Tinsley got the call, he was at his mother's house, down in Bedford County, about fifty miles southwest of Lovingston. It had rained an inch or two overnight in Bedford and the sky was clearing when Tinsley got on the Interstate in his private car, headed back toward Amherst to pick up his patrol car and a uniform. He wasn't listening to the radio, and the sun was shining, so he wasn't quite prepared for the shock when he came across the bridge over the James River in Lynchburg. "There must have been five hundred people on that bridge, watching the high water," he recalls. "One of the most amazing things about this storm was how *concentrated* it was—only a few miles down the road, in Bedford, it rained, but it wasn't much more than a summer storm. But by the time I got to Lynchburg, it was obvious that something really disastrous had happened."

When Tinsley got to Amherst, he learned from the dispatcher that there'd been a tremendous flood up in Nelson County and the northern edge of Amherst, and that "the rivers had risen to a height that had been unheard of before." Tinsley's sergeant—the one who ordered him back to duty—had been called out during the night and gotten trapped in the Piney River area when the bridges collapsed behind him; he was communicating now by police radio through the dispatcher. The sergeant gave Tinsley the task of attempting to determine the extent of the flooded area. It was a slightly quixotic mission—one trooper in a patrol car, trying to drive around a biblical flood—but all the phones were down, everything was chaotic, and the state police had no helicopters available to fly over the floodland, so there was really no other way to get a sense of its size. Trooper Tinsley began driving around the area, trying to grasp what had happened. Moved by what he saw, he started dictating into a tape-recorded diary each evening:

"I was getting some sense of what massive damage we'd had. Every low spot in the mountains had washed out from the very top of the mountain, down, which would indicate a terrific amount of rain involved . . . every gully, every little valley . . . had been washed out as if some giant claw had grabbed hold of it and pulled everything out of it. This was washed all the way down to solid rock.

"Everything gone! And as this built up going down the mountain to the streams and rivers and into the larger rivers, it carried everything with it . . . highways, roads, people, houses, cars, trucks. In one area alone, we lost two tractor-trailers which . . . had completely disappeared from the face of the earth."

Thursday morning, Tinsley had made his way by means of secondary roads towards the village of Massies Mill, which he had heard was one of the most devastated areas. All of the main roads and bridges to the town had been washed away. "In a lot of places," he remembers, the roads were washed away so completely that "other than the fact you might see a sign here and there, there was no evidence there had ever been a road there at all."

But somehow, by means of back roads and a general sense of direction, he'd made his way into the ruined town from the west, coming down out of the mountains. That's when he spotted the Raines boys, looking lost and alone, walking down the road. He stopped and got out of the patrol car. Because gawkers and sightseers had already become a problem in many flood-stricken areas, the state police were restricting access to anyone who did not have some legitmate reason for being there.

"Boys, where y'all going?" Tinsley asked them.

"We're going home."

"What do you mean you're going home—this is a restricted area. Y'all aren't supposed to be here."

"But this is our home! We live here."

"Well, where are your people?"

"We don't know. We sure wish we *did* know."

"What do you mean?"

"They got washed away in the flood and they're just gone. We can't find them anywhere."

"Do you have any other family in this area?" Tinsley asked.

"We have grandparents in Lynchburg. We have an older sister, Ava. She lives there, too."

"Okay, just hang on a minute," Tinsley told them, then got on the radio in his patrol car and talked to the dispatcher. When he was through he stepped back out of the car and told the boys, "I can get you down to the Piney River bridge, down on the Nelson-Amherst county line. I'll get another trooper to come pick you up there and take you down to Lynchburg."

Small and scared and silent, slathered in mud, the boys climbed into the back of the trooper's pristine patrol car. First he took them to their family home and let them go inside to take anything they might want to bring along. The brothers went into the house and emerged with nothing but a few family photographs. Tinsley was really touched by that. Then they rode silently all the way down to the Piney River bridge, where they saw a group of people standing along the railings over the river. Among them were their nineteen-year-old sister, Ava, their grandfather, and their great-uncle. It was strange, almost as if the whole meeting had been planned, but really it was just a happy coincidence: Having heard about the flood, the boys' relatives had come up from Lynchburg to see if they could find the family, or at least any information about them. The Piney River bridge was the closest the police would allow them to get to the Nelson County flood disaster area.

When the two scrawny Raines boys climbed out of Trooper Tinsley's patrol car, their relatives were overjoyed.

"Where's everybody else?" their grandfather asked.

"We don't know," the boys said. "We don't know where they are."

It was now almost a day and a half since the last time they'd seen their parents, sisters, and little brother alive. At this point it was increasingly unlikely they would ever be found, and though unspoken, this fact was apparent to everyone standing there on the bridge.

Thirty-five years later, in retelling the story, this is the place where Warren Raines's voice suddenly chokes up and he stops talking. He has related the rest of his extraordinary tale calmly and in great detail, with carefully controlled emotion. Now, just for an instant, the heart-break of that moment catches in his throat. It was the moment when their grandfather had broken down in tears, upon learning that it was now likely he had lost his beloved daughter, her husband, and who knew how many of his grandchildren. The great chain of family, stretching back into the past and on into the future, had been broken.

But what really shocked Warren and Carl Junior was when their great-uncle also broke down and started to cry. He'd been a war hero in World War II, a man the newspapers had called "Sergeant York the Second" because he'd captured large numbers of German soldiers single-handed, a warrior of extraordinary courage and composure under fire. Now, as he stood there on the Piney River bridge, tears poured down his face.

"I never would have dreamed I'd see the day when he'd break down and cry," Warren says today. "That really shook me up."

IN TRUTH, the rescue, recovery, and rebuilding of Nelson County began not long after daybreak the first morning after the flood. People woke up to the devastation and immediately began searching for family members, friends, or neighbors who might be trapped. Then they dragged out whatever equipment they could find and began cleaning up the rubble.

Vernon Lewis, the Baptist preacher who doubled as a band instructor at the county high school, described a scene that Wednesday morning to two reporters, Paige and Jerry Simpson, in a locally published book about the flood called *Torn Land*. Lewis had been up much of the night, having left the house just before dawn to rescue his son, who was stranded by the high water over in Lovingston. But he'd gotten only about a mile down the road when he came upon an amazing scene. In the gray, drizzly light just before dawn, downed trees and the smashed remains of some kind of barn or cabin were stacked up across the top of the bridge, three times the height of an automobile. A car had stopped in the rain up ahead, danger lights flashing, and a man was waving his arms frantically. Lewis got out of his car. In the dimness he could hear somebody yelling above the roar of the water. "Help! Somebody help us!"

Apparently, a car had washed off the road into the floodwater and somebody was stranded out there. Lewis moved his car to shine the headlights into the darkness, but still he could not locate the voices. Finally, about fifty yards downstream from the bridge, he spotted three young black men clinging to a tree in the middle of the muddy, raging torrent. Lewis and another man were able to throw a rope to the three men, who pulled themselves out of the river hand-over-hand. Another passenger in the car was not so lucky: After struggling several hours to free him, they finally pulled him ashore. He was dead.

By then, it was daylight, and men began gathering around the debris-choked bridge, which completely blocked traffic on a major north-south thoroughfare. It was obvious that something truly awful had happened, but nobody was quite sure what to do.

"Where's the highway department?" somebody asked. "Where are the police?"

Eventually, it became clear that nobody was going to come to help them clear the bridge. If they wanted it done, they'd have to do it themselves.

Lewis recalls: "I said, 'Fellows, there's only one thing we're going to have to do. We're going to have to get our own equipment, and dig out of here with our bare hands.' I said, 'I'm going home to change clothes. I'm coming back, and if you fellows want to help, you can join with me.'

"One of the men replied, 'I'll go home and get my power saw.' Another one said, 'I have a little tractor at home; I'll go get that.'"

So all the men dispersed, perhaps forty of them, then they came back and got to work digging out the bridge. It was in this way that the rescue and recovery of Nelson County began—by individual initiative, "all working side by side without regard to race, creed, or color, or things that had happened in the past," according to Lewis's account. Or as Cliff Wood later put it, "As far as rescue was concerned, most of the rescuing was just done neighbor-to-neighbor, without any real structure to it at all."

But there was work to be done that would require far more than mere goodwill and a couple of backyard tractors. There was, first of all, the grave possibility that an unknown number of people were stranded in remote hollows, perhaps injured, perhaps badly dehydrated or in need of medication. The only way to reach many of them was by air. That would require helicopters, which meant involving the state police, even the Marines, Army, Navy, or the Coast Guard. Many other residents—by Cliff Wood's estimate, at least four thousand people—needed to be fed. Then there was the grim task of recovering the bodies of those who had drowned or been buried in the landslides, swept away in the night and left sprawled in fields or buried beneath tons of mud, gravel, and debris. Body recovery would be a central task primarily because of their loved ones' need for closure and solace. But as a practical, medical matter, decomposing bodies in the August heat increased the risk of epidemic, which would create a whole new wave of problems. The truly exhausting work of clearing roads, rebuilding houses, buildings, and bridges—moving thousands of tons of debris—that would just have to wait.

By Thursday, a still-primitive information-gathering and rescue operation had begun to take shape. A short, level stretch of U.S. Route 29 outside of Lovingston, completely washed out at one end, had become a makeshift landing strip for fixed-wing aircraft provided by the state police, and for a couple of helicopters that had been sent down from the Marine Corps base at Quantico, Virginia, about ninety miles to the north. Dan Payne, who owned the Chevy dealership in Lovingston, brought over an old van and parked it beside the highway, to serve as a base of operations. Somebody else brought over an old schoolbus and a couple of card tables, and stretched a bit of canvas overhead for shade. This spot of shade between two derelict vehicles became known as "the strip," the "command center," or, jokingly, "Lovingston International." It was a jury-rigged, seat-of-the-pants operation, unglamorous but functional—just like so many command centers in war zones.

The situation was still so chaotic, and so many people were desperately seeking help and information—*Have you seen my wife? Should I boil the water? My family is still stranded up at Woodson! Where should I go? How can I help?*—that the command center was swamped.

Ham radio operators from Lynchburg had come in and set up a rudimentary system on the first day after the storm, so the center had a way of communicating with at least some people in the field. Florence Dawson, who worked as clerk of the general district court, found herself temporarily out of a job the morning after the flood, because the court system was completely shut down. When she ran into her old friend Cliff Wood, he asked her to come help, so in no time she was down at the command center, sitting at a card table in the August heat, taking incoming calls on the ham radio, jotting down messages coming in from rescue workers, and passing along plaintive requests for help or inquiries about lost family members. It was tedious, heart-wrenching work.

By early afternoon on Thursday, Cliff Wood "was desperate to find out what the heck was going on," so when the state police sent a fixed-wing plane over, he and Commonwealth Attorney Bob Goad went up to take a look around their county. Wood and his brother owned a plane, so they were familiar with the county's appearance from the air—in August, it was a green and bucolic landscape of mountain ridges, gentle foothills, wandering rivers, and tidy quilts of farmland and orchard. But what they saw from the air was "hard to believe," Wood recalls. Davis Creek "looked like a canyon, it was so gorged out. Bridges down, roads washed out, whole communities washed away. And everywhere you looked there were mudslides and landslides. It looked like those pictures you see of California."

As a practical matter, it was obvious that the James River, which was the southern boundary of Nelson County, was so swollen that either all the bridges or their approaches were completely washed out. It wasn't possible to get over the big river and reach the county from the south. All along the river and its tributaries, Wood could see immense piles of debris, "like beaver dams, only huge," and broken bridges, and the smashed remnants of houses. The small town of Amherst, across the James to the south, looked like a good staging area, if people had to be flown out of the county and then taken down to Lynchburg General Hospital farther south. From the air you could also see that huge sections of Route 29, the county's main north-south thoroughfare, were washed out, especially the area around Woods Mill just north of Lovingston. There was a house lying smack in the middle of the road, like a toy piece from a Monopoly game, completely blocking traffic north or south.

"The devastation was so profound—you lost the infrastructure, buildings, barns; you lost whole communities, a whole way of life," said Gene Ramsey, who lived in nearby Raphine and assisted in the rescue operation.

When Wood and Goad returned to land on the strip, a local man named Johnny Lee Wright came up to them. Wright, who lived on Davis Creek, was obviously distraught and exhausted, his face streaked with red mud. He told Wood that he had walked up the creek, assessing the damage, and talking to the few people who were left. Out of twenty-five homes that had been there, twenty-three had been swept away, he said. He knew all those people. And he knew how many were gone. As he stood there at the makeshift command center, he began reciting their names—dozens of names. There were George and Frances Martin, and their little boy, Robert. The whole Perry family, nine in all, including Betty and Carolyn, who were just teenagers, and Albert and Nelson and Emma. And the whole Simpson family, including all five children: Jimmy, Mike, Brenda, Paul, and Robert Junior. And old Charles Ramsey. And Roosevelt Burnley. And Mabel Wood and Henry Hudson. And then the Huffmans! Lawrence, Emma, Lottie, Annie Mae, Becky, and all the kids. Mitchell and James and Dale and David and Juanita and Brenda and all the rest! They were almost too many to count, and nobody knew how many more there might be.

"This was the first we really learned of the horrors of Davis Creek," Wood said later, and it was a sobering experience indeed.

Shortly after Wright delivered his sad litany, a man whom Wood had never seen before appeared. He had an air of authority and his manner was abrupt and forceful.

"I've been looking for you," the newcomer announced. "My name is Minor Hawley—I'm head of the state office of civil defense. I'm Jim Tribble's boss. You've got to take charge here. You represent county government, and you have a lot of authority and a lot of responsibility. You need to get things done, and you've got the legal authority to get it done. You've got to get organized here, you've got to start logging where you're sending these helicopters and recording who's on the flight, where they're going, what area they've covered, and all the rest. You've got to be a dictator. You've got to be an Adolf Hitler!"

It was, perhaps, an ill-chosen turn of phrase, but Hawley's point was simple: Somebody had to seize control of the situation.

"I don't know whether Minor passed the authority to me, or it already existed in the law somewhere, or I already had it," Wood says. "But anyway, now that I had it, I had to use it. You just had to get something done, and get it done *now*."

Everything was unfolding very rapidly and in a chaotic way. Volunteers and sightseers were showing up and crowding around. There were teenagers, eager to assist, jumping onto helicopters and going out on rescue missions. And there were who-knew-how-many people either injured, stranded, or in other ways in desperate need of help: people's children, their mothers and fathers, their uncles, cousins, and grandparents. Having been up in the air and seen what had happened, Wood knew that he was essentially looking at a war zone, with death, injury, and chaos on a massive scale. Body recovery alone would be an enormous task. There was the urgent problem of providing food, water, shelter, and medical care for large numbers of displaced persons, many of whom were probably injured or in shock. There was the enormous practical problem of transportation, with so many roads and bridges washed out, blocked by wreckage, or still underwater. And there was the continuing problem of poor or nonexistent communications—so far they had only a few ham radios, the state police radio, and a couple of local telephone lines that had been hastily installed at the command center just hours ago. Now, whether he liked it or not, Cliff Wood was in charge of the whole unholy mess.

A friend of Wood's, Boyd Tucker, who'd been in the Air Force in Korea, rode up on a bicycle and suggested that Wood put a rope around the command center to keep out the crowds. So Wood asked Boyd to do that. He also asked Florence Dawson, Virginia Peverill, and one Mrs. Delk to start jotting down the names of people going out on the planes, where they were going, and why. Jim Tribble returned from Amherst and pitched in. So did Austin Embry, who was clerk of the circuit court; attorney Bob Goad; Dan Payne; the reverends John Gordon and Vernon Lewis, and many others.

As the afternoon wore on, it was decided that they'd all meet up at the courthouse after dark "to give some structure to what we were doing," as Wood later described it. So that night, in the small room normally used for meetings of the board of supervisors, there was a meeting of about a dozen local citizens and a few public officials, with Cliff Wood presiding. They laid out command structure for the rescue and recovery of Nelson County.

In retrospect, it's not surprising that everyone who was put in charge had had military experience, either in World War II or in Korea.

Since Nelson County was now a war zone, the problems that would confront the rescuers were the problems of war. Even the helicopter pilots had military experience; many had recently returned from Vietnam. In the minds and experience of the rescuers, Massies Mill and Tyro, Lovingston and Schyuler were overprinted with images of chaos and destruction from Da Nang and Hiroshima, Dresden and Berlin.

Dan Payne later described the command structure as a "quasi-military organization," with Cliff Wood as the commanding officer. One of the first problems that needed to be dealt with were the newspaper, television, and radio people asking all kinds of questions. "We wanted to make sure they got facts and no rumors," Wood said, so he appointed Dr. Jim McDearmon, publisher of the *Nelson County Times,* to be the information officer. He'd be the "point man," providing information to the press; everybody else agreed not to talk to the reporters at all. Austin Embry would be the executive officer. Big Jim Tribble, who tended to tower over everybody in the room, would represent the state office of civil defense, along with Jack Saunders, a local orchardist. Bob Goad was put in charge of food and clothing, with a central collection and distribution center at Lovingston Elementary School. Sam Eggleston, another attorney, was put in charge of finding housing for those who'd lost their homes. And Dr. James Gamble, known to everybody in town simply as "Doc," would be the chief medical officer, working with Dr. Robert Raynor and several others. Other people took charge of transportation, dispatching helicopters from the command center and controlling traffic.

Conspicuously missing from this organizational chart was the sheriff of Nelson County, Bill Whitehead. He wasn't being deliberately overlooked, Wood said later, not at all. It was just that he was trapped in Roseland and couldn't get over to Lovingston. Somebody had to do something immediately. (Still, this oversight would explode dramatically the next day.)

One of the toughest jobs went to Dan Payne. He was a graduate of the ultra-conservative Virginia Military Institute, a major in the U.S. Army Reserve, and a veteran of the Korean War, where he served as a captain in the 39th Field Artillery Battalion of the 3rd Infantry Division. He took over the grim task of recovering bodies, which involved coordinating search-and-rescue missions, procuring earthmoving equipment if digging was required, and a multitude of other, even less-pleasurable chores.

But perhaps the toughest job of all was taken by Vernon Lewis, the soft-spoken Baptist preacher and band director. His assignment was to keep on top of the daily casualty lists, tabulate what bodies had been found, which ones were identified, whose family had been notified, and who was still missing. He was assisted in this task by another Baptist preacher, John Gordon, who was also a major in the U.S. Army Reserves. Lewis said later that one of the most difficult parts of his job was recruiting volunteers to notify families when the dead were identified.

"Will somebody come and help me?" he'd ask.

"Sure, I'll help you, what are you doing?"

"I'm notifying next of kin."

"Oh, no! I'll go back up in the mountains and I'll search and I'll traipse up and down, but I'm not going to tell anyone else that a relative is dead! I just don't have the heart to do it."

But it had to be done, and somebody needed to do it.

"We all did what we had to do, and none of it was pleasant," Florence Dawson said.

"This whole thing was such a local effort," Dan Payne's son Phil observes. "There was a kind of rump session of the board, responsibilities were divided up, and local guys directed the entire effort. If a disaster of this magnitude had happened today, we'd have two divisions of the National Guard out here, but then it was just a simple command chain of local people, and a pretty effective one at that. There was no sitting around, diddling or waffling, whining that the government won't send us this or that. People just did it. That's the way it worked."

Sometimes critical things are entirely hidden behind the veil of everyday life, like a gun beneath the carpet. Under normal circumstances you never notice them at all. It's only when catastrophe strikes—say, an armed intruder bursting through the window—that suddenly nothing is as important as the gun beneath the carpet.

Hurricane Camille brought out qualities in certain people that were absolutely critical to the survival of a community. But in the course of everyday life, these qualities could easily have gone unremarked. Payne said of the Reverend Gordon, who repeatedly performed heroic duties, including "the miserable, awful thing of getting a decomposed body into a bag": "He is a great, great guy. He's one of these low-key people who may give the wrong impression, of being simply easygoing—but when disaster struck he was capable of doing anything you might ask him to do." Or as Florence Dawson put it, "When other people have these tragedies in other communities, I just hope they have a Cliff Wood or a Jim Tribble to step in and take charge."

The group of people who came forward to rescue Nelson County was filled with individuals like this. Once it dawned on these ordinary folks that a catastrophe of extraordinary proportions had occurred, they quickly stepped up, organized themselves, and got busy.

CHAPTER FIFTEEN

Sunday, August 24
Nelson County, Virginia

Shelton's house near Floyd's store. A body found. Info from Mr. Lewis want help & body bag.

Farm of Mollie Owens 1 mi. Southeast of intersection 645 & 722 follow Rockfish River & see open field with white car & sheet for identification—need a boat—body in water.

Pls: check along Rockfish River below riverside church at Rockfish Depot—Smell: Human.

FLORENCE DAWSON normally spent her days as clerk of the general district court doing the paperwork for civil warrants and collecting fines for mundane offenses down at the old courthouse in Lovingston, a graceful white structure that sat up on a hill and dated back to 1808. She'd take her lunch at noon and sometimes, when the weather was pretty, sit outside in the dappled shade underneath the immense old trees that surrounded the courthouse, or beside the monument that celebrated all the young men of Nelson County who died fighting for the Confederacy during the War Between the States.

But after the night of August 19, Florence Dawson's daily routines were utterly altered, and she found herself living in a world she could not possibly have imagined only a few days earlier. Now the courthouse was shuttered and dark, without electricity or telephones. The streets of Lovingston were filled with mud, boulders, trees, and standing water. And half a mile down below the courthouse, alongside a short strip of U.S. Route 29, Florence Dawson found herself working with a team of exhausted volunteers, frantically attempting to rescue an entire community.

Seated at a card table under a tarp stretched between a derelict van and a bus, she scribbled desperate messages and "mission lists" coming in for the search-and-rescue teams, which were scouring the devastated county for the missing, the stranded, and the dead. Now, instead of calmly recording the paperwork for parking tickets or "DUIs" in a pleasant second-floor office, she was outside in the heat in a state of shock, recording the discovery of drowned bodies—many of them her friends and neighbors—scattered all across the county.

Less than a hundred yards from where she sat in the makeshift command center, small planes and helicopters were taking off and landing all day long, so many of them that somebody said they should apply for federal airport funding and start calling the place "Lovingston International." The aircraft were distributing food, water, and medical supplies to isolated areas, dropping off and picking up search parties, and retrieving bodies. When the choppers landed, they threw up so much red Virginia dust that the hem of one of Florence Dawson's white slips would become stained rust-red forever. When the choppers came in from some remote location and landed carrying a full body bag, the prop-wash blasting into the command center carried the sickly sweet smell of death—a smell that reminded Dawson so powerfully of rotting pineapples, she'd be repulsed by the smell of that fruit for the rest of her life.

Like Dawson, many of the volunteers had been working with little rest since Wednesday, the day after the flood, and state troopers had been on eighteen-hour days since then. Cliff Wood and Jim Tribble had been up for three days straight and had looked so exhausted the night before that Dawson had told them: "Tonight you're going to my house to sleep. Don't tell anyone where you are." The two men had gone home with her and slept in a guest room, but she heard them rolling and tumbling all night long. They just couldn't relax or release the thousand worrisome details of the rescue operation. The next morning, she cooked them breakfast and Jim Tribble joked, "I was so dirty, you'll never get the ring out of that bathtub!"

Trooper Ed Tinsley, who was also working at the command center, made an entry in his taped diary: "I had been assigned to the Radio Control at the Control Center. This is for the state police and involves taking all calls and relaying all calls we had from our post to the civil defense post on the county and state basis. It is very obvious by this time that the past four days of eighteen- to twenty-hour days are beginning to show on quite a few people. Tempers are cut pretty thin. People are saying a lot of things that they will probably regret later."

The county's information infrastructure had been so badly damaged that messages arrived at the center in any way that worked. Some came in on the ham radio system that local amateurs had set up on the first day. Sometimes messages were passed along by state troopers who had radios in their cars. A few of the search teams had walkie-talkies, and were able to communicate back and forth in this way. Long-distance phone service was down, except for two lines that had been hastily rigged up to serve the command center: one with a white telephone for incoming calls and the other with a red telephone linked directly to the governor's office, in Richmond. Jim Tribble would often call on the red phone and bark orders to the people in Richmond.

"This *is* the Governor's office!" Dawson heard him yell one day, apparently irritated that someone on the other end did not fully appreciate his authority.

"In those first few days we were just cut off from the world," says Phil Payne. "We are so accustomed to our amazing electronics today— cell phones and so on—that you forget about this. We had reverted to a pretechnological era. The sheriff from Augusta County flew over in a helicopter and saw our devastation and reported it because we couldn't. It was amazing how long it took us even to grasp what had happened, much less begin to communicate with people out in the field."

Most of the time, Dawson was taking information over the radio, but sometimes dazed-looking people would walk into the command center and speak to her directly. One day a man from Davis Creek, one of the Huffman family, came in. His clothes were stained with mud, his face ravaged with exhaustion.

"Somebody told me you could tell me where my family is," the man said, piteously.

Dawson knew by then that most of the Huffmans had been washed away, but she didn't have the heart to inform him. She sent him up to the courthouse to see Vernon Lewis, who was keeping track of the casualty lists. But she couldn't seem to get over the pain she felt, watching the poor man walk away.

Up at the courthouse, Lewis struggled mightily to keep track of the lists of confirmed dead, confirmed missing, and those whose whereabouts remained unknown. The situation was so chaotic, with new information coming in so fast, that names were continually being added or deleted in pencil, each stroke of graphite an anguished story of its own.

That Sunday morning, having been up all night—again—Lewis drew up his latest, most authoritative list. Neatly typed at the top of the page it read, "The following persons are officially listed as missing as of 6 AM August 24, 1969." A hand-scribbled note nearby read: "Names *not* to be be released to anyone." The roster was four pages long, with scribbled additions and deletions, so it was hard to tell if the total number of missing was ninety-two or ninety-three.

The list was heartbreaking in its brevity and hastiness. Whole familes were gone, such as Thomas and Mary Jackson and two children; Mr. and Mrs. Tom Burnley and two kids; couples Mr. and Mrs. Harry Wooten, George and Texas Giles, Mr. and Mrs. Dan Taylor, and John and Alice Oliver; and the children: Mallissa Cambell, the five-month-old child of Murphy Campbell; and the Huffmans, including an eighteen-month-old infant and a three-year-old boy. The deletions and corrections were especially poignant. The typed words "child of Robert Loving" were crossed out and marked "OK, in hospital, Lynchburg." And "Mrs. Carl (Shirley) Raines," typed on the missing list, was firmly crossed out and marked, simply, "dead."

In the initial hours after the flood, when the community was still in profound shock and very little outside help had yet appeared, local teenagers would simply appear at the command center and say, "What can I do?" A report or a rumor would come in of a body somewhere, and three or four kids, sixteen to eighteen years old, led by an older man as team leader, would hop on a helicopter supplied by the state police and fly out to try to recover it. Sometimes the body was buried so deeply in mud and debris that power tools were required to get it free. The volunteer rescuers struggled with this godawful task, sometimes succeeding and sometimes not, just trying to do the best that they could.

The search-and-rescue teams quickly discovered one rather re-markable thing: "There were almost no injuries of any kind and very little sickness—everybody was either alive and well or they were dead," said Nelson County Coroner Dr. Robert Raynor. People either had lived through that horrendous night or they had not. In Cliff Wood's wartime experience, he remembered being taught to expect something like 1,000 injuries for every 120 deaths. But when Colleen Thompson was wheeled into the emergency room at Lynchburg General Hospital, expecting the place to be jammed with injured survivors of the flood, her son and a couple of others were the only ones there. The rains had come so suddenly that many people didn't even have a chance to flee.

Not everybody who survived was eager or willing to be rescued. Mrs. Dora Morris, who was seventy-seven years old, lived alone at the head of the valley below Roberts Mountain, on high ground above the hollow of Davis Creek. There was a branch that flowed into Davis Creek just out back of her house. When she looked out the night of the storm, Davis Creek was fifty feet deep, tearing up the land to within twenty yards of her house. What she heard was "the awfulest roar, a horrible sound," that lasted for four hours or more, from about three in the morning until daybreak. "It was a fluke," she added. "I've never seen anything like it in my seventy-seven years in these mountains."

A couple of days after the flood, volunteer rescue workers landed a helicopter in her backyard, where her chickens were peacefully feeding in the grass near a walnut tree. The rescuers offered to give her a ride to safety.

"I appreciate your concern, but I'm not leaving," she told them, in a story later widely reprinted in local papers, because it represented a kind of mountain feistiness that many locals would find amusingly familiar. "I've lived up here alone most of my life. I haven't been out of the hollow in three years. I've got my wood stove and I've got plenty of wood—I never had electric lights. I figure if God had meant for me to go down the mountain, he would have sent me down in the flood. Now you boys get your flying machine out of here. It's scaring my chickens."

AS THE NEWS SPREAD, and the magnitude of the catastrophe became apparent, helicopters were sent into Nelson County by the Army, Navy, Marines, and Coast Guard, in addition to the state police. There were two types of helicopters, the big tandem-rotor Chinooks, built for hauling heavy loads and transporting people and weapons, and the smaller, more nimble Bell UH-1 series Iroquois, better known as "Hueys." The Huey, one of the most widely employed military helicopters in the world, was used in Vietnam for carrying men and matériel, as a gun ship, and for medical evacuations, or "MedEvac." Many of the pilots who came into Nelson County were Vietnam vets, able to drop one of these trim little choppers down on a narrow riverbed or a steeply inclined mountainside so gently it barely jingled the belt buckles on the canvas sling seats.

"When nobody's shooting at you, there's really nothing to it," said Major R.R. Bolen of Oak Ridge, Tennessee, who'd learned to fly with precision in tight spots during the siege of Khe Sanh. The flop-flop of the Hueys flying overhead, sometimes with black body bags suspended underneath their bellies, was one more way that the Camille catastrophe grimly echoed the American war experience, this time that of Vietnam. Adelaide Huffman later remembered fearing nothing as much as the helicopters, sometimes with body bags suspended from ropes, passing overhead like terrible insects.

That weekend, Virginia Governor Mills Godwin flew into Lovingston, and was taken up in a twin-engine State Highway Department plane to survey the damage.

"It's there. I see it. But it's almost too much to believe," he told a reporter on board, peering down at the spectacles of destruction below. Over Richmond, the governor watched frantic efforts to erect waterfront defenses along the James River, which was expected to crest at record levels later in the day. He saw all the little river towns along the James—Scottsville, Howardsville, Columbia, Bremo Bluff—completely inundated by muddy water. Over Buena Vista, he shouted, "look at the water line on the second story of that factory!" Then, later, "over there, beneath that washed-out bridge—that's a tractor-trailer on its side in the Maury River!"

But when they got farther west, into the hardest-hit areas in the hill country of west-central Virginia, in Nelson, Amherst, and

Rockbridge Counties, the scenes of devastation were so stark there was no suitable response but silence. Whole mountainsides had been ripped open, exposing bare, glistening rock. Beneath the gashes, you could see the rubble of the mudslides—rocks, earth, trees, houses, cars. Millions of tons of it. Buried in the rubble were the bodies of an unknown number of people.

Florence Dawson saw the governor's eyes well up with tears when he returned from his airplane tour of the county. "I just went over and gave him a big hug," she says. "You don't forget something like that. He was so compassionate." Later on, she learned that that day was the first anniversary of the death of the governor's twelve-year-old daughter, who'd been struck by lightning after a storm on the beach near Newport News.

Later that same day, Cliff Wood offered to take the governor up to see the damage at Woods Mill, a couple of miles north of Lovingston. A carload of high-powered officials, including the governor, his chief of staff, Carter Lawrence, and Major General Alfred Dennison, state coordinator of civil defense, stopped at the place where Davis Creek normally flowed underneath U.S. Route 29, a demure rivulet all but invisible to passersby. But after Davis Creek rose fifty feet in the night, Route 29 was completely washed out for about half a mile, and in its place was an immense pile of trees, boulders, and debris, perhaps thirty feet high.

Tinsley later described this scene in his tape diary: "Every field coming down out of the mountains where the road had crossed the valley . . . [was] completely filled, some of them to a depth of 30 and 40 and 50 feet with mud. At one particular location, there was a row of houses off of US 29. As the water and mud and debris and trees came down through, it picked up three of them and buried them."

Governor Godwin, Wood, Lawrence, Dennison, and the other officials got out of the car and walked over to the mountain of wreckage that blocked the road. People were climbing over the pile, looking for bodies.

"Did someone live here?" the governor asked.

"Yes, but the houses are all gone," someone answered.

"I don't want a single stick of this rubble burned until it's been completely searched for bodies," the governor said.

He turned to Cliff Wood.

"What do you think is the most urgent thing?"

"Keeping out the sightseers."

Wood's concerns were partly psychological—gawkers and curiosity-seekers seemed profane, almost ghoulish, to those who were searching for their lost brothers, sisters, mothers, or fathers. But it was also organizational—mobs of sightseers got in the way of police and the rescue teams. The governor nodded to a state police official, and within hours a more organized system for restricting access to the county was established. (Vernon Lewis would later say that the Sunday after the roads were reopened to outsiders, more than ten thousand cars passed one point in three hours.)

Within an hour after returning from the aerial survey, the governor declared the section ranging from Richmond to the western slope of the Blue Ridge Mountains a "major disaster area" and vowed quick and continuing state aid. He also asked President Nixon to make available all federal disaster assistance, and Nixon quickly complied.

The governor also declared Sunday a day of mourning throughout the state.

By late Sunday, the flood crest was passing through central Virginia, through the state capital of Richmond on its way to the Chesapeake Bay and thence out to sea. Now hundreds of people stood along the bridges and riverbanks of Richmond, looking for drowned bodies from upstream, since with the passage of time—as every reader of *Huckleberry Finn* knows—bodies swell and come to the surface. A group of convict camp inmates, accompanied by a deputy sheriff, were among those straining to see out across the big river; if they spotted bodies, boats or helicopters would go out to grab them and add them to the death toll.

"We are become fishers of men—and women and children and babies too," a preacher who was also a volunteer in the search told a reporter for *The Washington Post*.

One of the bodies that came floating by was a man wearing jeans and a tattered blue shirt. Face up, riding high in the water, he looked like a dreamy tourist out for an afternoon swim. When somebody went out to grab him from a boat, his eyes were open and cloudy. One observer said he looked surprised.

Far upstream, in Nelson County, search parties struggling through the wreckage around Woods Mill found enormous amounts of clothing and, oddly, a few baby bottles. But they also fought their own despair at the magnitude of the job. "It's sort of a useless battle we're fighting here," one of the exhausted searchers said. "We're just lucky if we stumble across one body."

The damage in the Davis Creek area was one of the most extreme. Once a shady hamlet of twenty-six small houses and trailers, with seventy-five or so inhabitants, it was now a geological cataclysm. So far, said civil defense officials in Lovingston, sixteen bodies had been recovered and forty-three people were missing and presumed dead. One observer of the scene in Davis Creek was struck primarily by the absence of any sign of man. Elsewhere, in Massies Mill and Piney River, there was a rubble of washing machines, clothes, children's toys, clothing, and houses. In Davis Creek, there were only rocks, mud, and huge tangles of fallen timber that the searchers took to calling "hummocks." They were so massive, sometimes three stories tall, that the very thought of trying to dig them all out was exhausting. Meanwhile, the Creek had returned to its pre-flood size, ten yards wide and hardly more than ankle deep.

One Davis Creek resident, Eldridge Harris, began to cry when searchers moved debris where a small dog had been sniffing. He was afraid his brother-in-law, Henry Hudson, was underneath the pile.

"That's his car over there," he told a reporter, pointing to a vehicle mired in mud.

"Where's his house?" the reporter asked.

"You're standing on it."

Meanwhile, dispatches from the Gulf Coast were growing increasingly incredible. There were little towns on the map that for all practical purposes no longer existed, like Boothville and Venice, just north of the mouth of the Mississippi. Most dwellings were completely gone, and what was left stood under five feet of water. Damage estimates now ranged from $500 million to $1 billion. Navy Seabees wearing gas masks were finding bodies "up in the trees, under the roofs, and out in the open" in Mississippi, as Camille's combined total death toll topped three hundred. Nat Cassibry, civil defense coordinator for the Mississippi coast, reported: "More bodies are buried in the beach sand—buried deep where they'll probably never be found. We've already pulled some bodies out of the water and there's no telling how many more have been swept out to sea."

"They're finding the young and the old in here," an Army sergeant helping to guard the evacuated town of Pass Christian observed. "The young said they were too tough for it to get them, and the old ones said it never happened before and it wouldn't happen now." The 1,700 Seabees working in the town stacked the bodies in the open and placed them in black plastic bags flown in by the Air Force. Local troops hauled them away to mortuaries without any attempt to count or identify them.

Farther south, it was reported that heavy rains from Camille had caused major flooding in Oaxaca State, on Mexico's Pacific coast, leaving at least one hundred thousand people homeless. Many of them, said Red Cross workers, were "poor people with no place to go."

THE SEARCH-AND-RESCUE SYSTEM in Nelson County became more sophisticated as time went on. By Sunday, according to Dan Payne, search parties of up to fifteen people would be sent out in a big twin-rotor Chinook, with one man in charge. Half the men were placed on one side of the river, half on the other, and the team was given perhaps three miles to search, along with a pick-up time and location. Every couple of hours, a plane flew over the party and if a body had been found, the searchers lit a safety flare, or communicated by means of a walkie-talkie. As the operation got more organized, every crew was sent out with body bags, a power saw, at least two gas masks, a shovel, rope, rubber gloves, and an odor-killing disinfectant. At night, the next day's searches would be planned for places where there had been reports of bodies, or people had seen buzzards, or smelled odors, or things had been spotted from the choppers. (Interestingly, circling buzzards turned out to be a false lead: They were always circling over dead animals, not humans.)

When the parties came back from these missions they'd be dog tired, mud slathered, and—due to the grim nature of their work—sometimes deeply changed, especially the teenagers, most of whom had never seen a dead body before.

Fifteen-year-old Phil Payne, Dan's son explained, "I got involved because any fifteen-year-old wants to be involved. In the beginning, local volunteers had not materialized, and in the summer I worked for my dad, so I ended up going out on some of the early search parties. It turned out to be the biggest event of my life—no comparison. Since

I have never been to war, it's the closest thing I ever experienced to it."

Payne went out in a party that included three of his best friends: Reid Embry (son of Austin Embry, the clerk of court), Mike Gamble (Dr. Gamble's son), and Buzz Goad (son of attorney Bob Goad). All of them, Payne remembers, "were looking for bodies but hoping we didn't find any." Fortunately or unfortunately, they found three. One was below the town of Schuyler, in the Rockfish River about five miles above the place it emptied into the James. All they could see were two feet sticking out of the mud and gravel in a great delta left by the flood. Once the corpse was dug out, it turned out to be a truck driver from North Carolina whose tractor-trailer had been swept off U.S. Route 29, probably around Woods Mill, seven or eight miles upriver. His truck was nowhere to be seen. Another body was that of a girl so deeply tangled in a hummock that chainsaws were required to cut her out of it, like a princess stuck in the enchanted forest in a fairy tale.

But the discovery that touched and frightened Payne and his friends most deeply was the first. It was the body of a sixteen-year-old boy named Mitchell Huffman, whom they all knew. They'd been to school together. He was their age. Now he lay on top of a heap of logs, dead in the August heat for more than thirty-six hours. At first they didn't even recognize him, because his nose had been crushed and his skin was turning black in the heat. But then they remembered him as he had been, a lively kid with buck teeth and freckles, a kid just like them, a kid who had been just a little bit less lucky than they had been on that awful night. They sent out a message on the walkie-talkie that a chopper was needed to fly the body out. But the experience of seeing that corpse was one Phil Payne would remember forever, whether he wanted to or not.

The next day Dan Payne decided it was probably unwise to allow these teenage boys to go out on the body searches, largely because the grisly work might be traumatic for them. And it *was* traumatic, no doubt about it. But "it got down to where they were the only ones willing to go," the elder Payne said later. So he started sending them out again. Many of these young men did heroic work at these ghastly tasks, but there was plenty of heroism to go around. "You just would not believe how this community came together," Florence Dawson remembers. Busloads of volunteers appeared: students from the

University of Virginia, church groups, the Red Cross, the Salvation Army, and ordinary individuals who simply felt compelled to help. Everyone was pitching in. "If you want a picture of who has helped, go up in an airplane and take a picture of this whole area," one woman said.

Perhaps the most remarkable group that showed up in Nelson County, for their selflessness, fortitude, and staying power, were the Mennonites. They appeared on the very first day, solemn and quiet, and immediately got to work. Nobody had called them. Nobody asked them to come. They just showed up.

In the first days there were as many as 150 Mennonites in the county, men and women, some from as far away as Canada. Some of the men wore traditional Mennonite dress—dark clothes, wide-brimmed black or straw hats, and shovel-shaped beards without moustaches. (Like the Amish, some Mennonites consider moustaches to be vain.) Others dressed simply as plain, working country men, with bib overalls, rubber high-top boots, and corn-seed caps. Most of the women wore prayer bonnets on their heads (after the biblical injuction that women must pray with their heads covered), and long dresses with aprons. Alltogether, they made for a quaint, old-fashioned sight. But the work they did evoked nothing but awe and gratitude. Gene Ramsey, the Augusta County schoolteacher who came to Nelson to help with the recovery, was impressed with the fact the Mennonites seemed to have only one question: "Can I help you?" They made no attempt to proselytize or to convert anyone; they just pitched in and did what needed doing. They'd help anybody, Ramsey noticed, "even one man who had lived a life most women shouldn't even know about."

Dr. Robert Raynor, working on body identification, said, "the Mennonites were fantastic. They were here by the next morning. The Salvation Army and the Red Cross and the Mennonites, all were fantastic. The Red Cross was much more organized—the first thing they wanted to know was where they could set up an office, a headquarters. The Mennonites just came in with sandwiches and coffee and set up places here and over here, one in Massies Mill and one in Woods Mill and one in Schuyler, and they just came in quietly and went to work helping people clean up or recover, find bodies, furnish food. They were unbelievable. Anywhere they could help, they were there."

Another physician, Dr. George Criswell, said the Mennonites did not shrink from some of the grisliest work that needed to be done, which involved working with decomposing bodies. "Its almost indescribable what it was like during that time," he recalled. "About the only people you could get to help you around the funeral home were the Mennonites, and they were wonderful."

"The Mennonites were beyond description," Phil Payne added. "They were so low key, they never made any effort to draw attention to themselves. They just came in and did it—digging, searching, rebuilding houses, restoring, repairing. They were as friendly as anyone wanted them to be—but they never kicked back and rested. They didn't chew the fat; they worked. If you wanted to talk to them, you had to work beside them."

The Mennonites and the Amish grew out of a doctrinal dispute dating back to sixteenth-century Europe, when a small group of believers challenged the reforms of Martin Luther and others during the Protestant Reformation, protesting that those reforms were not radical enough. In particular, they believed that only adults who had confessed their faith (not infants) should be baptized. This breakaway group became known as the Anabaptist movement. The Anabaptists became better known as Mennonites under the leadership of a young Catholic priest named Menno Simmons; but later, another group led by a Swiss bishop named Jakob Ammann broke away, becoming known as the Amish. Amish and Mennonite churches still share many doctrinal beliefs, but differ in dress, language, and technology. Old Order Amish men dress like Abraham Lincoln and travel by horse and buggy; Mennonites drive cars and tend to be at least a bit more "worldly" in appearance.

For the Mennonites, the Nelson County floods came at a fortunate moment because most of them were farmers and at that time of year, things were relatively slow on the farm. The crops were not yet ready for harvest, and the schools had not yet opened. So when the word went out that the people of central Virginia needed aid, the Mennonites saw it as "a great chance to help our fellow man, and a great chance to restore people's faith in humanity," according to Kevin King, executive coordinator of the Pennsylvania-based Mennonite Disaster Service.

The MDS was born at a Sunday-school picnic in Kansas in the

summer of 1950 when a group of young Mennonite men, many of whom had been conscientious objectors during World War II, decided they needed to make themselves of service to humanity. The Mennonites and the Amish, most of whom lived in isolated farming communities, had a long history of mutual aid symbolized by the barn-raising. If a farmer's barn burned down, a hundred or more of his neighbors would show up at dawn on a designated day, and before nightfall a new barn would be built in its place—an uplifting American scene.

The Mennonite Disaster Service brought the ethos of the old-fashioned barn-raising to communities across the United States and even abroad, responding to floods, fires, earthquakes, tornadoes, hurricanes, and whatever other calamity might befall humanity. In Nelson County the efforts of the MDS (sometimes knowingly referred to as "make do somehow") were coordinated by Jonas Kanagy, a bearded, square-jawed farmer who lived in nearby Stuarts Draft. Kanagy later estimated that the Mennonites put in fifteen thousand man-hours and three thousand five hundred woman-hours helping to rebuild the county; some of them were coming back on weekends as much as a year later.

That the Mennonites seemed only interested in helping, rather than in saving souls, was deliberate, according to King. A famous quote from Saint Francis of Assisi sums up their general attitude: "Preach the Gospel at all times and when necessary use words." (In other words, rebuilding a house for a homeless neighbor usually says all that needs to be said.) A Bible passage that was particularly meaningful to the Mennonite rescuers is a parable in the book of Matthew, in which Jesus admonishes his followers: "For I was hungry and you gave me food, I was thirsty and you gave me drink, I was a stranger and you welcomed me, I was naked and you clothed me . . . Truly I say to you, as you did it to one of the least of these my brethren, you did it to me."

Gene Ramsey was a Presbyterian at the time the Mennonites showed up in Nelson County. But he was so impressed with their unassuming good works that he became a Mennonite himself. "I was waiting for something like this," he says today. "This was my view of missions. This was my view of faith."

To anyone who was not actually there helping with the rescue and recovery, it was difficult to convey the physical and psychic exhaustion that had begun to set in by now—an exhaustion that perhaps only faith could carry the body through.

"This is my sixth day now in excess of sixteen hours" [trooper Ed Tinsley reported wearily to his diary on Monday, August 25].
"Our job now seems to be mainly operating in the outlying areas and cutting off the traffic that's coming in. I can understand the people wanting to come in and visit their families, but I will probably never understand the curiosity seekers that want to come in and see the area that has been destroyed by the flood . . ."

"It's just hard to believe that the damage that I'm looking at, the damage that I've seen, the damage I've flown over and walked through could be so great and so extensive. My honest feelings are that there could never be an accurate description or record in the history books as to what goes on here . . . Pictures will show part of it. Words will tell part of it. But it will never be accurately described or made a part of history except by the people that looked at it."

CHAPTER SIXTEEN

Wednesday, August 27
Nelson County, Virginia

THAT WEDNESDAY AFTERNOON, a week after the night of the great flood, a funeral was held for the four members of the Raines family who had been found so far. Carl Junior and Warren's father, their older sister Johanna, and their little brother, Sandy, who used to play *Combat* in a plastic helmet in the backyard, had been found together, sprawled in the riverbed about a mile and a half downstream from the place Warren last saw them the night of the flood. Their mother was not found until several days later, about a mile farther downstream. She was "in pretty bad shape," Warren said, and was identified by the initials engraved on her wedding band. Their sister Ginger, Donna Fay Wood, and her brother Gary had still not been found. Search parties were still looking: At one point during the funeral service, the *flop-flop-flop* of a Huey passing overhead drowned out the preacher's voice.

"My father, sister, and younger brother could have been fixed up for a funeral, but we didn't want to get into any of that," Warren said. "I just wanted to remember them as they were." The caskets were closed.

All the local papers were filled with death stories.

A photograph of a freshly dug double grave, with a shovel lying nearby, appeared on the front page of the paper in nearby Waynesboro. The grave had been prepared for a mother and son. The father and four other children were still missing.

Sam Johnson of Massies Mill said his wife was on her knees, praying, when water started coming through the upstairs window. "All at once I was floating through a hole around the eaves—I remember going past the store on a log. Then another log knocked me off and I went under. The next thing I knew I was in a tree. I was naked like the day I came into the world—I had lost my glasses, my teeth, everything."

Search parties later discovered the bodies of his wife, a mile downstream near Fleetwood School, and his thirteen-year-old daughter, a few yards away from where he was found in the tree.

"I reckon the Lord just wanted to see what he could do with me without killing me," Johnson said. When asked if he'd come back to Massies Mill, he responded: "All I got is gone. I ain't got nothing to live here for. If I built a house here, I'd think about my wife and daughter every time I saw it. It don't make sense for me to come back."

Already, the flashbacks had begun: Mrs. Harmon Small Jr. told an interviewer: "The terror is at night. You wake up and you can see the water and the trees still coming at you. But we've got to pull ourselves together. We have got to keep going . . ."

Mrs. Small, her husband, and their four children survived, though their six-room house on Buck Creek, not far from Woods Mill, was destroyed when an avalanche of mud and rocks came through the back door. Even their pony survived. But fourteen-year-old Robert Simpson, a close friend of one of Mrs. Small's sons, was drowned. The boy had been buried with his mother on Tuesday.

Yet all the stories of death were also tableaus of life. They painted a picture of everyday existence in this small rural southern county that was in many ways a world preserved in amber, far removed from the raw and recent killings of Bobby Kennedy and Martin Luther King Jr., generational strife, Vietnam and anti-Vietnam, Woodstock, rock 'n' roll, race riots, and all the other discontents of modern life in 1969.

The storm killed whole extended families because in Nelson County families tended to be intact, close-knit, and living close together. The mother would live up on the hill, the sons and daughters in the next hollow, and the grandchildren would shuttle in between. Lila Huffman, the matriarch of the Huffman clan on Davis Creek, had nine children; most of them also had large families, and nearly all of them came back to settle down along Davis Creek close to the old family homeplace. They liked each other and wanted to stay there. They enjoyed being close to their roots. "I never saw nothing much but Nelson County—but I never saw anything I'd trade it for either," said Junior Thompson, whose family had lived in the little town of Piney River for seven generations. Even his daughters who were up and grown still came back on weekends. Piney River was like a home star, drawing people back into its orbit no matter how far away they might roam.

In Nelson County, people were not unlikely to take over the family business, or just to live in the house their daddy and mother lived in, and their parents before them. They tended to express their satisfaction with life by simply staying put, generation after generation. They "voted with their feet." Down at the cemetery, you were apt to see gravestones bearing the family name, with a couple of praying hands and the inscription "How Great Thou Art," flanked by a pair of blank panels, awaiting the death of the owners. People knew where they lived, and they knew where they were going when they died.

The storm took a snapshot of a kind of American life that had long since vanished in the frantic, industrialized, hyperkinetic urban regions of the country, where kids would grow up and move away to California or Connecticut; Granny would wind up in a nursing home rather than a house on the hill above the family farm; and broken marriages and broken families were more the norm than an anomaly. In that world, nobody had even *heard* of the word "homeplace," except on television shows like *The Waltons,* which were a kind of electronic echo of real life in Nelson County.

Russell Huffman gave an interview to a local paper not long after the flood. Russell had a great rural Southern face, like something out of the Depression-era photographs of Walker Evans: tough but not unkind, sun-creased and narrow, slightly lantern-jawed, with close-together eyes and thick hair clipped up high above the ears. "I'm one of the lucky ones—I only lost one child," he said. He, his wife, and eight other children were able to get out before the flood swept his house away, but his 16-year-old boy, Mitchell, who was staying up the creek with another family, was not so lucky. Unluckiest of all was Russell's brother James, who was working up near Charlottesville the night of the flood. Though James survived, he lost his wife, three sons, a brother, two daughters-in-law, two grandchildren, and a father-in-law.

"I'm moving a little farther up the creek into an empty house that was higher than the water," Russell said. "I've lived here all my life. This is my home." But, he added, "some of the other families from up the creek won't be coming back here to live; they have nothing to come back to."

To say that they were not coming back to Davis Creek—breaking the chain of connection to this place and the generational web of family and friends who lived here—was to say something indeed.

THE AMERICAN RED CROSS had moved into Nelson County, preparing for what one official called "a long stay in the area." Two disaster relief offices were set up and immediately began taking applications for aid and dispensing "personal emergency kits"—toothbrushes, soap, razors, shaving cream, and other comforting toiletries. On his fourth trip in five days to the County, Governor Godwin flew into Massies Mill and landed in a Marine helicopter in the center of what was left of town. Massies Mill, the governor stated, "looks like the most completely devastated area I have seen." The devastation was so widespread that an unanswered question hung in the air, as it hung over Davis Creek: "We businessmen have got to decide whether we are going to put this town back together again or leave it down the creek," resident Jack Young told a reporter.

The answer was still not known. David Lea, postmaster and storekeeper in the village, said, "most of the people here are still dazed. They don't know yet what they will do."

Search parties found seven more bodies in the debris that Wednesday. Vernon Lewis issued his daily updated casualty totals, raising the total number of dead to sixty-three. He issued an appeal for more information about the missing, who included E.B. "Buzz" Thompson, little Bonnie Thompson, Donna Fay Wood, Gary Wood, and Ginger Raines.

A FEW DAYS LATER, Cliff Wood and the rest of the rescue leaders announced a "gigantic, all-inclusive Labor Day weekend search for at least sixty-six people still missing in the flood disaster of August 20."

Over five hundred people, many of them trained in rescue and recovery, arrived from all across Virginia to take part in the holiday weekend effort to find the rest of the Nelson County dead. Rescuers were assigned to teams, concentrating on the great, chaotic, debris-choked delta along the Tye River downstream from Massies Mill; and in the Rockfish River watershed downstream from Davis Creek and Woods Mill. Most of those still missing were from these two areas. Down at the command center on U.S. Route 29, Florence Dawson scribbled a new mission list:

ORDER FOR TOMORROW

5,000 hot dogs & rolls
200 lbs. onions
10,000 paper plates—rush
10,000 cups
10,000 spoons & forks
5 tons ice for Tuesday
500 gallons H$_2$O

By the end of the holiday weekend, the army of volunteers had found twenty more bodies, raising the toll of dead to eighty-three, with fifty-three still missing. (The number of people missing fluctuated from day to day; sometimes it went down because people had merely been away on vacation or in the hospital, much to the relief of those who thought them dead.)

It was during this big Labor Day push, eighteen days after the flood, that Buzz Thompson's body was found, buried in sand, underneath a hummock of debris as high as a room. He was perhaps five hundred yards downstream from the place where Lena Thompson's house had been ripped to pieces by the floodwater.

Colleen Thompson's husband, Jake, and his nephew had spent two days right after the flood hunting along the wreckage-filled river channel of what had once been Muddy Creek, looking for Buzz and Bonnie's bodies. At that time Jake had called up to Fort Eustis, where he worked as an aircraft mechanic, to explain to his boss why he was gone, and the colonel had called back to ask if there was any way the folks up at the fort could help.

"The only thing you could do is to put together a search party for our daughter," Jake replied.

Shortly afterwards, a search party with twelve people and a plane had arrived to look for Bonnie and Buzz. Jake had a little bit of specialized knowledge that might be helpful, he told the searchers: He knew what a decomposing human body smelled like. He'd been a flight engineer in the Air Force, and they used to fly bodies from overseas. Once the Air Force left six improperly packed corpses on a plane in the Azores for twenty-four hours and Jake had the unforgettable experience of inhaling that. "The smell is different from a dead animal," he said. "It's kind of a sweet, sickening smell."

Eventually, Jake and his group located a place on the riverbed where he could detect that ominous stench.

"I found this body, but it's buried in the riverbed and I can't get it out," Jake told Dan Payne, who was coordinating the body-search teams, including the task of locating earth-moving equipment. Payne sent a front-end loader down there and the operator began carefully excavating sand and gravel in the riverbed, slice by slice, like an archeologist, so as not to disturb the body. Eventually they uncovered Buzz, buried in the wet sand and perfectly preserved except for his head, which had decomposed. Buzz was a big man, over two hundred pounds, still wearing all his clothes, including one of the sleeveless shirts he always favored, and with $600 still in his wallet.

Because there had been rumors of some looting around the county, Reverend Gordon, the pastor on the aircraft, warned the searchers, "I know he's got six hundred dollars in his billfold and it better stay in that billfold." It did.

"Buzz was the hero of that flood," Jake Thompson said later, "because even though he was terrified of water, he kept coming back."

DURING THE FIRST WEEK after the flood, so many bodies were being discovered that the local funeral homes were overwhelmed. Once the roads were opened, the Morton Frozen Food company sent a refrigerated tractor-trailer over to Lovingston. It was parked outside the Sheffield Funeral Home to serve as a temporary morgue, and also as a kind of grisly showroom, where family members came to see if those they had lost had been found.

Sometimes it was an easy enough matter to identify the dead. Often the search teams who found them recognized them right away, since it was a small community and everybody more or less knew everybody. But as time went by and the trailer-morgue began filling up with the bodies of people who had been dug out of the riverbed or dragged from underneath piles of debris in the August heat, it became more and more difficult to identify them. Ultimately, there were thirty-seven bodies that proved difficult to identify, some of them so badly crushed or decomposed that only by means of an autopsy could it be determined whether they were male or female.

The importance of identifying them was both profound and simple: "When death comes, rest doesn't come until the body is found, or an unidentified body is identified," Reverend Gordon said.

A team of local doctors set up a makeshift outdoor laboratory a few yards from the refrigerator truck and began conducting autopsies. Dr. Robert Raynor was pressed into service as a member of the medical/forensic team identifying bodies because he was one of three medical examiners in the county, whose job was to investigate suspicious or unexpected deaths. He was assisted by a state deputy medical examiner, Dr. Walter Gable; by the two other county medical examiners, Dr. James Gamble in Lovingston and Dr. Russell Smith in Piney River; and by local dentist Dr. George Criswell, who helped identify the bodies from dental records.

This was not a line of work that Bob Raynor particularly cared for—in fact, he stated, "it's not the kind of thing that would appeal to me at all!" But after Camille, plenty of people had to do things that did not appeal to them at all. At the time, Dr. Raynor was a thirty-eight-year-old family practitioner doing what he always wanted to do in a place he had always loved. When he was six years old and having his tonsils removed in the hospital he recalls, "I sort of fell in love with one of the interns, because I thought he was one of the nicest young men I'd ever met. I decided that's what I wanted to be when I grew up and I never changed my mind." Now he reveled in his busy small-town practice, treating everything from sore throats to sprained ankles, and even delivering babies. The morning after the flood (which didn't do much more than submerge his basement), he drove over the mountain to Waynesboro, did his rounds at the hospital, and then headed back to Lovingston to do an ob-gyn clinic for the local Health Department. He was stopped on Route 151 by a sheriff's deputy, who was blocking traffic. Dr. Raynor knew the deputy—a patient of his named Tim Nelson.

"Hey, Doc," Nelson said, leaning into the car window. "You can't get through up ahead—all the roads are washed out. I can't even get back to the sheriff's office in Lovingston. You'll have to turn around and go back."

Just then a state trooper pulled up. He told them that the roads to the south, through Piney River, were also washed out and impassable. As the three talked, a message came in over the state trooper's radio.

"There's been a body found in the Rockfish River, over near Nellysford," the dispatcher reported. "They need a medical examiner over there, right now."

It was at this point, Dr. Raynor recalled later, "that I realized for the first time that the county had a catastrophe on its hands."

He parked his car, got in the trooper's police cruiser, and drove over to the place where the body had been found, beside a bridge where the south fork of the Rockfish passed under Route 151. It was the sort of scene that would become wearyingly familiar in the days ahead. A house beside the creek had been swept away and crushed to pieces against the bridge, like a house made of drinking straws. In the midst of the wreckage they found a dead woman, sprawled face-down in the river. Not far away, they found a man. Doc Raynor knew them both—they were husband and wife.

One of his primary concerns as a medical examiner was to determine whether a death was due to suspicious circumstances, but clearly, there was no human transgression involved (other than the inability to predict the weather). It was just one of those things the insurance companies call "an act of God." So he officially ascribed their cause of death as drowning.

"The thing happened at night and everybody was in bed asleep," says Dr. Raynor. "So their house was just destroyed while they were sleeping in it. Whether they were killed when the house hit the bridge, or because of trauma or drowning, I didn't feel it really made that much difference. You knew it wasn't a criminal death. So we didn't do autopsies; we just called it drowning and let it go."

Determining a cause of death was much less important than determining the identity of the dead. And often that was not easy.

"The floodwater and the mudslides were so strong that most of the bodies did not even have jewelry on," Dr. Raynor explained. "It took their clothes off; it took their jewelry off. If they had a wedding ring on, we could identify them, because it usually had some initials or a message on it. But most of them didn't even have their rings on.

The older people had taken their dentures out before bed, so they had no teeth at all to check against the dental records. They were just naked bodies, stripped and battered and bruised, and even if you knew them well, it was difficult to say for sure, 'Yeah, that's who it is.' "

Dr. Criswell was no more eager to take on the grisly task of body identification than Dr. Raynor was. He was just a small-town dentist accustomed to joshing with patients while filling cavities and capping teeth—until six days after the flood a state trooper walked into his office and pressed him into service. Dr. Criswell never claimed to be an expert in dental forensics, but like so many others he was forced into his task. Since many of the bodies were so far gone that the only real way to identify them was through dental bridgework or cavities, it was a job that had to be done. So he did it.

The state's deputy medical examiner, Dr. Gable, performed the autopsies and then turned the bodies over to Dr. Criswell. Volunteers from the Mennonite Disaster Service, who were unfailingly cheerful and willing to help, assisted him in cleaning up the faces of the dead, and then held the bodies upright so he could take eight-by-ten-inch X-rays and left and right angles of the teeth. Once the X-rays were developed, Dr. Criswell hung them up around his office on clothesline, trying to match fillings and crooked teeth from the X-rays of the dead with those of his patients. A palpable sadness hung in the air over many of these cases. Some of the bodies were of children only four or five years old, who were too young to have had any dental work at all.

Eventually, the team identified all of the bodies lying in the refrigerated tractor-trailer except for eight. To this day, these eight people remain unidentified. Only one thing about them seems certain: "There was no question in our minds but what these eight people were not from the county," Dr. Raynor said. Still, they haunt those who tried so hard to find out who they might have been. "I think it bothered all of us," Dr. Raynor says today. "It still does."

There was the teenage boy with longish blond or light-brown hair, found on August 24, four days after the flood. He was a good-looking young man with high cheekbones, heavy eyebrows, and a thin blond moustache. He stood 5 feet, 8 inches and weighed 155 pounds. He was circumcised. He had no noticeable scars on his body.

And he might have been a bit of a nervous fellow—his fingernails were bitten down to the nubs. When his stomach was opened during the autopsy, it revealed the remains of his last meal: red beans and meat. It also showed the boy had roundworms, something that might be associated with growing up poor. Then again, it might not.

Another young white male was twelve to fourteen years old, just over five feet tall, with long dark-brown hair. He, too, had eaten red beans just before he died.

There was a stocky, muscular man in his late fifties, bald on top, with a fringe of black hair and sideburns. His teeth were ground down and deeply stained, like those of a tobacco-chewer (none too unusual among country men in those parts). He was found in the Rockfish River near where it empties into the James, at Howardsville. Some people theorized he might have been a truck driver whose rig was washed off U.S. Route 29 upriver at Woods Mill.

Two little girls whose bodies were eerily similar were found miles apart. One, about ten years old and with a nimbus of long, curly blond hair, was discovered in the Rockfish River about two miles above Howardsville. The other girl was younger, perhaps six or eight, and weighed only sixty pounds. She still had her baby teeth. The medical examiner's report noted that the girls' hair was "identical," that they were physically similar in other ways, and that their stomachs both contained red beans. Though some speculated that they might have been sisters, or at least related, the smaller of the two girls was found on an island in the James River in Fluvanna County, more than ten miles away from the other child.

Another body, that of a woman in her late forties or early fifties, weighing about 150 pounds and five feet tall, was found in the Rockfish about a mile below the bridge over Route 29. She had one remarkable characteristic: Her left breast was about three times larger than her right one.

There was the old, toothless white woman, around seventy, with long white hair. She was about five-foot-two and had had both an appendectomy and a hysterectomy. Her stomach contained nothing but "a large amount of mud."

The last unidentified body was found at Woods Mill on September 6, eighteen days after the flood. She was a white woman in her late thirties, 5 feet, 5 inches, weighting around 140 pounds. She had scars on her back and belly, but what was most striking about her was how well manicured she was. Her nails were done. She was wearing makeup. Her legs and armpits had been freshly shaved. She was attractively and fashionably dressed. And unlike the others, she'd had a nutritious, well-balanced last meal: green beans, tomatoes, and corn.

Who was she? Who were any of them?

Seeking answers, Dr. Criswell put together detailed dental descriptions of all eight and sent these out to ten thousand dentists across the United States, asking them to see if they could match these with patients of their own. The response rate was poor. Only about ten dentists replied (all in the negative). The University of Virginia Hospital sent over a portable X-ray unit, so that the medical team could X-ray the bodies to check for healed bones from past breaks, and (in the women) evidence of a hysterectomy. If somebody stepped forward to claim they knew who the people were, these things could be compared to the person's medical and surgical records. But nobody ever did.

At one point, information about the eight mystery bodies was sent out on radio and television all up and down the East Coast. Trooper Ed Tinsley recalled that a man came down from somewhere in New England, claiming that the teenage boy was his lost son. But a police investigator named Dave Jones grew suspicious, and under intense questioning it emerged that the man—who really did have a son who was lost—was just trying to claim a body in order to cash in a life insurance policy.

Increasingly frustrated by their inability to identify the eight, the medical team decided to seek the help of the Federal Bureau of Investigation. On September 19, the hands were cut from the adults, packed in salt, and sent to the FBI's Latent Fingerprint Section. But the fingerprints of the severed hands did not match any of those in the Bureau's files.

Unable to procure a conclusive identification, or match the bodies with an existing medical record, the team was left with little more than rumors and theories.

Who was the young blond man, for instance? In the days before the storm, several local people had talked to a young Frenchman who was hiking and camping around the county, so there was some suspicion that the body might have been his. Others suggested he might

have been a young traveler, perhaps a hitchhiker, passing through
Nelson on his way to Woodstock.

Dr. Raynor described several of the others as "dark-skinned, good-
looking, Mexican-type people." They may have been Mexican or
Central American migrant workers, possibly come north to central
Virginia for the peach and apple harvest. A last meal of red beans
would seem plausible for a migrant worker. Then again, almost anybody could have eaten red beans, especially in the rural South.

It's conceivable that a happy-go-lucky teenage boy might have
been passing through the county on his own that night. But what
about the two little girls? They could not possibly have been traveling
alone. Were the rest of their families (or family) killed that night? If so,
how many other people are buried ten or twenty feet beneath the
Nelson County mud, whom nobody will ever know of? If the families
survived, why didn't they report the girls missing? What about the
families of the others? Why didn't *their* relatives or employers or land-
lords or coworkers or friends or neighbors miss them? Who were
these people? Had they ever written a love letter? Done a friend a remarkable favor? Betrayed someone? Longed for something? Written or
painted or done something beautiful?

Still, hard as it is to believe that eight people could essentially
walk off the face of the earth and not be missed, the same thing had
happened a few days earlier, when Camille made landfall on the Gulf
Coast of Mississippi. There, in the ravaged town of Pass Christian, the
storm left the bodies of three white women who remain unidentified
more than thirty-five years later. For the first decade after their deaths,
the women lay in unmarked graves at Evergreen Cemetery in
Gulfport, Mississippi. Every August 17, Civil Defense Director Wade
Guice and his staff would come by to bring flowers and pray over
these drowned, lost women whose husbands or mothers or children
had never come to claim their bodies. Eventually the gravesites grew
over with grass and the simple wire markers provided by the funeral
home disappeared. Guice felt the women needed a more respectful
remembrance, so he started a memorial fund to which people could
contribute a quarter for a headstone.

Guice's wife, Julia, remembers that Guice always felt, "these three
women were human beings who deserved names, not just Woman
Number One, Woman Number Two, and Woman Number Three." So

he chose the names "Faith," "Hope," and "Charity", in lieu of their real names. A local monument maker enscribed the gravestone with these names for free, and the collected money was put into a perpetual fund to pay for flowers.

"Faith" was a woman in her early sixties found wearing a paisley pullover. "Hope," a woman in her early thirties, weighed about 135 pounds and was wearing a green and white blouse, green slacks, and black rubber boots. Charity was a small woman, about 5 feet, 2 inches, thought to be between forty and fifty. Among the four rings on her hand was a wedding band. A coroner's inquest ruled that all had died by drowning. Although they were found in Pass Christian, nobody knew if they knew each other in life. The three women are now remembered on the Camille Memorial Wall in Biloxi, and every year a memorial service is held at their gravesites.

"We honor these three women because no one has contacted us about them after all these years," said Tammy Bagwell, chairwoman of the memorial service committee. "We've kept doing this out of respect for Wade Guice. He felt it's important to keep people aware of hurricane preparedness, so that this many people won't die again."

Wade Guice always took the storm very personally, and he also took the deaths of these three women personally—as well as the lives of everybody else who died. "I hope no one in the whole world has to go through another Hurricane Camille," he said later, before his own death from cancer. "We lost a hundred and thirty-two precious lives in the storm. I consider each of them a personal failure. The ghosts of my failures cry out to me every time I drive down the beach, and that's a heavy burden indeed."

It's a hard, lonely thing to imagine: that someone could die without being missed by anyone. That somebody you noticed yesterday in the grocery store, or stopped at a red light, or waiting for a bus, could be so tenuously connected to the human community that his death would not register a single blip, anywhere, despite intense efforts to find someone, somewhere who knew or who cared about him.

There remains one narrow sliver of hope. Tissue samples of liver, heart, and other organs from the eight bodies found in Nelson County were mounted on slides and are still on file at the State Anatomical Lab in Richmond. At the time of Camille, DNA testing was not available; but today, if someone stepped forward claiming to be related to one of the eight—a brother, child, sister, cousin—DNA tests could confirm or rule out this claim.

Ultimately, the eight bodies of what is sometimes called the "Camille family" were cremated, and the ashes buried in an unmarked grave in Richmond, where they remain, awaiting the return of someone who loved them, hated them, or even just knew who they were.

But in the nearly four decades since Camille came hurtling out of the night, that person has never appeared.

~

PART THREE

AFTERMATH

*"I think the storm had a great deal to do
with a lot of us regaining our perspective
as to really what life is all about and what it is
that will really bring joy."*

—Dr. Marion Dodson

CHAPTER SEVENTEEN

DURING THE FIRST week of September 1969, while bodies were still being pulled from the wreckage along the devastated Gulf Coast, two sociologists from Mississippi State University began walking through the ruined neighborhoods of Harrison County looking for people to interview.

They wanted to know how people had responded to the warnings as Hurricane Camille bore down on the Coast, especially on Sunday, August 17, as the predictions of wind speed and storm surge grew increasingly dire and the storm began veering to the west, shifting its projected target away from Florida and heading directly for Pass Christian. What factors influenced people's decisions to stay or to leave, in the face of a storm of unprecedented violence? How were the people who chose to flee different from those who chose to stay? Had the warnings been adequate? And did either group fully grasp the danger they were in?

A couple of previous studies had revealed some intriguing clues about human behavior in the face of extreme danger from hurricanes. One study, conducted by sociologist Harry Estill Moore, looked at how people responded to warnings of Hurricane Carla, a massive Category Three that slammed into the Texas-Louisiana coast with 120-mile-an-hour winds during September 1961. Moore compared people's behavior in Cameron Parish, Louisiana, and in Chambers County, Texas, two similar areas that laid directly in the projected path of the storm. People in Cameron Parish were much more frightened of the approaching storm, and virtually all of them (97 percent) evacuated their homes. But only 65 percent of the people in Chambers County chose to flee—even though their community had actually experienced *more* hurricane destruction over the years. Why? Because Cameron Parish had had more *recent* experience with terrifying storms, especially Hurricane Audrey, a Category Four that had killed over four hundred people only four years earlier.

A fresh scare is far more motivating than a stale scare.

In this and other hurricane-prone coastal communities, Moore also found what he described as a "disaster culture." That is, attitudes and behavior that included not only calm and rational preparations for hurricanes (building storm shelters, establishing evacuation routes, and the like), but he adds, "an attitude of defiance and of pride in the ability to 'take it' expressed in vehement refusal to flee before the winds."

Did "disaster culture" defiance contribute to the deaths in Hurricane Camille? To answer this and other questions, sociologists Kenneth Wilkinson and Peggy Ross succeeded in interviewing 384 heads of households, drawn randomly from the heavily damaged coast of Harrison County, which included Pass Christian. They chose to focus on the area between the coast and the railroad tracks, which ran parallel to the shoreline about a half mile back from the beach, and where most of the destruction was concentrated. They also secured death certificates for 123 people who were among those who died in the storm. Except for a few who died of head injuries caused by flying debris or falling objects, almost all of these people "were drowned while trying to ride out the storm in a residence near the waterfront," Wilkinson said.

Obviously the people who died were impossible to interview, so one can only guess why they chose to do what they did in those terrifying last hours when the atmosphere turned dead black and Camille lifted the sea itself onto the shore. The dead were probably not idiots; among those who chose to ride out the storm and survived, 90 percent still had habitable, standing houses after the storm passed, suggesting that they were either lucky or knew what they were doing.

"Given all the forces, values, [and] miscalculations . . . which weigh upon human decision-making during periods of crisis," Wilkinson and Ross noted, "it must be concluded that for an indeterminable number of persons, including some presumably among the dead, the most logical choice, perhaps even the only choice, was to stay."

In the fear, panic, and chaos of that Sunday afternoon, of course, it was not immediately clear whether one should stay or go. Desperate dramas played out, as the wind began shrieking in the telephone lines and two-hundred-year-old live oak trees started pitching over. Several people said that during the day, Sunday, many women were more anxious than their husbands to evacuate. But towards evening, as the window of opportunity rapidly closed, men were inclined to want to "make a run for it" and their wives were the ones who refused to leave. The deadlock was often broken by favoring the view of the person who had lived on the Coast the longest.

(Janice Stegenga described these terrifying moments from her own experience: "Once you're trapped, once the storm takes hold and you realize you've made a mistake, it's just too late to correct that mistake. It is too late to get help in flying debris and rising water—you are trapped, and your only choice is to pray. Once that water rises, once your exits are cut off, once the building starts to fall apart, it's too late to say, 'Let's leave.' ")

Was there any difference between the people who chose to stay and those who chose to go? Surprisingly, the researchers concluded that in terms of age, marital status, education, race, or the fanciness of their homes, there was really no significant difference between the two groups. It didn't even matter if they were new arrivals on the Gulf Coast, or storm-chastened, longtime residents. Given roughly the same information, about half chose to stay and half chose to leave. (In interviews with survivors, Julia Guice found that the three most common reasons people gave for staying were that pets were not accepted at the shelters; they thought the buildings they were in were safe; or they had to stay to assist elderly people or those who could not or would not move.) Beyond these factors, what mattered most was their internal perception of how much danger they were in. And one of the startling findings of this study was that almost *nobody* truly grasped the level of danger they were in as Camille hurtled toward the Coast.

One problem was that in some ways, people were misled by their own experience. Most of the respondents were longtime residents of the Gulf Coast, having lived there on average twenty-two years. More than 80 percent of them said they'd lived through at least one previous hurricane; 20 percent said they'd lived through three. They considered themselves to be battle-scarred hurricane veterans.

But on closer questioning, it also emerged that, though many of these people had "lived through" hurricanes, only a few (less than one fifth) had experienced serious injury or property damage. They had not actually looked death in the face or had the bejeezus scared out of them. It also turned out that only about half knew how high their houses were above sea level, even though this number is as critical a bit of information on the low-lying Gulf Coast as one's blood pressure or cholesterol reading. (Quite a few people *thought* they knew their homes' elevation, but got the number wrong.) In short, people were not actually as experienced or as knowledgeable as they thought they were.

"There is, in fact, a question as to whether 'having been in an area where a previous hurricane hit' had a positive or negative effect on adaptive behavior," Wilkinson and Ross wrote. "The fact that [Camille] was a uniquely severe storm coupled with successful previous experiences with lesser storms on the part of some residents created a situation in which many people were aware of the predictions but unable, or unwilling, to translate this awareness into a conception of personal danger commensurate with the facts."

Nobody knew how bad it was going to be, because nobody had ever experienced such an event. This storm was without precedent; there were no benchmarks for comparison, even among people who had lived on the Coast all their lives. "It is doubtful," the researchers added, "that even those making the predictions could have foreseen the severity of destruction."

Many people said that they used their experience of the great hurricane of 1947 as a mental reference point by which to judge the warnings about Hurricane Camille. The '47 storm was a ferocious Category Four, which struck the Florida, Mississippi, and Louisiana coasts with 150-mile-an-hour winds, driving a 15-foot storm surge over the seawall and submerging downtown Biloxi. As Camille drew closer to the coastline, one television station urged listeners to recall the high-water marks of the '47 storm or talk to old-timers about it to help understand the warnings about Camille.

When questioned, people tended to envision even a twenty-foot storm surge as a slow rise in water level, followed by a slow subsiding. They considered it dangerous, but something they could survive without serious injury or property damage. In fact, they failed to grasp the crucial connection between high winds, high tides, and storm surge, which created a massive battering ram of water and debris that pulverized miles of coastline.

Were the warnings adequate? Wilkinson and Ross concluded that "the area was saturated with official warning information during the thirty-six hours preceding the storm." But the warnings weren't perfect, they were sometimes contradictory, and in some cases they were barely warnings at all. For instance, by Sunday afternoon a "highly emotional plea to get out" along with specific local detail was being issued on a Biloxi television station. At the same time, the U.S. Weather Bureau was issuing calmer and more generalized bulletins from far-away places. Even during the final hour, just before midnight, the Bureau predicted landfall "near Gulfport," which was accurate— but it wasn't accompanied by a high-pitched scream: *Get out or take shelter, now!* Some complained that even Nash Roberts's forecasts from New Orleans, while uncannily accurate, did not adequately convey how urgent the situation had become, perhaps partly because he was broadcasting from sixty miles west of the place where Camille was about to make landfall.

Incredibly, one informant reported listening to a station on the Coast most of the day Sunday without hearing any news about the coming storm at all. Some out-of-town papers delivered Sunday morning carried headlines indicating that the Florida Panhandle or Alabama would be the target; some people went to bed Sunday night still convinced the storm would continue moving east into Florida. There were undoubtedly those who died in their beds, still convinced of this.

In general, though, the study showed that people's belief that the storm would actually hit the Mississippi coast grew dramatically as the warnings became increasingly strident that Sunday. According to the recollections of those surveyed, at 8:00 A.M. Sunday morning, only about 34 percent were convinced it definitely would hit the coast; by noon, 55 percent were convinced; by 6:00 P.M., 87 percent thought it would hit; and by 8:00 P.M. Sunday night, almost everyone (93 percent)—whether they chose to stay or to flee—was convinced that Camille would definitely hit the Mississippi coast. Four hours later, she did.

Was there evidence of a "disaster culture" on the Gulf Coast? Yes, in the sense that most people were extremely reluctant to leave, even

when they were in great danger. Many left only when they were
forced to do so, against their will. Even Sunday night, when virtually
everyone knew that a potentially lethal storm was about to hit the
Coast, most people reported feeling that leaving was only something
to do "as a last resort."

A few wild and reckless souls reveled in the chance to defy the
wind. The alcohol-besotted "hurricane party" is an old tradition in
storm-threatened coastal areas, at least among the young and foolish,
and Camille was no exception. The researchers found thirty-six people who said they knew of someone having a hurricane party the
night of the storm. (Some of these stories came from news reports.)
One man in Gulfport reported that a drinking party in a trailer near
his house only broke up around 10:00 P.M. Sunday night when a wall
caved in. Another Gulfport man, who had built a supposedly "hurricane-proof" house after Betsy in 1965, had been planning to have a
hurricane party in it ever since. Both he and his wife died when
Camille crashed the party, and the hurricane-proof house proved to
be no such thing.

But the most famous hurricane party—or *alleged* hurricane
party—took place in the Richelieu Apartments in Pass Christian that
Sunday night. This was the party described by cocktail waitress Mary
Ann Gerlach, whose husband, Fritz, was killed when the entire apartment building was lifted off its foundations and swept away in the
world-record storm surge. Researchers Wilkinson and Ross (interviewing residents only a few weeks after the storm) said they found four
people who had either been invited, or knew someone who had been
invited, to the party at the Richelieu.

Yet, in the months and years after the storm, reporters have asked
whether the party even occurred at all. Some suggested that Mary Ann
Gerlach had more or less made it all up, and had also left the erroneous impression in her many press interviews that she was the only
survivor of the Richelieu. In fact, there were two other known survivors: business school student Ben Duckworth and NASA engineer
Richard Keller. (Keller's wife, who wanted to stay to cook a roast, was
killed.)

The Richelieu hurricane party story really got its legs when no less
a personage than Walter Cronkite, the most respected newsman in

America, was flown into Pass Christian to broadcast from the site in the early days of the recovery.

"This is the site of the Richelieu Apartments in Pass Christian, Mississippi," Cronkite intoned, in the world's most believable baritone, as the camera panned across the windswept foundation, all that remained of the building. "This is the place where twenty-three people laughed in the face of death. And where twenty-three people died."

It was a good line. But it does not appear to have been precisely true. Though news stories at the time reported that at least twenty bodies had been recovered from the wreckage of the building, later reports suggested that perhaps as few as eight people died in the Richelieu that night, all the others having fled before Camille made landfall. It's possible that some of the recovered bodies came from nearby houses or buildings; the Richelieu itself was completely destroyed and the scene around it totally confused. (One person known to have died was apartment manager Merwin Jones, who had told Gerlach that the Richelieu was "the safest place to be on the beach.")

To this day, Gerlach maintains that she was getting ready to go up to a hurricane party on the third floor, but never got there because the storm intervened. She challenges the stories of one survivor, who claimed to have clung to trees through that long, long night. "The Richelieu was in this very low-lying area, called the rice fields, and I know for a fact all the trees there were underwater. When I washed out the window, I thought I was out in the Gulf because there were no trees above the water. There was no way that man could have been holding on to a tree."

In any case, the true story of the Richelieu may never be known, and if there are any other survivors they may never be heard from. "I can understand why Richelieu survivors aren't coming forward," Civil Defense Director Julia Guice said. "It was such a horrific experience, no one wants to relive it."

IN THE DAYS shortly after the storm, as the shock and disbelief wore off, people awoke to the sheer physical devastation of their surroundings. The Gulf Coast, with its white-columned mansions and stately, Spanish moss-bearded live oak trees, was now a horriffic, chaotic mess. The harbor had been reduced to rubble. Disemboweled boats lay strewn on residential streets. Houses were simply gone. And in the sticky heat, snakes, vermin, and then the fetid smell of death began to appear.

Beachcombers poking in the rubble along the north shore of Ship and Horn Islands found large numbers of outlandish, perfectly round objects, some bigger than basketballs, formed when Camille's fantastic wind and surf spun seagrass and debris into spheres so tightly packed they could not be pulled apart by hand. They had to be cut open with a saw. These strange storm orphans, once thought to have magical power against gout and plague, have been known by many names in many languages—"drift balls," "newt nests," "bezoarsteine." They were evidence of forces at work in the storm that were so extreme and bizarre that they appeared to come from another world.

The other-worldliness of the storm's destruction began taking its toll on people's states of mind. "The next day it was a sorrowful experience looking at a very pretty community that was ugly, and looking at a lot of sad people who had lost a lot of things," said Dr. Marion Dodson. "All the big trees were gone. It was just an ugly place to live. And we talked about it then: It would be ten years before it would look nice." Though he was able to bury himself in a busy medical practice, his wife was not so fortunate. Like so many others, she began to slip into a paralyzing depression. The big giveaway was when Dr. Dodson came home from work one day and she had painted the bathroom black.

In many ways, how people responded to the hurricane's devastation and the aftermath revealed more about themselves than about the storm itself. Some saw in the storm a chance for selfless gallantry, and for a community to be bound together by calamity. The Mennonites saw it as a chance to serve God. Harrison County Civil Defense Director Wade Guice, one of the true heroes of the hurricane, said later, "I know for a fact that disaster brings out the very best in people." It certainly brought out the best in *him,* and in many other less-heralded individuals. But it also brought out the worst in people. Looters and profiteers, of which there were a fair number on both the Gulf Coast and in central Virginia, simply saw it as a chance to make a quick buck. Others displayed an almost unspeakably ghoulish picture of their souls—like the mysterious man who showed up in

Nelson County and tried to use a young boy's body as an unwitting tool in an insurance scam.

Some people adopted an attitude of utter defiance after the storm, almost like a post-hurricane "disaster culture." Frances Fitzergerald, who with her husband and baby survived the deluge only by climbing into the rafters, still lives in the same low-lying house within a couple of hundred yards of the Tye River—even though the house has been repeatedly inundated by floods in the years since Camille. In 1985, she had five inches of mud in her kitchen—there are still waterline stains on the kitchen cabinets—and in 1996, during Hurricane Fran, severe flood damage caused the whole house to be gutted. After the Fitzgeralds got nearly ten thousand dollars in flood insurance payments, Frances reports, "a county supervisor suggested that we move somewhere else, but I said, 'I don't want to move anywhere else. This is my home. You do something about that river!'" To this day, she states, if it rains for a couple of days, her husband can't sleep. "He gets in his truck and drives up the road to check the river. He's terrified. He'll just sit here at the kitchen table and drink coffee all night."

For others, a close encounter with a Category Five hurricane triggered spiritual doubt or spiritual revelation. Jungian analyst David Schoen, a Louisiana native who witnessed Camille's destruction in Bay Saint Louis, observes, "there seems to be a powerful transforming wisdom that comes to humans as they approach the hurricane experience—a fear and stirring of the spirit that has been absent from their everyday lives."

As a therapist who has counseled hurricane survivors, Schoen says that "because the hurricane has such gigantic energy potential, because it is so potent, so numinous, so primitive, it forces people to realize that they are in the presence of a power much greater than themselves, whether as an individual or as a society. It has the ability to trigger spiritual experiences, and often does."

In some cases, the terror and destruction wrought by Camille raised the most ancient of religious doubts and questions. At Nelson County High School, band director Vernon Lewis later recalled that students began asking: Why has God allowed this to happen? Why has God done this to me? Where is God? Is there a God at all?

"Most of these people were pretty religious, but many of them had questions after the storm," Dr. Robert Raynor said. "One guy in particular, I remember him just stopping and looking up at the sky and saying, "God, dammit, *why?*"

For other people, the experience of having earthly possessions utterly stripped away led to a different kind of inner transformation. Alma Anderson, who lived on the Gulf Coast in comfort and affluence but lost nearly everything in the storm, remembered that "I was just as worldly as the next one. We had the Cadillacs at a young age, we had three or four furs, we had everything. A lot of people envied us because of what we did have as young as we were, but it was all taken."

As Dr. Dodson put it: "I think the storm had a great deal to do with a lot of us regaining our perspective as to what life is all about and what it is that will really bring joy."

Many people's psychological experience of Camille is difficult to discern, because they have refused to talk about it at all. Tinker Bryant, who lost his beautiful wife, Grace, and three daughters—Louise, Patricia, and Frances—has not spoken publicly about it since that awful August night in 1969. Even if unexpressed, the emotions that surround Camille still remain as potent as if the storm had happened last year. Martha Connor, wife of Nelson County superintendent of schools Henry Connor, said in an interview more than thirty-five years after the fact: "It's hard to talk about the emotional part without breaking down." Adds Gene Ramsey: "A lot of people don't want to talk about it and never will. Even I, who didn't lose anybody, get upset when I think about it after all these years."

The emotional impact of the storm was so powerful that even today, residents of Nelson County and the Gulf Coast speak of life "before Camille" and "after Camille."

FOR MARY ANN GERLACH, "after Camille" began when an immense black man carried her out of the swamp where she'd been deposited by the storm, after the Richelieu apartments exploded in the storm surge and she was swept out to sea. (A meteorologist who studied the storm later estimated she'd been transported twelve miles, out into the raging Gulf and then, miraculously, back onto shore.) She was shivering uncontrollably in the rain, crouched atop a pile of debris two stories high. Her knee had been ripped open by a nail; she'd used her bra as a tourniquet to stop the bleeding. After she was found, she was taken to a temporary medical center in a school and then to a nursing home, where a doctor sewed up her knee. In the chaos of the storm's aftermath there was no running water, so the wound was closed without being sterilized. Within a couple of days Gerlach's knee swelled up "to the size of one of those icebox watermelons." Because her husband was in the military, she begged to be taken to Keesler Air Force Base in Biloxi. There doctors operated on her knee twice, trying to save it before a staph infection spread throughout the leg, which would have required amputation.

Eight days after the storm, Fritz's body was found in the top of a tree underneath a soggy mattress. The body was so badly decomposed it was almost impossible to identify; but a friend of the Gerlachs, George Smith, thought he recognized a little diamond ring—it looked just like one Mary Ann had given Fritz for their second anniversary. Smith convinced Mary Ann to come down to the meat locker where the body was being stored, to identify her husband. She was warned that there was no way she could go inside the locker to see the body—it was so black and swollen that it "didn't even look human." But, she recalls, "I was bound and determined to see my husband's body. I said, 'just want to touch him one one time, please let me get in,' and I was fighting them." The doctors gave her a shot of Demerol to calm her down. One odd thing about the body, they told her, was that it was fully clothed—it was the only body they'd found that had not had its clothes stripped off by the storm. She told them what Fritz had been wearing—what kind of shoes, what kind of belt. Eventually, Mary Ann got inside the meat locker and identified the swollen, disfigured body, still wearing his pants, shirt, and loafers. Fritz's body was eventually sent to his parents, but because his widow was still under close medical supervision, she could not even attend the funeral.

After Mary Ann was released from the hospital, she moved into a little three-bedroom house with her friend Eva, but after a few months, continually upset, ill, and taking nerve pills, she said, "I've got to get out of town." So she moved to Houston, then to suburban Chicago, then, eventually, back to the Gulf Coast.

When her cast was removed, Gerlach found that her once-beautiful leg had "a real bad scar" on the knee, and her "muscles were caved in on one side and all." Still, she was grateful to have legs at all. For a year after Camille, she remained deathly afraid of water. She wouldn't even get in a swimming pool. She'd drive over a bridge and start shaking. Eventually, a friend dragged her back into a pool and helped her overcome her fear of submersion. Finally she got back into the ocean on a calm day and, over time, even began going out day-sailing in small boats.

But Gerlach's luck, never the best, did not seem to improve. In an interview ten years after Camille, she mentioned that she'd had mul-tiple operations on her kidneys (a preexisting condition exacerbated by Camille), had had brain surgery after a car accident, and that her daughter had recently killed herself. "It just seems like so much tragedy has happened to me, until I just don't see why He keeps me alive . . . I don't know what God keeps saving me for, but it seems like He has some purpose."

Though God's interest in Gerlach's life may have remained mys-terious, the criminal justice system's interest in her was completely un-ambiguous when, on a January night in 1981, she picked up a .357 Magnum and shot her ex-husband five times. Lawrence Kietzer, a thirty-six-year-old offshore oil worker, had been Gerlach's eleventh husband before she divorced him seven weeks prior to the shooting. In the trial that followed his murder, she admitted killing him. But she blamed the murder on her own physical pain from various injuries and operations, and on the emotional scars she bore from her expe-rience in Hurricane Camille. Her explanation did not satisfy the court. She served more than ten years in prison at the Central Mississippi Correctional Facility before her release in December 1992. In the years afterwards, she married her twelfth and then her thirteenth husband—James Troy, an inmate she'd met in prison.

Reached by phone in the summer of 2005, Gerlach told a caller she was rushing off to a prayer meeting. Now sixty-seven, she had re-cently moved to a small town near Jackson, Mississippi, where her life revolved around her Christian faith and new friends at the First Baptist Church. "I don't drink or party anymore," she said. "I had strayed so far away, but now I am back with the Lord. He is giving me a second chance to get it right."

SHERIFF WILLIAM WHITEHEAD is invariably interviewed when the local newspapers do a retrospective on Hurricane Camille. Reporters come to his ancestral home at Willow Brook, down in a hollow above Hat Creek, to listen to him talk and to take a look at his impressive collection of photographs of the storm. Life has not been particularly gentle to the sheriff. He lost his wife, Catherine, in a car accident, and spends much of his time shuttling around the kitchen in a motorized wheelchair, the result of injuries caused by that accident. He was not reelected to office after the storm—neither was Cliff Wood—partly due to their constituents' displeasure with the recovery efforts. It is probably unfair to blame anyone for failing to recognize that an ordinary summer thundershower is about to turn into a once-in-a-thousand-years storm. But that's what sometimes happens in a democracy.

Over the years, Warren Raines has also given innumerable interviews about that night of endless rain, the night he became an orphan. But he doesn't share such intimacies lightly. On a summer afternoon in 2004, the phone rang as he manned the front desk at Raines Electronics, his small video rental and electronics store in Piney River, Virginia. The woman on the other end of the line was complaining about problems she was having with her video dish.

"Looks like we've got some bad weather coming, with that hurricane down south," she added.

In the front room of Raines's store, on a TV tuned to Fox News, a reporter broadcasting live from Mississippi noted that Hurricane Ivan, a Category Three, was bearing down on the Gulf Coast with 135-mile-an-hour winds. The hurricane, the reporter said, could disrupt the weather as far north as Virginia.

"I heard there was a real bad hurricane up here in these parts, a long time ago—Camille, I think it was," noted the woman on the phone, who was a recent arrival in Nelson County.

"Yeah, it was a bad one," Raines replied, without elaboration or emotion. "Want me to come out there and fix that dish?"

Warren Raines was forty-nine, though he seemed older than his years. His eyes were penetrating and a little sad. He spoke in the broad, melodious drawl common in rural Virginia. (Storm became "stawm," corn became "cawn," and the Southern familiar "y'all" found its way into every few sentences.) On this particular summer afternoon, business was slow. As he sat chatting with a visitor in a back room of the store, sometimes twenty minutes would go by before somebody walked in. Suddenly the front doorbell jingled and a small girl of about seven walked into the store to make a beeline for the cartoon video section. Warren got up and walked over to greet her.

"*Scooby-Doo* just came in yesterday," he told the little girl gently. "It's only ninety-nine cents overnight."

In the days immediately after the storm, as Warren and his brother Carl Junior woke up to the fact that they no longer had a family, they were forced to figure out who would take care of them. The only surviving immediate family member was their sister Ava, who was only nineteen, barely older than they were. Their grandparents couldn't take care of them, nor could their father's half-sister. So one of their father's customers, a man named Jack Young, let the boys stay with him for a few weeks while he tried to straighten out the legal loose ends of their new situation. Young wound up becoming the administrator of the boys' estate, such as it was.

"I liked Jack Young," Warren said. "He was a kind of fill-in father figure."

Until someone officially became the brothers' legal guardian, Young suggested they go to private boarding school. At least that would give them a place to live. Carl decided he wanted to go to Woodberry Forest, in nearby Orange, Virginia, but at the last minute, a "dream come true" occurred—a family named the Harveys, who lived near Roseland and had never had children of their own, offered to let the boys come live with them on their farm. Carl decided to accept their offer and go to public high school. But for Warren, that option had already vanished. He had made the decision to enroll at Staunton Military Academy, in nearby Staunton, Virginia.

"It was one of the worst decisions I ever made," he said in 2004. "The people advising us should never have let me do that."

Warren Raines was fifteen years old and newly orphaned. He was separated from his brother for the first time in his life. What he needed was nurturing, warmth, and support; but what he got was a kind of sadistic boot camp, where troubled boys received a heavy dose of military discipline. He had to rise at the crack of dawn, wear a uniform, and was subjected to continuous harassment and humiliation by upperclassmen. Once, when a student was suspected of stealing, the young cadets were forced to stand at attention for hours on end, until some of them began to faint from exhaustion. The academy (now defunct) was only thirty miles from Virginia Military Institute, one of the nation's most hard-core military boarding schools, but, Raines recalls, "People who went to Staunton and then later to VMI said VMI was a cakewalk compared to what we did in that place."

After a brutal year of military school, Warren joined his brother at the Harvey farm for a couple of blessed years. When he was seventeen, incredibly enough, Warren moved back to the family home in Massies Mill, living there alone, cooking and taking care of himself, for two years.

"You know, it's a funny thing, but sometimes I felt my mother in that house, or it seemed like I could feel her. Maybe it was just a wish or a thought. It was a tough thing, though, living there all by myself and with all those memories."

Not long after he began dating a girl named Sharon, she casually mentioned that her mother was a Huffman and that she'd lost two brothers and their entire families on Davis Creek during Camille. A few months later, she and Warren were married; he was nineteen years old. They have now been married for thirty years and have two children. Sharon plays the organ at the local Baptist church. "Faith and family are the two most important things in my life," he states. "I guess you could say I really depend on my faith more than anything."

"The big question, though, is *why?*" His voices trails off. "In the hereafter or whatever, those questions will be answered. But for now, you can't help wondering."

IN THE YEARS after Camille, Nash Roberts's reputation only continued to grow. In September 1998, still broadcasting on New Orleans television at the age of eighty, he predicted that Hurricane Earl would come ashore at Panama City, Florida—a full sixteen hours before it made landfall in exactly that spot. A few weeks later, he did it again. At a time when the National Weather Service predicted that Hurricane Georges was aiming almost directly at New Orleans, and record numbers of people had already evacuated, Nash Roberts insisted it would come ashore well to the east, near Biloxi. And it did.

In 2000, Nash Roberts closed up his meterological consulting service and retired. After a half century of forecasting hurricanes, he was tired. But he was also tired because Lydia, his beloved wife of more than sixty years, had become an invalid and required full-time care. He tried for almost a year to take care of her himself, but finally had to hire nurses working round the clock to assist him. Nevertheless, during the summer of 2004, when Hurricane Ivan began drifting up "hurricane alley" toward New Orleans on a path that was eerily reminiscent of Camille's, Roberts agreed to do a storm-track projection, just for his family and a few friends. He no longer had the benefit of a top-notch meterological staff or the tools of modern science. So he decided to do it the old-fashioned way.

"I just went back to the old days without all that fancy scientific input, no satellite images and little or no radar. I just plotted and examined what was changing from one report to the next. You get lazy after fifty years—I was surprised I still remembered how to do it that way. And it was surprising how well it worked."

It was also surprising how quickly Nash Roberts's "private" prediction got around town. Huge numbers of people, having heard through the grapevine that Roberts was predicting landfall far to the east, chose to ignore the National Weather Service predictions, which forecast landfall unnervingly close to New Orleans—so close, in fact, that thousands of people did evacuate that low-lying city. In the end, Ivan came ashore as a Category Three at Gulf Shores, Alabama, about a hundred miles east of New Orleans.

Nash Roberts was right again.

THE STORY does not end here. In fact, in many ways, it is just beginning. For another storm was soon to be born, a storm, like Camille, that would become the stuff of legend.

Her name was Katrina.

EPILOGUE

AT THE CALVARY Baptist Church in Lovingston, Virginia, parishioners have created a scrapbook of photographs to remember those lost in the great flood of 1969. For a visitor paging through this book of sorrows, some of the faces stand out. There's Audrey Zirkle's little brother Gary "Giggy" Zirkle, a kid with a hugely enthusiastic smile and a crooked, broken tooth. There's Edward "Buzz" Thompson, a big, big man—Pastor John Campbell says he weighed over two hundred pounds—who was deathly afraid of water. Then there's Clyde Mitchell Huffman, with buck teeth and freckles, as American as Dennis the Menace. Some faces are especially beautiful, like Tinker Bryant's wife, Grace Marshall Bryant, all in soft focus, with 1940s hair and a sweet, beatific smile. And Emory "Red" French, with his wife, Elizabeth Campbell French—in a scratchy black-and-white photo, he's wearing a sharp suit and has the craggy good looks of an old-time movie star, like Kirk Douglas.

It is impossible to measure the depth of anguish suggested by these faces of the dead. But some hint of it is suggested by two gray stone monuments that stand on the tree-shaded lawn of the Nelson County Courthouse.

One monument, topped by an intrepid young soldier in battle dress, is inscribed: "In Memory of the Heroic Confederate Soldiers of Nelson County Who Served in the War Between the States, 1861–1865. Love Makes Memory Eternal." Twenty paces away, is another memorial—a simple, upright engraved stone. Its inscription reads, "Dedicated to the memory of the citizens of Nelson County who lost their lives during Hurricane Camille August 19–20, 1969."

In the South, the Civil War is less a historical event than a raw, living wound. To say that Camille had an impact on the collective memory of this small Southern community comparable to that of the War Between the States is to say something remarkable indeed. But the impact is not only symbolic. It is also literal—blood, body, and bone.

According to Robert E.L. Krick, eminent historian of the Richmond National Battlefield Park and an expert on the Army of Northern Virginia, Nelson County probably raised eight companies during the war, amounting to about one thousand men. Assuming that casualty rates were about the same in Nelson as they were elsewhere in the South, probably 100 to 150 men were killed in that bloody war, and about 300 wounded. By comparison, the final death toll from the Camille floods in Nelson County came to 124—84 bodies recovered and identified, 32 people missing and never found, and eight bodies recovered but never identified. That represents about one percent of the population of this small rural county. (The storm killed 26 people elsewhere in the state, raising the total deaths in Virginia to 150.)

It could well be argued that Hurricane Camille was actually even more traumatic to Nelson County than the Civil War. Everybody knew the war was coming, and it lasted five years. But the hurricane struck almost completely without warning, in the dead of night, and it lasted all of eight hours. In the war, mostly young men who had chosen to fight died; but Camille killed indiscriminately, taking the lives of men, women, and children, including a little blond-haired girl who still had her baby teeth and was probably frightened of thunder.

The string of small communities along the Mississippi Gulf Coast was no less traumatized by Hurricane Camille. And the human sorrow of the storm is remembered in Biloxi, Mississippi, in a lovely monument called the Hurricane Camille Memorial Wall. The wall is a semi-circle of black granite inscribed with the names of 175 people—131 dead and identified, 41 missing, and three bodies that were never identified: "Faith," "Hope," and "Charity." The granite wall wraps around a shallow pool, and beneath the water a swirling mandala of blue and white tiles represents the hurricane. One is struck by the beauty, grandeur, and wholeness of the great storm itself, a kind of celestial mandala, at the same time one is moved by the names of the dead. (The memories of Camille are still alive and full of pain on the Gulf Coast; and the memorial is also a living thing, continuously visited by people who stroll by and pause quietly to read the names on the wall.)

The monument sits on the shady, contemplative grounds of the

Episcopal Church of the Redeemer, overlooking the waterfront in Biloxi and surrounded by great old live oak trees, many of them bearded with Spanish moss gently stirring in the Gulf breeze. The original church, built in 1874, was regularly attended by Jefferson Davis, president of the Confederacy, during the latter years of his life. The church building, along with the rectory, was destroyed by Camille (and has since been rebuilt). But a two-story bell tower that stands separate from the church survived the storm. A historical marker on the tower notes that "throughout that harrowing night, the frantic tolling of this bell could be heard over the din. Miraculously, this tower and its bell survived. . . ."

Including those lost on the Gulf Coast, Camille's total known death toll (as best it can be determined) comes to 325. Considering that Camille was one of the most violent hurricanes in modern history, this number is remarkable chiefly for how small it is. As National Hurricane Center Director Dr. Robert Simpson later wrote: "If the twelve or fifteen hours of explicit warning of a record storm had been later in coming, or if the evacuation authorities had been less efficient in conducting the evacuation, it has been estimated that thousands of additional lives would have been lost . . . We survived Camille by the grace of God. It could have been a much greater tragedy."

Still, life goes on, and people forget. Many current residents of the Gulf Coast are either too young to remember Camille or did not live there then. In the almost forty years since that frightful summer midnight in 1969, the Coast has dramatically changed. Riverboat casino gambling was legalized in 1990, and enormous, multi-story, Las Vegas-style resort-casinos, including Biloxi's $700 million Beau Rivage, have sprung up along the Coast in Harrison and Hancock Counties, glittering through the night like lurid promises. Due to a deal struck with anti-gambling interests, casinos are only legal if they're "on the water," so they have been built either on pylons over the Gulf, or on floating barges. Camille survivor Janice Stegenga, whose husband lost three family members in the storm, can only shake her head at this. Camille, she points out, picked up an enormous barge like a child's toy and tossed it across Highway 90 a quarter mile away.

Casino gambling has triggered a building boom all up and down the Gulf Coast. In Pass Christian, a Winn-Dixie grocery store stands on the spot where the Richelieu Apartments once stood. Catatonic Muzak now plays in aisles of frozen food and baked goods, where, in the moments before death, people once plunged through collapsing walls into chaos and darkness. Only a couple of hundreds yards away, closer to the beach, a seventy-unit condominium complex was under construction in the summer of 2004. A gaily painted sign advertised the new "Island Breeze" complex featuring "West Indies/Caribbean-style living one hour from New Orleans." There is no apparent memory of the unforgettable night of thirty-five years earlier when the Gulf of Mexico exploded into second-floor bedrooms of a very similar building, obliterating the entire structure almost as effectively as a nuclear bomb. And apparently without irony, the builders of the swanky new complex had chosen as their slogan, "For Once in a Lifetime."

AFTERWORD:
KATRINA WAS NO LADY

"OVER THE YEARS, Hurricane Camille's legend grew, and it was not uncommon when I was a child and student in Mississippi to hear horrific tales from coast residents who had survived it," best-selling author John Grisham wrote in an op-ed piece in *The New York Times* in September 2005. "For almost 40 years, it was a well-established belief that the Gulf Coast had taken nature's mightiest blow, picked itself up, learned some lessons and survived rather well. There could simply never be another storm like Hurricane Camille."

Then came Katrina.

Shortly after dawn on August 29, 2005—thirty-six years and twelve days after the terrible midnight when Camille came ashore—Hurricane Katrina made landfall near the mouth of the Pearl River, on the low-lying coast at the border between Mississippi and Louisiana. A couple of days earlier, hurtling up through the superheated Gulf, she had accelerated into a frighteningly large Category Five. She was huge by almost any measure, darkening the entire region with her vast spiral of storm clouds and feeder bands. As her wind speeds revved up to 175 miles an hour and her barometric pressure began dropping precipitously, hundreds of thousands fled the Coast. Mayor Ray Nagin ordered the first-ever mandatory evacuation of New Orleans. Katrina was, he said, "the storm that most of us have long feared." Because of Katrina's extraordinarily low barometric pressure and wind speeds, the National Hurricane Center made the chilling declaration on Sunday, August 28, that she was "comparable in intensity to Hurricane Camille of 1969 . . . only larger."

By the time Katrina made landfall just after 6:00 A.M. the following morning, her sustained winds were still screaming ashore at 125 miles an hour, making her a strong Category Three. She drilled through the tiny bayou town of Buras, Louisiana, in Plaquemines Parish, which hangs down into the Gulf like a tonsil. She scattered shrimp boats, piers, and cold storage plants like so many toothpicks, briefly crossed back out over open water, and a few hours later came howling ashore onto the mainland, black as death, bringing with her the greatest natural horror in American history: An immense dome of water that was more than eighty miles wide and in some places thirty feet high, stretching from New Orleans to Mobile, Alabama. In some low-lying areas the storm surge inundated the Coast for up to three or four miles inland, simultaneously running up rivers, bayous, and estuaries so that some coastal cities were slammed from two sides at once, as water poured in from the Gulf to the south at the same time it poured in from the back bays and bayous to the north. Where the two walls of water met, almost nothing remained.

Katrina was the third-most intense hurricane ever to strike the United States, according to the National Weather Service. Her barometric pressure, taken moments before landfall by a U.S. Air Force recon plane at dawn that Monday, was measured at 27.11 inches of mercury. By comparison, Grisham wrote, "I suspect that Hurricane Camille will soon be downgraded to an April shower."

Well, not hardly. In fact, Camille was actually a dramatically more violent (though smaller) storm than Katrina. Camille's central pressure dropped to an astounding 26.84, the second-lowest ever measured for a landfalling hurricane in the United States. And her wind speeds, at nearly 200 miles an hour, were also far higher than Katrina's. (Don't forget that the damage inflicted by hurricanes increases *exponentially* as wind speed increases, so the difference between 145-mile-an-hour winds and 200-mile-an-hour winds is enormous.) The only other storm to eclipse Camille's central pressure was the small and freakish Labor Day storm of 1935, which hit a record 26.35 and is still the most intense of all landfalling hurricanes in U.S. history.

Because the Labor Day storm crossed the Florida Keys, it can fairly be said that Camille was the most intense hurricane ever to strike the *mainland* of the United States—and it still is, despite the devastation wrought by Katrina. Nevertheless, due to her great size and her trajectory, Katrina was a disaster without precedent.

"Although its intensity at landfall was less than that of Hurricane Camille, which devastated coastal Mississippi in August 1969, the size of Katrina, with hurricane force winds extending 120 miles from its center, was much larger and the destruction more widespread than

Camille," the National Oceanic and Atmospheric Administration said in a statement. Katrina's ferocious core, with winds of maximum speed, was about thirty miles wide. By contrast, Camille had a core of maximum winds about nine miles wide.

One of many eerie similarities between the two monster storms was that they made landfall on the Gulf Coast within less than fifty miles of each other. Camille came ashore up the mouth of Saint Louis Bay, nearly obliterating the little towns of Bay Saint Louis and Pass Christian, which stand on opposite sides of the channel. Katrina collided with the mainland less than an hour's drive to the west, in Hancock County, Mississippi. But because she was so enormous, her dreaded right-front quadrant—the most terrifying and destructive leading edge of the cyclone—brought astounding wind and storm surge ashore to the east of that point, in the Mississippi towns of Waveland, Bay Saint Louis, Pass Christian, Long Beach, Gulfport, and Biloxi, and as far east as Pascagoula. Her storm surge even flooded into Mobile Bay and inundated Mobile, Alabama.

But some of the saddest and most sordid scenes of destruction occurred to the west, in New Orleans. The city so vulnerable to catastrophic flooding that it's sometimes described as "a sand castle built at low tide" had finally succumbed to what had long been feared. In some ways, Katrina became the storm that Dr. Robert Simpson feared that August day in 1969 when he was watching Camille hurtling toward shore on the National Hurricane Center satellite monitors. His greatest worry was that she'd make a direct hit on New Orleans. As it turned out, Camille gave the Big Easy a pass. And Katrina did too, veering to the east at the last minute and thus sparing the city a bulls-eye landing. Even so, her immense storm surge drove massive amounts of seawater into the east-facing mouth of Lake Pontchartrain, overtopping and then breaching the city's fragile ring of levees in at least three places. Within twenty-four hours, about eighty percent of the city was flooded up to 20 feet deep. A few weeks later, adding sadness to sadness, vulnerable parts of the city were reflooded by Hurricane Rita, another frightful storm that briefly became a Cat Five during her passage through the Gulf.

In retrospect, Katrina's devastation of New Orleans can be seen as a ghastly illustration of exactly what Simpson feared—except that Camille could well have been worse. If a storm that didn't even hit the city could do as much damage as Katrina did, imagine what would have happened if Camille—a hurricane of dramatically greater feroc-ity—had come smashing straight down Bourbon Street. There might have been almost nothing left.

When it was all over, NOAA had officially listed Katrina as "the most destructive hurricane to ever strike the U.S," with damage esti-mates ranging over $100 billion. (The previous record-holder was 1992's Andrew, with damage estimates around $45 billion.) In fact, Katrina was probably the costliest and most destructive natural disas-ter of any kind ever to strike the United States. In Louisiana alone, an estimated 160,000 buildings were rendered uninhabitable. Over ninety thousand square miles were declared a federal disaster area. More than a million people were displaced by the storm, a humanitarian cri-sis unseen since the Dust Bowl days of the Great Depression, or per-haps even the Civil War. As of this writing (in October 2005), the death toll has topped thirteen hundred but is sure to go higher.

To many people on the Gulf Coast, all of this came as an enor-mous shock. It wasn't that they were unprepared for hurricanes, of course. It was that, as long as anyone could remember, people be-lieved that if they had survived Camille, they could survive anything. Those who had survived Camille felt magically protected by this ex-perience—immune, in some mystical way, to any future catastrophe that nature could possibly conjure. Longtime New Orleans resident Patty Still, who fled the city in the face of Katrina, observed in a news-paper column that "there are those who wear the litany of hurricanes they have survived like an amulet, with extra protection given if they can invoke the name 'Camille.' "

In the end, though, all of this magical thinking proved to be no more useful or protective than a handful of smoke. In fact, it was dan-gerously in error. And it had all happened before.

When Camille was bearing down on the Coast that August 1969, many local residents judged their level of personal danger based on the only other "Big One" in their experience, the legendary storm of 1947—or perhaps 1965's Hurricane Betsy. At that time, these previous storms seemed to confer a magical amulet of invulnerability. If your house had survived either one, people thought, it would be safe to stay there now because this latest storm couldn't possibly get any worse.

In truth, though, it *could* get worse.

Much worse.

Camille proved that once and for all.

Yet not long after people woke up to the nearly unimaginable destruction wrought by Camille, they quickly came to think that *she* was the worst that could possibly happen. Once again, they learned the wrong lesson. In a radio interview shortly after Hurricane Katrina, one longtime Gulf resident summed up the danger of this seductive psychological fallacy.

"Camille has killed a lot of people," he told the talk-show host.

"You mean *Katrina,*" the host corrected. "Katrina has killed a lot of people."

"No, I mean Camille," the man said. "A lot of these people didn't evacuate because they figured that if they survived Camille, they could survive anything."

What had actually occurred was simply a failure of the imagination, an inability to conjure nightmares. There is no way of knowing how many of these Camille survivors were later found crushed beneath the wreckage of their houses or washed up on the beach in the wake of Katrina, bloated and limp as dolls.

As people began to grasp the enormity of the devastation wrought by Katrina, former Louisiana senator John Breaux remarked in an interview, "If we don't learn from this disaster, it's a double disaster."

Yet in many ways, Hurricane Katrina was a double disaster the moment it happened. Because one of the most striking things about the whole terrible story was how little had actually been learned in the nearly four decades since Hurricane Camille. Just as individuals seemed to learn incorrect or misleading lessons from that tragedy, so did whole communities and even a nation.

Prior to Camille, many Gulf Coast communities did not have any planning or zoning in place at all. According to one retrospective report, "the development and building practices in existence at the time of Camille had been greatly influenced by the gradual uncontrolled and disorganized growth which had taken place in the coastal communities for the previous hundred years." Many homes and businesses were built in low-lying areas particularly vulnerable to storm surge, many buildings were poorly constructed to withstand hurricane-force wind and water, and only twenty percent of them were covered by flood insurance. Yet in the rush to rebuild after Camille, "the same characteristics which led to absolute destruction of homes and businesses were repeated in the months immediately following the hurricane." The pattern continued in ensuing years until today there has been such a massive rebuilding of the entire Gulf Coast that the region has become dramatically *more* vulnerable to hurricanes than it was in the days before Camille. What seems particularly lunatic is the building of massive, three-story-high casino barges sitting directly on the water squarely in the center of hurricane alley.

Perhaps most ironic of all is the fact that the Federal Emergency Management Agency (FEMA) was created almost directly as a result of the confused and disorganized response to Hurricane Camille. Yet it was FEMA that seemed to bear the brunt of the criticism after its slow, confused, and disorganized response to Hurricane Katrina almost four decades later. The sensible effort to create a single federal agency to coordinate disaster response teams from state and local government as well as volunteer organizations seemed to have failed in a dozen different ways. In a radio interview, former FEMA director Jane Bullock summed up the situation succinctly: "The state, local, and federal emergency response system is broken."

What makes this all the more remarkable is that Katrina's phenomenal devastation did not come as a complete surprise. Far from it, in fact. Compared to the terrorist attacks of 9/11, Katrina was almost as predictable as a train. In the summer of 1999, hurricane experts Roger A. Pielke Jr., Chantal Simonpietri, and Jennifer Oxelson produced a retrospective paper called "Thirty Years After Hurricane Camille: Lessons Learned, Lessons Lost." In it they observed:

> For many, Camille is a distant memory, an historical footnote
> from a time long gone. But Camille is also a harbinger of
> disasters to come. Another storm of Camille's intensity will strike
> the United States, the only question is when. When this future
> storm strikes, it will make landfall over conditions drastically
> different from those in 1969. The hurricane-prone regions of
> the United States have developed dramatically as people have
> moved to the coast and the nation's wealth has grown.

Estimates of potential losses from a single hurricane have topped
$100 billion.

The only place these expert observers erred is that they did not go far enough. Incredibly, Katrina's damage now appears to be closer to twice the size of their most far-fetched estimate.

THE MAGNITUDE of Katrina's destruction is difficult to grasp, even in the era of CNN, high-quality newsmagazines, and the Internet. So in late September 2005, about three weeks after she made landfall in Mississippi—and two months after I submitted this book to the publisher—I returned to the Gulf Coast a second time. Almost exactly a year earlier, while doing research for the book, I'd visited this seductively balmy place, with its lorldly live oaks and magnolias, its grand oceanside homes, and its sense of leisurely gentility. Now I needed to bear witness to the aftermath of the disaster with my own eyes, to talk to people, to be fearful and uncomfortable, to get close enough to *smell* it, and if possible to lend a helping hand.

New Orleans was still closed, virtually empty, and partially flooded, and no phone service was there (or almost anywhere else along the Gulf Coast, for that matter). So my attempts to locate legendary meteorologist Nash Roberts, who still lived in the Big Easy, were unsuccessful. Instead, I went to visit the small Gulf cities of Pass Christian, Long Beach, Gulfport, and Biloxi.

Driving down from the north, I began seeing evidence of Katrina two hundred miles from the coast: Pines trees snapped off like matchsticks, collapsed billboards, roofs peeled back like sardine tins. The damage seemed surprisingly discontinuous, with huge stands of trees nearly flattened, followed by a stretch that seemed almost untouched. But the farther south I traveled, the more severe and continuous the devastation became. By the time I arrived in Gulfport, near dark, the only proper response to what I was seeing was silence. The picturesque little city seemed to have been deliberately brutalized by some demonic god, who'd scattered cars, trees, houses, telephone lines, brightly colored children's toys, beds, mattresses, and garbage in every direction. I tried to drive down to the beach—Ground Zero— but was turned back at a police checkpoint. The entire half-mile-wide downtown area between the railroad tracks (which paralleled the

Coast) and the beachfront had been sealed off to everyone but local residents and disaster-response teams. Razor-sharp concertina wire had been unrolled along the tracks, to prevent entry. It was as if the beachfront were an open tomb, sacred and secret, to be glimpsed only by rescue teams and the families of the deceased.

Armed police and National Guardsmen cruised the empty, littered streets. After looting broke out in some places within hours after the storm, strict curfews had been placed into effect and violaters were being hauled off to jail. There was no electricity or phone service. No hotel rooms were available for 150 miles in any direction. Throughout the city, emergency operations centers had been set up under enormous tents, like circus tents, where church groups and others dispensed food, water, medical care, tetanus shots, comfort, and information. A feeling of danger and profound desolation was in the air, a sense that there was no comfort to be had anywhere. I slept in the van in a mall parking lot, uneasy and exposed.

The next morning, I met a weary-looking middle-aged woman named Sherrie Nance, picking through a heap of donated clothes in a strip-mall parking lot in Long Beach. She'd lost everything, she said, including her car, her oceanfront condo, all her clothes and possessions—even all her important documents, which she'd dutifully tucked away in a safe deposit box at the bank. "They always tell you to do that," she said, "but they don't tell you what to do if the bank washes away too." Even her ten-year marriage had washed away, when her husband went "cuckoo" ten days after the storm and asked for a divorce.

Still, she offered to take me into the restricted beachfront disaster zone because she wanted to pick through the rubble around her condo one last time, to see if there was anything left to salvage. She took me into a small temporary office where the police were issuing beach access passes to residents. When we walked in, a fight was in progress. A fierce-looking man, taut and muscular, was screaming at an officer working behind the desk.

"Don't refer to my home as a 'debris-field'! That's my home! That's my life! Have some respect for people's feelings!"

When the man stormed out, the desk officer confided quietly to another policeman: "Well, that's what it is—a debris-field. That's what my house is too."

Sherrie had just bought an old used car, so she drove through the police checkpoint, flashing her access pass at the cops, and down into the beachfront disaster zone. What we saw simply beggared belief. For the most part, there was simply nothing left at all—no house, no grocery store, no bank, no gas station, no cars, no garages, no flowers or gardens or front lawns. There weren't even any street signs left, so people had posted hand-lettered cardboard signs on what trees were still standing—Magnolia, Beach Park Place, Island View—to give disoriented residents their bearings. Several people had spray-painted their names and addresses on pieces of tin or wood and propped them beside what were once lavish oceanfront homes, some with expansive patios, tennis courts, and pools, but which could now fairly be described as, well, debris-fields. One sign said, "Berry, 516 Trautman," though it was almost impossible to tell that a house had ever been there at all. Another said, more plaintively, "Whitney Are U OK? Call Brazil."

Sherrie was grateful that the streets—at least, the streets that were left—had now been partially cleared of toppled trees and rubble, so she could drive all the way down to the beach where her old condo used to stand. She loved her condo, the middle unit in a cluster, with a fabulous view right across Beach Boulevard and out onto the Gulf, which was not three hundred yards from her front door.

She parked her car and walked over into what was left of the Beachwood Condominiums—now just five bare cement slabs arranged around a swimming pool filled with trash and stinking, putrid water. The monstrous storm surge that Hurricane Katrina brought ashore utterly destroyed this entire complex, ripping down ceilings, walls, snapping off all the plumbing and heating pipes, even peeling back linoleum and parquet off the concrete slab. In place of Sherrie's home lay nothing but a chunk of broken brick wall the size of a card table, a few splintered boards, a tangle of electric wires, and a puddle of discolored water. Everything else was gone. On previous trips here, Sherrie had found a few things scattered in the sand that were not hers but that her neighbors might want—a chipped Lenox china dish, a ceramic cup, a concrete pelican with a loopy grin. She'd gathered them into a little pile and marked the spot with a blue plastic fly swatter stuck upright in the sand. It was as if a nuclear bomb had gone off, and all that was left of civilization was a blue fly swatter stuck in the sand around a scatter of broken dishes.

Out here in the sun-blasted disaster zone, there was no escaping the smell. It was a scent of burning, of dank rot, of dust and plaster, and of death. In the distance could be heard the sound of the front-end loaders and bulldozers, shoveling up the wreckage of people's lives and loading it into dump trucks to be hauled away. Almost the entire beachfront was being bulldozed to the ground. There was simply nothing left to salvage. Except for the distant growl of 'dozers, a kind of stunned hush lay over the place. Almost nobody was here; the people who once lived here had come, surveyed the wreckage, wept, collected a few things, and left.

As far as one could see in any direction, the scene was the same: rubble-strewn concrete slabs where homes used to stand. A nightmarish jumble of downed trees, smashed and overturned cars and boats, houses reduced to heaps of kindling wood. The trees left standing had had their bark battered up to twenty feet off the ground, where the debris-choked storm surge inundated the coast. In the lower branches, ghostly as floating, disembodied children, hung tattered clothes and long, trailing shrouds of plastic, now stirring eerily in the Gulf breeze.

I WENT to find Janice Stegenga, who lived in Pass Christian and whose eyes had welled with tears when she remembered the aftermath of Camille. I remembered her sitting at her kitchen table then, shaking her head in disbelief while showing me a photograph of an immense ocean-going barge that Camille had tossed across the highway as dismissively as a paper cup.

A couple of streets back from the beach, I found the modest brick Stegenga home, still standing, but empty. In the front yard—as in the front yards of so many other homes in the area—was an immense heap of whatever furniture, clothing, bedding, and other possessions could be salvaged from the flooded house. A note was pinned to a tree in the front yard: "Harry, Janice, Dawn, Polly, Steven, Jessica, Ana, Maryellen, Tammy, Shane, Jose, Savannah, and Jade All Alive Praise God."

But nobody answered a knock at the door.

Even so, this neighborhood looked almost livable compared to the beachfront itself, only a few blocks south. To view this area was to understand meteorologists' comparison of a Cat Four or Five hurricane to the almost inconceivable power of a nuclear explosion (in fact, a whole series of nuclear explosions). Almost all of downtown Pass Christian was an unrecognizable pile of rubble. The cute little harborside Bed and Breakfast where I'd stayed the year before was now a pile of bricks. Next door, still standing but ripped open like one of those cutaway dollhouses in a museum, was a Victorian home with an enormous sign posted outside: KEEP OUT. The building was clearly in danger of collapse, and the bulldozers, already fast at work, would probably soon return it to dust. What numbed the mind was how extensive the damage was—block after block, mile after mile, from New Orleans all the way to Mobile.

Nearby I found Trinity Episcopal Church, where Paul Williams lost thirteen family members during Camille. The superstructure of the church, with its vaulted window casements and high ceilings, was still standing. But everything else had been destroyed. One could look straight through gaping walls of the building and see all the way down to the glittering Gulf, where six-inch wavelets now pattered on the sand, docile as kittens. Across the street, the cemetery where Williams rode out Camille in a tree was filled with toppled gravestones, battered air-conditioning units, bits of roof, and other unrecognizable objects that once may have been comforting touchstones in some person's home.

A couple of blocks away stood a cement marker in front of what had been Pass Christian Middle School. A bronze plaque celebrated the rebuilding of the school following Hurricane Camille. Atop the flagpole was a tattered red, white, and blue rag, barely bigger than a dishtowel—all that the hurricane wind had left of the Stars and Stripes. Behind it, nothing was left except a great sea of brick, cinder block, twisted wire, and wooden auditorium chairs.

Closer to the beach, the Island Breeze condominium complex, built a couple of hundred yards from the site of the Richelieu Apartment buildings, was also devastated. Though the three-story structure with poured concrete uprights was still standing, the bottom two floors had been completely blown out by the storm. It was obvious that the storm surge in this spot—which was considerably higher than sea level—had been at least twenty feet high. The second floor, made of poured concrete and rebar, had been ripped out and now hung down from the second floor into thin air like a bit of tattered lace. Fortunately, the building was unoccupied at the time of the storm, so no deaths were reported. Even so, in an odd echo of the Richelieu Apartment disaster, one of the largest clusters of deaths occurred in the Quiet Water Apartments in Biloxi, where about thirty people were killed when the entire building was blown off its foundations and completely destroyed.

IN BILOXI, about twenty miles east of Pass Christian, a black Gambian man named Abdoulie Jatta took me on a tour of the devastated beachfront, home to some of the glitziest casinos on the Gulf. What Janice Stegenga had foreseen had come true. Immense three-story casino barges had been lifted up and flung across Highway 90 a quarter mile or more inland. The barge from the President Casino landed on top of a Holiday Inn. At the Grand Casino Pier, two barges broke in half. One ploughed across the yacht club north of U.S. Route 90; another landed in the middle of the highway. As a consequence, state and local authorities have begun considering new regulations to allow casinos to be built on land.

Jatta's friend George Kidd lived nearby in a small house on Division Street. Kidd had served two tours in Vietnam—he remembered watching news coverage of Hurricane Camille on television in Da Nang—but he'd never lived through anything like Katrina. He looked out his window as the storm surge came in shortly after dawn and saw an enormous uprooted tree go flying by, completely airborne. He saw cars and trucks being swept down the street in the surge, moving so fast it looked like they were going fifty or sixty miles an hour. The scene echoed Warren Raines's experience in Massies Mill, riding out the night on a fallen willow tree while watching cows, houses, and cars fly past in the torrent.

"I'd never, ever try to ride one of these things out again," Kidd said. "You can call me 'Chicken George' if you want to. But next time a hurricane is coming in here, I don't care if it's a Category *Zero*—I'm outta here!"

Not far down the beach, Beauvoir, the historic home of Jefferson Davis, had been badly damaged and some of it totally destroyed.

But one of the saddest sights of all was what remained of the lovely, contemplative Hurricane Camille Memorial Wall, on the grounds of Biloxi's Episcopal Church of the Redeemer. The graceful old wooden church was completely gone. All that remained was a steel superstructure, bent and twisted by the storm surge, as if it had been built of pipecleaners. The freestanding bell tower that had tolled through the night during Camille was now just a nondescript heap of bricks. And about half the memorial, bearing the names of the 175 people on the Gulf Coast who died in Camille, had been peeled away and broken by the wind-driven storm surge.

Shattered pieces of black granite, each inscribed with names of the dead or missing, had been stacked in the empty fountain at the center of the memorial, on top of the great swirling mandala of tiles that represented the power and beauty of the storm. Now a new storm had risen up and ripped the memorial to shreds. It was as if, even though survivors had stopped to praise the mystery and the magnificence of the storm, clearly the grand forces in the ocean and the atmosphere were fiercer than anything humans could imagine, much less anticipate. In the face of a biblical tempest such as Camille or Katrina, it seems, the proper human reponse is to be overcome with a kind of divine and humble awe.

And then to run for dear life.

SOURCES

Bell, Dolph, ed. "Mending a Torn Land: Recollections of the Extraordinary Efforts Made to Repair Nelson County From the Devastation of the Hurricane Camille Flood 25 Years Ago." Special supplement to the *Nelson County Times,* August 18, 1994.

Biel, Steven, ed. *American Disasters.* New York: New York University Press, 2001.

Caire, R.J., and Katy Caire. *History of Pass Christian.* Pass Christian, Mississippi: Lafayette Publishers, 1976.

Charles, Nick. "Gale Force: When It Comes to Tracking Hurricanes in the Gulf, No One Matches Meteorologist Nash Roberts." *People,* November 30, 1998.

Coastal Studies Institute, Louisiana State University, Baton Rouge. "Meterological Aspects of Hurricane Camille: Bulletin Number Four." National Oceanic and Atmospheric Administration, February, 1970.

Committee on Public Works. "Federal Response to Hurricane Camille: Hearings Before the Special Subcommittee on Disaster Relief of the Committee on Public Works, United States Senate, Ninety-First Congress, Second Session." Roanoke, Virginia, February 2 and 3, 1970.

Criswell, M.E., and R.S. Cummins. "Survey of Gulf Coast Structural Damage Resulting from Hurricane Camille." U.S. Army Engineer Waterways Experiment Station, Vicksburg, Mississippi, April, 1970.

Davies, Pete. *Inside the Hurricane: Face to Face with Nature's Deadliest Storms.* New York: Henry Holt, 2000.

Davis, Jefferson. "The Autobiography of Jefferson Davis." *Belford's Magazine,* January 1890.

Division of Mineral Resources, Department of Conservation and Economic Development, Commonwealth of Virginia. "Natural

Features Caused by a Catastrophic Storm in Nelson and Amherst Counties, Virginia." *Virginia Minerals,* special issue, October 1969.

———. "Road Log—Storm-Damaged Areas in Central Virginia." *Virginia Minerals.* Vol. 16, No. 1, February 1970.

Drye, Willie. *Storm of the Century.* Washington, D.C.: National Geographic Society, 2002.

Dubuisson, Mary L. "Drift Balls." *Down South* magazine, January-February 1970.

Eaton, L. Scott, Christopher M. Bailey, and Amy K. Gilmer. "The Debris Flows of Madison County, Virginia." Report for 34th Annual Virginia Geological Field Conference. September 24–25, 2004.

Ellis, Dan. *All About Camille.* Privately published, 2000.

———. *Pass Christian Tri-Centennial 1699–1999.* Privately published, 1997.

Embrey, Austin. Private papers donated to the Nelson County Historical Society.

ESSA (Environmental Science Services Administration). "The Virginia Floods, August 19–22, 1969: A Report to the Administrator." U.S. Department of Commerce, Washington, D.C., 1969.

———. "Hurricane Camille August 14–22, 1969." Preliminary Report. September 1969.

Executive Office of the President. "A Year of Rebuilding: The Federal Response to Hurricane Camille." Office of Emergency Preparedness, 1970.

Fisher, David E. *The Scariest Place on Earth.* New York: Random House, 1994.

Funk, Ben. "Swept Away." *The New York Times Magazine,* September 18, 1977.

Guice, Julia C. List of Hurricane Camille Fatalities on the Gulf Coast.

Hamner, Earl, and Ralph Giffin. *Goodnight John-Boy.* Nashville: Cumberland House, 2002.

Hearn, Philip D. *Hurricane Camille: Monster Storm of the Gulf.* Jackson, Mississippi: University Press of Mississippi, 2004.

Johnson, Robert Allen. "Stream Channel Response to Extreme Rainfall Events: The Hurricane Camille Storm in Central Nelson County, Virginia." Master's thesis, Department of Environmental Sciences, University of Virginia, August 1983.

Junger, Sebastian. *The Perfect Storm.* New York: W.W. Norton, 1997.

Kilgannon, Corey. "Forecaster Is Right On for Gulf Storms." *The New York Times,* Sunday, October 4, 1998.

Larson, Erik. *Isaac's Storm.* New York: Vintage Books, 1999.

Makower, Joel. *Woodstock: The Oral History.* New York: Doubleday, 1989.

Mennonite Disaster Service. "MDS Report 1969–70." Akron, Pennsylvania, 1970.

Michaels, Patrick C. "Camille: The Twentieth Anniversary." *The Virginia Climate Advisory,* Virginia State Climatology Office, Department of Environmental Sciences, University of Virginia. Vol. 13, No. 2, Summer 1989.

Miles, Barry. *Hippie.* New York: Sterling, 2004.

Morgan, B.A., G. Iovine, P. Chirico, and G.F. Wieczorek. "Inventory of Debris Flows and Floods in the Lovingston and Horseshoe Mountain, Va. 7.5′ Quadrangles, From the August 19/20, 1969, Storm in Nelson County, Virginia." Department of the Interior, U.S. Geological Survey, Open-file report 99–518, 1999.

Morison, Samuel Eliot. *Admiral of the Ocean Sea.* Boston: Little, Brown and Company, 1942.

Oliver, John. "The Tropical Cyclone Surge." Natural Hazards and Reinsurance, 1989, proceedings of a conference sponsored by Sterling offices (Australia) Ltd.

Oral histories. *The Mississippi Oral History Program of the University of Southern Mississippi,* by R. Wayne Pyle. Hattiesburg: McCain Library and Archives. Histories cited: Anderson, Alma (vol. 256, 1979); Breath, Charles and Mary (vol. 228, 1984); Gerlach, Mary Ann (vol. 223, 1981); Guice, Wade (vol. 183, 1981); Longo, John Jr. (vol. 269, 1979); Peralta, Gerald D. and Marie (vol. 224, 1984); Stegenga, Piet and Valena (vol. 201, 1982); Taylor, Robert L. (vol. 275, 1979); Tully, Rosemary (vol. 268, 1980); Williams, Paul Sr. (vol 231, 1984).

Payne, P.D. third. Private papers.

Piddington, Henry. *The Sailor's Horn-Book for the Law of Storms.* London: Williams and Norgate, 1855.

Pielke, Roger A. Sr. *The Hurricane.* London: Routledge, 1990.

Pielke, Roger A. Jr. and Roger A. Sr. *Hurricanes: Their Nature and Impacts on Society.* New York: John Wiley & Sons, 1997.

Pielke, Roger A. Jr., Chantal Simonpietri, and Jennifer Oxelson. "Thirty

Years After Hurricane Camille: Lessons Learned, Lessons Lost."
University of Colorado Hurricane Camille Project Report, July 12,
1999.

Pinder, Eric. *Tying Down the Wind: Adventures in the Worst Weather on Earth.* New York: Jeremy P. Tarcher, 2000.

Rappaport, Edward N., and Jose Fernandez-Partagas. "The Deadliest Tropical Cyclones, 1492–1996." National Oceanic and Atmospheric Administration technical memorandum NWS NHC 47, May 28, 1995.

Rienike, Irma. "Miss Camille—The Devastating Female." Fennell's Coast Litho Printing Co., Inc. 1969.

Roberts, Nash C. Jr. *The Story of Hurricane Camille,* Gulf Publishing Company, Gulfport, Mississippi, 1969.

———. Private papers, Booth-Bricker Special Collections and Archives at the J. Edgar and Louise S. Monroe Library, Loyola University, New Orleans, Louisiana.

———. "The Story of Extreme Hurricane Camille, August 14th through 22nd, 1969." Privately published account, 1969.

———. "Is the Hurricane Threat Increasing?" *New Orleans Magazine,* November 1969.

Rochell, Anne. "Weatherman Right On When No One Else Is." *The Atlanta Journal and Constitution,* October 2, 1998.

Schoen, David E. *Divine Tempest: The Hurricane as a Psychic Phenomena.* Toronto: Inner City Books, 1998.

Schwartz, Francis K. "The Unprecedented Rains in Virginia Associated with the Remnants of Hurricane Camille." *Monthly Weather Review.* U.S. Weather Bureau. Washington, D.C., November 1970.

Scotti, R.A. *Sudden Sea: The Great Hurricane of 1938.* Boston: Little, Brown and Company, 2003.

Sheets, Bob, and Jack Williams. *Hurricane Watch: Forecasting the Deadliest Storms on Earth.* New York: Vintage Books, 2001.

Shenk, William E. "Nimbus 3/ATS 3 Observations of the Evolution of Hurricane Camille." *Journal of Applied Meterology,* Vol. 17, Issue 4, 1978.

———. "Satellite Observations During the Rapid Intensification of Hurricane Camille." *Significant Accomplishments in Sciences,* proceedings of a symposium held November 7–8, 1972, at the NASA Goddard Space Flight Center. Washington, D.C.: NASA, 1973, p. 196.

Simpson, Paige Shoaf, and Jerry H. Jr. *Torn Land*. Lynchburg, Virginia: J.P. Bell & Co., 1971.

Simpson, Robert H., ed. *Hurricane! Coping with Disaster: Progress and Challenges Since Galveston, 1900*. Washington, D.C.: American Geophysical Union, 2003.

———., and Herbert Riehl. *The Hurricane and Its Impact*. Baton Rouge: Lousiana State University Press, 1981.

———., Arnold L. Sugg, and staff. "The Atlantic Hurricane Season of 1969." *Monthly Weather Review*. Vol. 98, No. 4, April 1970.

"Southern Meets the Challenge of Hurricane Camille." *Ties, The Southern Railway System Magazine*, September-October 1969.

Spitz, Bob. *Barefoot in Babylon: The Creation of the Woodstock Music Festival, 1969*. New York: W.W. Norton, 1979.

Sullivan, Charles L. *Hurricanes of the Mississippi Gulf Coast*. Gulfport, Mississippi: Gulf Publishing Company, 1987.

Swift, Earl. "When the Rain Came." Special supplement to *The Virginian-Pilot*, Norfolk, Virginia, August 15–22, 1999.

Wiebe, Katie Funk. *Day of Disaster*. Scottdale, Pennsylvania: Herald Press, 1976.

Williams, Garnett P., and Harold P. Guy. "Erosional and Depositional Aspects of Hurricane Camille in Virginia." Geological survey professional paper 804. Washington, D.C.: U.S. Government Printing Office, 1973.

Tannehill, Ivan Ray. *The Hurricane Hunters*. New York: Dodd, Mead & Co., 1963.

Toomey, David. *Stormchasers*. New York: W.W. Norton, 2002.

U.S. Army Corps of Engineers. "Report on Hurricane Camille, 14–22 August 1969." New Orleans, Louisiana, May 1970.

U.S. Department of Commerce, ESSA's Climatological Data, National Summary. "Hurricane Camille August 5–22, 1969." Vol. 20, No. 8, 1969.

Virginia State Water Control Board, Bureau of Water Control Management. "Flood Plain Information: Tye River, Nelson County." January 1976.

Wieczorek, G.F., G.S. Mossa, and B.A. Morgan. "Regional Debris-Flow Distribution and Preliminary Risk Assessment from Severe Storm Events in the Appalachian Blue Ridge Province, USA." *Landslides*. Heidelberg: Springer-Verlag. Vol. 1, No. 1, March 2004.

Wiegand, William Green. "Pass Christian of All Places." Pass Christian Historical Society & heirs of W.G. Wiegand, 2003.

Wilkinson, Kenneth P., and Peggy J. Ross. "Citizens' Responses to Warnings of Hurricane Camille," Social Science Research Center, Mississippi State University, State College, Mississippi. October 1970.

INDEX

Abruzzi, William, 66
Abyssinian Plateau, 8–9
Acceleration of Camille, 35, 38–39
Aftermath of Camille, 257–72
Agnew, Spiro, 212
Air Force, U. S., 39–42, 67, 246
Airplane reconnaissance. *See* Reconnaissance planes
Air temperature, 61. *See also* Sea-surface temperature
Air Weather Service, 41–42
Aldridge, Edward "Pete," 116
Aldrin, Edwin Eugene "Buzz," 26, 116
Alfonzo, Nathan, 84–87, 113
Alfonzo, Vincent, 84–87, 113
Allen, Calvin, 175, 178
American Cyanamid Plant (Piney River), 138–39, 190
American Red Cross, 80, 106, 110, 211–12, 237–38, 244
Amherst, Virginia, 214–15
Amish, 237, 238–39
Ammann, Jakob, 238
Anabaptist movement, 238
Anderson, Alma, 112, 266
Anemometers, 73
Aneroid barometers, 94–95

Apples, in Nelson County, Virginia, 124
Armstrong, Neil, 26
Army, U.S., 231
Ashley, Roger, 132–33
Associated Press (AP), 210–11
Atomic bombs, 37

Back Bay, 62–64
Baltimore Colts, 211
Barometers, 94–95
Barometric pressure, 35–38, 76–77
   Hurricane Camille, 10, 42, 52, 67–68, 94–95, 115
   Hurricane Katrina, 277, 278–79
Barrett, Billy, 62–63, 74–75, 84–87, 97–99, 112–14
Bathymetry, 76
Battle, William, 129, 139
Bay Saint Louis, Mississippi, 84–87, 94–97, 107, 212, 279
Beachwood Condominiums (Long Beach), 285–86
Beauvoir (Pass Christian), 22–23, 288–89
Belcher, Mrs., 200
Bell helicopters, 231

Bermuda High, 9, 10
Bielan, Mike, 71
Biloxi, Mississippi, 23, 48–49, 58,
    105–16, 274–76, 283–84,
    288–89
Binder, John, 105
Bolen, R. R., 231
Bond, George, 181
Bowling, Duval, 189–90
Bowling, Johnny, 165
Bowling, Sadie Thacker, 189–90
Bowling's Store (Massie's Mill),
    189–90
Bragg, Braxton, 21
Breath, Charles, Jr., 94–95
Breaux, John, 281
Bruguiere, Tom, 213–17
Bryant, Grace Marshall, 180, 266,
    273
Bryant, Tinker, 169–70, 180–84,
    194, 266
Buffalo Bills, 211
Bullock, Jane, 282
Burnley, Tom, 200

Caire, Ronnie, 212
Calvary Baptist Church
    (Lovingston), 273–74
Campbell, Edna, 190–92
Campbell, Gordon, 190–91
Campbell, Iris, 190–92
Campbell, John, 273
Campbell, Ward, 190
Cardin, Pierre, 26
Carson, Johnny, 141–42
Casino gambling, 275–76,
    288–89
Cassibry, Nat, 234

Castro, Fidel, 25–26
Casualty lists, 227, 228–29, 244
Category One hurricanes, 36
Category Three hurricanes, 36
Category Five hurricanes, 36–38
Cauls, 16
CBS, 24–25
Central Virginia Electric
    Cooperative, 131, 197
Chappaquiddick Island, 116
Charlottesville *Daily Progress*,
    129–30, 211
Church of the Redeemer (Biloxi),
    274–75, 289
Civil defense, 29, 32–33, 45, 49,
    79–80, 107–10
Civil War, 273–75
Clark, Robert Lee, 67–69
Clifford Forge, Virginia, 183
Climate, 48, 60–61
Cline, Isaac, 43
Closed systems, 9
Cloud seeding, 40
Coast Guard, U.S., 47, 231
Cocker, Joe, 67
Colley, Mr. and Mrs., 174
Command center, 219–28, 245
Communications, 219–20,
    222–23, 227–28
Communism, 29–30
Connor, Henry, 266
Connor, Martha, 266
Corpus Christi, Texas, 43–45
Country Joe and the Fish, 51
Cove Creek, 166–67
Covington, Virginia, 183
Crabtree Falls, 122
Criswell, George, 238, 247–54

Cronkite, Walter, 262–63
Cuba, 25–28, 34–35
Cuban Civil Defense Committee,
    26

Daily Herald (Gulfport,
    Mississippi), 24, 25, 26, 27,
    105–6
Dambrink, Anna, 91–94, 103–4
Dambrink, John, 91–94, 103–4
Davis, Jefferson, 22–23, 288–89
Davis Creek, Virginia
    August 19, Tuesday, 141–50
    August 20, Wednesday,
        197–98, 204, 206
    August 21, Thursday, 220–23
    August 24, Sunday, 230,
        231–34
    August 27, Wednesday,
        242–44, 245
Dawson, Florence, 219–20,
    222–29, 232, 236–37, 245
Death toll, 115–16, 211–13, 224,
    229, 245, 275
Deer Island, 63
DeLisle, Mississippi, 81–82
Delk, Mrs., 222
Dennison, Alfred, 232–34
Dickens, Charles, 16
Disaster culture defiance, 257–62
DNA testing, 253–54
Dodson, Marion, 111, 264
Dorsey, Sarah, 22–23
Downdraft, 56
Drinking water, 109–10
Drumheller, Buren, 132–33
Duckworth, Ben, Jr., 69–72,
    262

Easterling, Albert, Jr., 75
Eggleston, Sam, 223–25
Eglin Air Force Base, 47
Ekman spiral, 77
Elkemer, Dr. and Mrs., 113
Ellington Air Force Base, 68
Elliot, Rona, 105
Embry, Austin, 222–25
Embry, Reid, 236–37
Emergency Operations Center,
    79–80, 110
Emergency shelters, 106
Ethiopia, 8–9
Evacuation, 45, 79–80, 277–78
Evans, Walter Scott, 195
Eye of Camille, 40–41, 55–56,
    58–61, 67–69, 95–96
Eyewall of Camille, 55–56,
    58–61, 67–69, 76–77

Falwell, Jerry, 137–38
Federal Bureau of Investigation
    (FBI), 251
Federal Emergency Management
    Agency (FEMA), 282
Feeder bands, 42
Ferguson, A. W., 211
Fiddler crab, 53–54
First Baptist Church (Gulfport),
    108
Fisher, David E., 37
Fitzgerald, Angie, 176, 178
Fitzgerald, Anita, 176, 178
Fitzgerald, Frances, 174–79, 265
Fitzgerald, John Henry, 174–79
Fitzgerald, John Henry, Jr.,
    175–79
Flippin, Bill, 195

Florida Keys, 14, 25, 38, 278
Florida Panhandle, 46–49
Floyd, Bobby Ray, 132–33,
     171–74, 200
Floyd, Chris, 173–74
Floyd, Herman, 173
Floyd, Margaret, 171–74
Floyd, Susan, 173–74
Fly-by images, 39
Forensics, 246–54
Fort Eustis, 245–46
Fortune, Berks, 132–33
Fortune, Jimmy, 170
Fort Walton Beach, Florida,
     46–47, 48, 49
Fox News, 269
Francis of Assisi, Saint, 239
French, Elizabeth Campbell, 273
French, Emory, 273
Freshwater Cove Creek, 205–6

Gable, Walter, 247–54
Galveston storm of 1900, 43, 78
Gamble, James, 223–25, 247–54
Gamble, Mike, 236–37
Gannon, Mike, 71
Gathright, Thomas, 203–5
Generators, 110
Gentry, Cecil, 40
Geological Survey, U.S., 166
Geological time, vs. human time,
     4–6
Geology, 203–5
Gerlach, Fritz, 19–21, 69–72,
     88–90, 262–63, 266–68
Gerlach, Mary Ann, 19–24,
     28–29, 69–72, 88–90,
     99–100, 262–63, 266–68

Giles, George and Texas, 229
Giles, Mac, 181
Goad, Bob, 205–6, 220–22,
     222–25
Goad, Buzz, 236–37
Godsey, Jimmy, 169, 180–84
Godwin, Mills, 231–34, 244
Gordon, John, 222–25, 246, 247
Grand Bahama Island, 14
Grand Cayman Island, 8, 17
Great Abaco Island, 14
Grisham, John, 277, 278
Guadeloupe, 8
Guice, Charles, 31
Guice, Judy, 109
Guice, Julia Marie Cook, 29–30,
     32–33, 49, 109, 252–53,
     259, 263
Guice, Wade, 29–33, 49, 53,
     76–80, 107–10, 252–53,
     264
Gulfport, Mississippi
     August 17, Sunday, 57–58,
          62–64, 73–87
     August 18, Monday, 97–99,
          105–8
     August 21, Thursday, 211–13
     Hurricane Katrina, 279,
          283–84
Guthrie, Arlo, 50

Halverson, Jeffrey B., 61, 157
Hamner, Earl, Jr., 122–23
Hancock General Hospital
     (Gulfport), 111
Hardin, Durrie, 101
Harris, Eldridge, 234
Harrison County Civil Defense,

29, 32–33, 49, 76–80,
    107–10
Hat Creek, 148–49, 182
Hattiesburg, Mississippi, 115
Havens, Richie, 51
Hawley, Minor, 206, 221–22
Heat engines, 59–61
Henderson, John, 80–81
Henderson, Louisa, 80–81
Hendrix, Jimi, 104–5, 141
Higgins Industries, 12–13
Hill, Billy, 132–33, 171–74
Hiroshima, 37
Hoffman, Walter, 195
Hog Farm, 66
Holton, Linwood, 129, 139
Howardsville, Virginia, 199–200
Howell, Henry, 129, 139
Hudson, Henry, 221, 234
Huey helicopters, 231
Huffman, Adelaide, 141–45,
    228–29, 231, 242–43
Huffman, Ann, 142, 143–44,
    228–29, 242–43
Huffman, Jesse, 141–45, 228–29,
    242–43
Huffman, Lila, 242–43
Huffman, Maude, 144–45,
    228–29, 242–43
Huffman, Mitchell, 145, 228–29,
    236, 242–43, 273
Huffman, Russell, 141–45,
    228–29, 242–44
Huffman, Tommy, 141–45,
    228–29, 242–43
Human time, vs. geological time,
    4–6
Hurricane Andrew, 95, 280

Hurricane Audrey, 13, 258
Hurricane Betsy, 13–17, 33, 69,
    280
Hurricane Camille
    Katrina compared with, vii–ix,
        277–89
    naming of, 17–18
    origins of, 7–17
    remnants of, 156–62
    timeline. See Timeline of
        Camille
Hurricane Camille Memorial Wall
    (Biloxi), 274–75, 289
Hurricane Carla, 10, 257–58
Hurricane Condition Three, 47
Hurricane Debbie, 40
Hurricane Earl, 271
Hurricane Fran, 265
Hurricane Georges, 271
Hurricane Gilbert, 95
Hurricane Gladys, 25
Hurricane-hunter planes. See
    Reconnaissance planes
Hurricane Ivan, 269, 272
Hurricane Janet, 39
Hurricane Katrina, vii–ix,
    277–89
Hurricane parties, 28–29, 69,
    262–63
Hurricane rankings, 35–38
Hurricane track projections,
    45–47, 52–53
Hurricane warnings, 46–47, 48,
    257–62
Hurricane watch, 46–47
Hurricane Watch (Sheets), 68
Hurricane Wilma, vii
Hydrogen bombs, 37

Hydrology of the Weather
    Bureau Office, 5, 115

Indonesian tsunami (2004),
    77–78

Jackson, Thomas and Mary,
    229
Jackson River, 183
James River, 198–200, 210–11,
    220, 231–32
Jatta, Abdoulie, 288–89
J.C. Penney, 26
Jefferson Airplane, 66–67, 141
Jet stream, 158–61
Johnson, Sam, 241–42
Johnson, Walter, 212–13
Jones, Buddy, 70–71
Jones, Dave, 251
Jones, Merwin, 69–72, 263

Kanagy, Jonas, 239
Keesler Air Force Base, 23, 92,
    267
Keller, Luane, 70
Keller, Richard, 70, 262
Kennedy, Edward, 116
Kennedy, John F., 129
Kent, John, 196
Kidd, George, 288–89
Kietzer, Lawrence, 268
King, Kevin, 238–39
KISS (Keep it simple, stupid)
    system, 32–33
Kopechne, Mary Jo, 116
Korean War, 24, 201, 222, 223
Krick, Robert E.L., 274
Kukulkan, 17

Landslides, 203–5, 232
Lawrence, Carter, 232–34
Lewis, Vernon, 133, 179, 217–18,
    222–25, 229, 244, 265–66
Little, Marvin A., 67–69
Live Oak Cemetery (Pass
    Christian), 80–81, 100–102
Live Oak Society, 22
Long Beach, Mississippi, 66,
    90–94, 107, 212, 279,
    283–86
Longo, Johnny, 58
Looting, 112–13, 114, 213, 246,
    264–65
Lovingston, Virginia, 273–74
    August 19, Tuesday, 135–39
    August 20, Wednesday,
        171–74, 193–209
    August 21, Thursday, 210–11
    August 24, Sunday, 226–27
Lovingston Elementary School,
    132–33, 223
Lovingston Formation, 203–5
Lovingston Volunteer Fire
    Department, 171–72
Luther, Martin, 238
Lynchburg General Hospital,
    187, 209, 220, 229, 230

McCarthy, Joe, 29–30
McCarthy, John, 202
McDearmon, Jim, 223
McInnis, Mrs., 113–14
Mckay, Parnell, 212
Major disaster areas, declaration
    of, 212
Martial law, 211–13
Martin, Frances, 221

Martin, George, 221
Martin, Robert, 197–98, 221
Massies Mill, Virginia
    August 19, Tuesday, 119–34
    August 20, Wednesday,
        151–66, 184–86, 200, 207–9
    August 21, Thursday, 210–11,
        213–17
    August 24, Sunday, 234
    August 27, Wednesday, 244
Matecumbe Key, 38
Mechanics of hurricanes, 59–61,
    76–78, 158–60
Mennonite Disaster Service
    (MDS), 238–40, 249
Mennonites, 237–40, 264
Merritt, Dick, 111–12
Merritt, Jonathan, 111–12
Meteorology, 35–38, 48, 58–61,
    76–78, 156–62
Michaels, Pat, 47–49, 53–54,
    56–58
Miller Chemical Company
    (Massies Mill), 124–25,
    185–86, 195, 214
Mission lists, 227, 245
Mississippi River, 14–15, 47,
    106
Monticello, 122
Moon landings, 26, 116
Moore, Harry Estill, 257–58
Morgan 34, 62–64, 73
Morris, Dora, 230
Morton Frozen Food, trailer-
    morgue, 246–54
Mountainslides, 203–5, 232
Mountain View Tearoom (Tyro),
    174–75

Muddy Creek, Virginia, 170–71,
    186–90, 245

Nagin, Ray, 277–89
Nance, Sherrie, 284–86
Napier, Bobby, 169, 180–84
National Guard, 110
National Hurricane Center
    (NHC), 15–18, 25, 27–28,
    56–57
National Weather Service, 115
Navy, U.S., 39–41, 47, 75, 231.
    See also Seabees
Nelson, Tim, 247–48
Nelson County, Virginia, 3–6,
    119–254
    August 19, Tuesday, 119–50
    August 20, Wednesday,
        151–209
    August 21, Thursday, 210–25
    August 24, Sunday, 226–40
    August 27, Wednesday,
        241–54
Nelson County All-Stars, 132–33,
    171–72
Nelson County Board of
    Supervisors, 198
Nelson County Courthouse,
    273–74
Nelson County High School, 119,
    133, 139, 265–66
Nelson County Times, 223
Nelson County Water and
    Sewage Authority, 166–67
New Orleans, 7–17, 106
    flooding dangers in, 14–15
    Hurricane Betsy and, 14–15
    Hurricane Katrina and, 277–89

New Orleans *Times-Picayune*, 15
Newspapers, 210–11, 241
New York Times, 277
Nixon, Richard, 24–25, 26, 212

Ocean Springs Laboratory,
    48–49, 56–58, 105–6
Oliver, John and Alice, 229
Orographic effect, 3–4, 159
Oxelson, Jennifer, 282–83

Paleofloods, 5
Pass Christian, Mississippi,
    262–63, 275–76, 279
  August 15, Friday, 19–24
  August 17, Sunday, 57–59,
    64–66, 80–90, 96–97
  August 18, Monday, 99–104,
    108–12, 130
  August 21, Thursday, 212
  August 24, Sunday, 234–35
  August 27, Wednesday,
    252–53
  Hurricane Katrina, 286–89
Pass Christian Garden Club, 22
Pass Christian Middle School,
    287
Payne, Dan, 219, 222–25,
    235–37, 246
Payne, Phil, 205–6, 224, 228,
    235–37, 238
Peaches, in Nelson County,
    Virginia, 124
Pensacola, Florida, 47, 49
Peralta, Gerald, 58, 70–71, 101–2
Personal emergency kits, 244
Peverill, Virginia, 222–25
Picayune, Mississippi, 202

Pielke, Roger A., Jr., 282–83
Piney River, 135–40, 142–43,
    145–48, 202, 216, 234, 243
Plane reconnaissance. *See*
    Reconnaissance planes
Plaquemines Parish, Louisiana,
    212–13
Pontchartrain, Lake, 14–15,
    279–80
Ponton, Al, 171–74
Ponton, Herman, 172
Ponton, Johnny, 171–74
Pressure gradients, 61
Profiteering, 213, 264–65
Project Stormfury, 40
Protestant Reformation, 238
Psychological experience of
    Camille, 265–66

Quarles Elementary School
    (Long Beach), 66, 90–94

Racial segregation, 23
Radar, 39, 56–57, 156–57
Raines, Ava, 125, 216, 270
Raines, Carl, Jr., 119–25, 134,
    151–56, 164–66, 184–86,
    195, 207–9, 213–17,
    241–42, 270–71
Raines, Carl, Sr., 124–25, 151–56,
    164, 185–86, 195, 207–9,
    241–42
Raines, Ginger, 125, 134, 152–56,
    164, 207–9, 241–42, 244
Raines, Johanna, 125, 151–56,
    164, 207–9, 241–42
Raines, Sandy, 125, 134, 152–56,
    164, 241–42

Raines, Sharon, 271
Raines, Shirley, 152–56, 163, 164, 207–9, 229
Raines, Warren, 119–25, 133–34, 151–56, 163–66, 184–86, 195, 207–9, 213–17, 241–42, 269–71
Rainfall, 4–5, 159–62, 201–4
Rain meteorology, 156–62
Ramsey, Gene, 220–21, 237, 239–40, 266
Ranking hurricanes, 35–38
Raynor, Robert, 223–25, 230, 237–38, 247–54, 266
Reconnaissance planes, 17–18, 39–42, 52–53, 67–69
Recovery operations, 210–54
Red Cross, 80, 106, 110, 211–12, 237–38, 244
Rescue operations, 109–10, 130, 201, 210–54
Richelieu Manor (Pass Christian), 21, 69–72, 96–97, 108, 130, 212, 262–63, 266
Roberts, Lydia, 7, 15, 272
Roberts, Nash C., Jr., 7–17, 47, 52–54, 73, 261, 271–72, 283
Rockfish River, 166–67, 196–200, 236, 245, 250
Rodriguez, Dr., 27–28, 34–35
Romney, Hugh, 66
Roseland, Virginia, 139–40, 166–70, 180–84
Ross, Peggy, 258–62

Saffir, Herb, 35–38
Saffir-Simpson Hurricane Damage Potential Scale, 35–38
St. Charles Hotel (New Orleans), 7–8, 15
Salvation Army, 110, 237–38
Satellite images, 39, 42, 58–59, 61
Saunders, Jack, 223
Schoen, David, 265
Schwarz, Francis K., 201–2
Scott Air Force Base, 41–42
Scottsville, Virginia, 211
Seabees, 23, 110, 234–35
Search-and-rescue operations, 227–30, 233–42, 244–46
Sea-surface temperature, 8, 42, 59–61, 67–68
Sebastian, John, 51
Seeding, 40
Shankar, Ravi, 50
Sheets, Bob, 68
Sheffield Funeral Home, temporary morgue, 246–54
Simmons, Menno, 238
Simonpietri, Chantal, 282–83
Simpson, Jerry, 217–18
Simpson, Joanne, 40
Simpson, O. J., 26
Simpson, Paige, 217–18
Simpson, Robert, 17–18, 25, 34–47, 56–57, 67–69, 96, 242, 275, 279–80
Slick, Grace, 66–67
Small, Mrs. Harmon, Jr., 242
Smith, George, 267
Smith, Russell, 247–54
Smothers Brothers Comedy Hour (TV show), 24–25

Soap Box Derby Championship, 211
Sources, 291–96
Spiral, 59, 77
SPLASH (Special Program to List Amplitudes of Surges from Hurricanes), 68
Staunton Military Academy, 270–71
Stegenga, Elizabeth, 91–94, 103–4
Stegenga, Harry, 64–66, 90–94, 102–4
Stegenga, Janice, 64–66, 90–94, 102–4, 259, 275, 286–87
Stegenga, Joey, 91–94, 103–4
Stegenga, Loretta, 65, 103–4
Stegenga, Piet, 65, 91–94, 103–4
Stegenga, Valena, 65, 91–94, 103–4
Stevens, Ivanhoe, 131
Still, Patty, 280
Storm surge, 35–38, 68, 76–77
    Hurricane Camille, 76–79, 96–97, 107–8
    Hurricane Katrina, 279–80
Storm-track projections, 45–47, 52–53
Super Constellation WR-121s (Connies), 40–41

Taylor, Beverly Ann Glass, 62, 74
Taylor, Dan, 229
Taylor, Robert, 62–64, 73–75, 84–87, 97–99, 112–14
Temporary morgue, 246–54
Thermodynamic efficiency, 59–61, 158–60

Thompson, Bonnie, 135–39, 142–43, 145–48, 187–89, 244, 245–46
Thompson, Colleen, 135–39, 142–43, 145–48, 170–71, 186–89, 230
Thompson, Dale, 135–39, 142–43, 145–48, 187–88
Thompson, Eddie, 135–39, 142–43, 145–48, 187–89
Thompson, Edward B. "Buzz," 136, 138–39, 142–43, 145–48, 170–71, 187–89, 244, 245–46, 273
Thompson, Grace, 136, 138–39, 142–43, 145–48, 187–89
Thompson, Hampton, 138
Thompson, Jake, 135–39, 142–43, 145–48, 187–89, 245–46
Thompson, Lena, 135–39, 142–43, 145–48, 187–89, 245–46
Tidal wave, vs. storm surge, 77
Timeline of Camille
    August 14, Thursday, 7–17
    August 15, Friday, 19–33
    August 16, Saturday, 34–54
    August 17, Sunday: 5:00 AM, 55–72; 8:00 PM, 73–87; 10:30 PM, 88–90; 10:45 PM, 90–94; 11:15 PM, 94–97
    August 18, Monday, 97–106; 12:00 Noon, 107–16
    August 19, Tuesday: 8:00 AM, 119–29; 1:00 PM, 129–31; 6:00 PM, 131–33; 8:00 PM, 133–40; 9:00 PM, 141–50

August 20, Wednesday: 2:00 AM, 151–62; 3:00 AM, 163–79; 5:00 AM, 180–84; 6:00 AM, 184–92; morning, 193–209
August 21, Thursday, 210–25
August 24, Sunday, 226–40
August 27, Wednesday, 241–54
Tinsley, Ed, 214–17, 227–28, 240, 251
Tipping point, 204
Tonight Show, The (TV show), 141–42
Torn Land (Simpson), 217–18
Tribble, Jim, 206, 221–25, 227–28
Trinity Episcopal Church (Pass Christian), 80–84, 100–102, 287
Tropical cycles, viii–ix, 8–9
Tropopause, 48, 60–61
Troposphere, 48, 60–61
Troy, James, 268
Tsunamis, 77–78
Tucker, Boyd, 222
Tucker, Walter, 200
Tully, Rosemary, 58, 96, 110–11
Tye River, 4, 120–22, 151–56, 166–68, 174–75, 182, 193–94, 196–200, 202, 207–8, 244–45
Tyro, Virginia, 174–79, 193–94

Unitas, Johnny, 211

Veil babies, 16–17
Vietnam War, 24–25, 116, 129–30, 231

Virginia Department of Civil Defense, 183–84
Virginia Division of Mines, 203–4
Virginia Military Institute (VMI), 223, 271
Virginia State Climatology Office, 203
Volkswagen Beetle, 26, 121–22

Wallace, Mary Evelyn, 74–75, 84–87, 97–99
Waltons, The (TV show), 122–23
Warm core, 61–62
Washington Post, 233
Waveland, Mississippi, 279
WDSU-TV, 11–14, 49
Weather balloons, 160
Weather bulletins, 28, 45–46, 53, 57, 68–69, 115
Weather Bureau, U.S., 156–58, 201–2, 261
Weather satellites, 39, 42, 58–59, 61
Whirlpool galaxy, 59
White, Sandy, 183–84
White, Wilson, 169–70, 180–84
Whitehead, Catherine, 126, 128, 139–40, 148–50, 168–69, 269
Whitehead, Dick, 126, 128, 149–50, 167–70, 180–84
Whitehead, John, 126, 128, 149–50, 169, 180–84
Whitehead, Lucy, 173–74
Whitehead, Mildred, 173–74
Whitehead, Nancy, 126, 128, 149–50

Whitehead, William "Bill,"
126–31, 139–40, 148–50,
167–70, 180–84, 194–98,
223, 269
Wilkinson, Kenneth, 258–62
Williams, Bridget, 101
Williams, Esther, 101
Williams, John Bell, 211–13
Williams, Malcolm, 100–101
Williams, Myrtle, 81–84, 101–2
Williams, Paul, Sr., 80–84,
100–102, 287
Paul William's daughter Myrtle
Mae, 101
Paul William's granddaughter
Bridget, 101
Willoughby, Hugh, 38
Wind speeds, 35–38, 60, 75,
107–8, 115
Hurricane Katrina, 277,
278–79
Wood, Buen, 155
Wood, Cliff, 198–201, 205–6,
218–25, 227–28, 230,
232–34, 244–46, 269
Wood, Donna Fay, 153–56, 241,
244

Wood, Francis, 153
Wood, Gary, 153–56, 241, 244
Wood, Lola, 155
Wood, Louise, 198–99
Wood, Mabel, 221
Wood, Mike, 125, 153–56, 195
Wood, Page, 153
Wood, Ron, 139–40, 167–68
Wood, Teresa, 153–56, 195
Woods Mill, 233–34, 245, 250–51
Woodstock (documentary), 51
Woodstock Aquarian Music and
Art Fair, 27, 49–52, 66–67,
104–5, 116, 129–30
Wooten, Mr. and Mrs. Harry, 200,
229
World War II, 32, 75, 81, 127,
201, 217, 239
Wright, Garland, 195
Wright, Johnny Lee, 221–22

Yasgur, Max, 50, 104–5
Young, Jack, 244, 270

Zirkle, Audrey, 179, 273
Zirkle, Gary, 273